The Humanitarian Fix

This book investigates how humanitarians balance the laws and principles of civilian protection with the realities of contemporary warzones, where non-state armed actors assert cultural, political and religious traditions that are often at odds with official frameworks.

This book argues that humanitarian protection on the ground is driven not by official frameworks in the traditional sense, but by the relationships between the complex mix of actors involved in contemporary wars. The frameworks, in turn, act as a unifying narrative that preserves these relationships. As humanitarian practitioners navigate this complex space, they act as unofficial brokers, translating the official frameworks to align with the often-divergent agendas of non-state armed actors. In doing so, they provide an unofficial humanitarian fix for the challenges inherent in applying the official frameworks in contemporary wars.

Drawing on rich ethnographic observations from the author's time in northern Iraq, and complemented by interviews with a range of fieldworkers and humanitarian policy makers and lawyers, this book will be a compelling read for researchers and students within humanitarian and development studies, and to practitioners and policy makers who are grappling with the contradictions this book explores.

Joe Cropp is a delegate with the International Red Cross Red Crescent Movement and a researcher and lecturer in humanitarian and development studies.

Routledge Humanitarian Studies

Series editors: Alex de Waal, Dorothea Hilhorst, Annette Jansen and Mihir Bhatt

The Routledge Humanitarian Studies series in collaboration with the International Humanitarian Studies Association (IHSA) takes a comprehensive approach to the growing field of expertise that is humanitarian studies. This field is concerned with humanitarian crises caused by natural disaster, conflict or political instability and deals with the study of how humanitarian crises evolve, how they affect people and their institutions and societies, and the responses they trigger.

We invite book proposals that address, amongst other topics, questions of aid delivery, institutional aspects of service provision, the dynamics of rebel wars, state building after war, the international architecture of peacekeeping, the ways in which ordinary people continue to make a living throughout crises, and the effect of crises on gender relations.

This interdisciplinary series draws on and is relevant to a range of disciplines, including development studies, international relations, international law, anthropology, peace and conflict studies, public health and migration studies.

International Humanitarian NGOs and State Relations
Principles, Politics, and Identity
Andrew J. Cunningham

Crisis Management Beyond the Humanitarian-Development Nexus
Edited by Atsushi Hanatani, Oscar A. Gómez and Chigumi Kawaguchi

Urban Poverty in the Wake of Environmental Disaster
Rehabilitation, Resilience and Typhoon Haiyan (Yolanda)
Edited by Maria Ela Atienza, Pauline Eadie and May Tan-Mullins

Disaster Public Health and Older People
Emily Chan

Humanitarianism and the Quantification of Human Needs
Minimal Humanity
Joël Glasman

The Humanitarian Fix
Navigating Civilian Protection in Contemporary Wars
Joe Cropp

The Humanitarian Fix

Navigating Civilian Protection in Contemporary Wars

Joe Cropp

Routledge
Taylor & Francis Group
LONDON AND NEW YORK

First published 2021
by Routledge
2 Park Square, Milton Park, Abingdon, Oxon OX14 4RN

and by Routledge
52 Vanderbilt Avenue, New York, NY 10017

Routledge is an imprint of the Taylor & Francis Group, an informa business

British Library Cataloguing in Publication Data
A catalogue record for this book is available from the British Library

Library of Congress Cataloging-in-Publication Data
Names: Cropp, Joe, author.
Title: The humanitarian fix : navigating civilian protection in contemporary wars / Joe Cropp.
Description: Milton Park, Abingdon, Oxon ; New York, NY : Routledge, 2021. | Includes bibliographical references and index. | Identifiers: LCCN 2020024919 (print) | LCCN 2020024920 (ebook) | ISBN 9780367440916 (hardback) | ISBN 9781003007500 (ebook)
Subjects: LCSH: Humanitarian law. | Humanitarian intervention. | War (International law)
Classification: LCC KZ6471 .C758 2021 (print) | LCC KZ6471 (ebook) | DDC 341.6/7–dc23
LC record available at https://lccn.loc.gov/2020024919
LC ebook record available at https://lccn.loc.gov/2020024920

ISBN: 978-0-367-44091-6 (hbk)
ISBN: 978-1-003-00750-0 (ebk)

Typeset in Baskerville
by Taylor & Francis Books

MIX
Paper from responsible sources
FSC™ C013985

Printed in the United Kingdom
by Henry Ling Limited

Contents

Preface

Before starting this ethnographic account, it is worth pausing for a moment to identify my position in the research. Personal experiences have motivated this research, are reflected in the questions I set out to answer and colour the methodological approach. In hindsight, the field experience on which this study is based began in 1994, when I was a 25-year-old ex-soldier, aspiring freelance journalist and lost traveller in eastern Zaire. With no idea of the scale of the humanitarian crisis unfolding, I hitchhiked across the border from Uganda to see the camps where some two million refugees had sought safety from the Rwandan genocide. Memories have faded over time, but I still clearly recall my journey from the border, past a growing column of refugees, and that first sight of one of the camps. Set against the magnificent backdrop of an active volcano was a sea of blue tarpaulins extending out to the ends of the valley. In the centre was a small compound of white tents surrounded by wire, more a prison camp than a haven for the refugees. A seemingly endless line of people snaked through the blue tarpaulins and up to the front gate of the compound, now lit up like a sports stadium as night approached. A column of Land Cruisers was leaving for the relative safety of nearby Goma before night set in and militia groups took control.

Staying in a cheap hotel in the town, I spent my days travelling with people involved in the response, under the guise of journalism, sometimes riding in the water trucks as they shuttled between the shores of Lake Kivu and the chaos of the camps, sometimes hitching a ride with an aid convoy as it made the journey from the border with Uganda. I watched from the back seat of a Land Cruiser as the local United Nations fixer handed over cash at each military checkpoint to get relief supplies through – the more senior the soldier, the bigger the stack of notes. Listening to the stories of the aid workers and contractors in local hotels at the end of the day, my interest was in the day-to-day, the musings of individuals, which said so much about what was happening. I left Goma by ferry after a few weeks, but there is something about a humanitarian crisis that is addictive. Over the next two years I stumbled through a number of humanitarian crises, including Sudan and the Balkans, visiting camps, following the route of refugees, and hanging out with aid workers and humanitarian contractors. It was these complex emergencies across the 1990s that led the humanitarian community to develop the raft of codes of conduct and professional standards that form part of this research.

After working as a journalist for some 15 years – a career that is in part responsible for the narrative style of this book and my interest in people's stories – I began working for the International Red Cross and Red Crescent Movement. Working as a communications adviser in development programmes, I juggled the contrasting narratives that appeared between the policies I read in head office and the stories I heard from field staff as I travelled around Asia and the Pacific. Participatory development, almost mandatory for every policy document at the time, was routinely adapted and changed by field workers to suit the context. Yet their official reports reflected the authorised policy of the institution and major donors. This experience gave me an appreciation of ethnographic comparisons of development policy and practice when I returned to my studies. Later, when I began working in complex emergencies, it raised the seemingly obvious question: If there are discontinuities between policy and practice in development, do similar ones exist in the humanitarian sector with its international laws and humanitarian principles?

These experiences have shaped my academic interests. Working in today's conflicts and complex emergencies, I have witnessed the benefits of the institutionalisation of humanitarianism and the related frameworks and codes of conduct that followed the failures of 1994, when humanitarianism potentially caused more harm than good. I have also seen the shortcomings of the models we work with in ever-changing political environments, motivating me to look beyond the frameworks that are the focus of much humanitarian scholarship. These experiences position me between humanitarian practice and research, which colours my perceptions. While I have aimed to incorporate the level of objectivity and academic rigour that is required of the ethnographic researcher, I am also part of the group at the centre of this study. All that follows should be read in this context, for as well as the unique insights that come from being an insider, there are also biases that cannot be fully cast aside.

Acknowledgements

This book is the culmination of a long journey, which like many journeys has proven alternately fascinating, challenging, frustrating and rewarding. There have been many encounters along the way, some brief, while at other times people have travelled with me for some time. I take this opportunity to acknowledge as many of them as a page will allow. First, I thank my family, who have been there from the beginning and have always kept me going with their belief, encouragement and support; I particularly thank my sister for showing the way.

Thank you to my thesis supervisors, Violeta Schubert and Bart Klem, who provided patient guidance from the moment I arrived at university with a somewhat random collection of experiences, stories and half-baked ideas. I would have become lost without the two of them. Throughout the journey they helped me see what I was trying to argue and introduced me to the conceptual tools to express my ideas. Also, looking further back, I want to thank all those who have been my teachers over the years. There are too many of you to mention here, but it was your faith in that somewhat shy, uncertain student that kept me going each step of the way.

In addition, I have been fortunate to be part of a community of early career academics, both in Australia and internationally, who have listened to my thoughts and read my material from the beginnings of this project. Your knowledge, encouragement and friendship were invaluable on the journey.

Finally, my thanks go to the humanitarian workers who have been so generous with their time and knowledge throughout my research. Any moments of insight and clarity in the following pages are due to them. Any errors of fact, judgment or otherwise are all mine.

1 Introduction

The improvised roadblock comes as a surprise, bringing us to a halt on the road to Sinjar. The gunman stands in the middle of the long stretch of road, his face masked by a balaclava, his assault rifle in the carry position. To one side, another black-clad figure disappears silently into the low scrub; to the right a third masked man crouches, waiting just off the edge of the road, assault rifle to his shoulder. We stare at each other across 50 metres of asphalt, our Land Cruiser now idling on the single lane road in northern Iraq. My Iraqi Red Crescent colleague Mohamed places his hands on the passenger-side dashboard, in clear view, following the practiced security script. Making no other movement, the big Sunni silently looks through the cracked windscreen, across the dusty bonnet marked with the two distinctive red emblems, the universal symbols that we are not part of the fight. I reach from the back seat and place my hand on Faisel's shoulder. "We are good?" I ask, searching for reassurance from the local Shia driver. This will play out differently depending on who this gunman is, where he is from, what he is part of. Different actors in this world play by different rules at different times.

This is the complex space of contemporary conflicts in which modern humanitarianism operates, with few fixed boundaries and multiple actors with shifting, often opaque agendas. The Iraqi Government army is far to the south, recently routed by ISIS, which now occupies Mosul, some 80 kilometres to our east. The thousands of displaced people who last week filled the roads out of Mosul have largely dispersed, either sheltering in relief camps in Sinjar, where we are now heading, or travelling further north across open country to the apparent safety of the mountains. That leaves the Peshmerga – the military forces of the autonomous region of Iraqi Kurdistan who now control this part of the country – and the Iranian-backed Shia militia. The Kurds have taken the opportunity to push further south to extend their political and economic territory and build a buffer against ISIS. The Shia – who call both ISIS and the Kurds their enemy – are mobilising for a fight, their strategy as yet unclear. To further complicate matters, somewhere hidden in this mix of armed actors are US and Australian special forces, supporting and training various factions. Many of these armed actors follow the rules of war that work to protect civilians and allow free access to neutral humanitarian actors.

On the road to Sinjar, the man in black waves us forward with a casual flick of the hand. "We are good; we are good," Faisel says quietly, first in Arabic then in

English, as he slowly drives forward. They are Shia, he quickly explains before we reach the temporary checkpoint. "They know we are going to Sinjar, they know we are here to help their people." Based on an understanding of the context and its different actors, his reasoning focuses on the motivations of the gunmen. We are here to support "their" community, so are likely to be provided access. His reasoning is slightly different to mine, which follows the established Red Cross script of combatants respecting the neutrality and impartiality of the emblems and allowing access. Two days in the field, new to Iraq in particular and humanitarianism in times of war in general, this legal lens I have had repeated to me throughout my Red Cross career is how I view protection in armed conflict.

From this view, reflected across humanitarian scholarship and policy, it is the official frameworks that drive humanitarian protection in war. In this understanding, these laws limit the behaviour of armed actors towards civilians and provide access to neutral and impartial humanitarians. This state-based, legal approach to protection has remained relatively consistent over the years, slowly extending to accommodate intra-state conflicts and non-state armed actors. However, in today's wars these legal frameworks seem fundamentally at odds with the on-the-ground realities they are supposed to govern. This dissonance has only become more apparent as various non-state armed actors have increasingly asserted their authority, drawing on cultural and religious traditions that are often different to these Western inspired legal frameworks. Yet the international frameworks persist despite the myriad of contradictions and the buoyancy of a range of actors that have an uneasy relationship with these legal norms.

This book seeks to resolve this puzzle by studying the everyday negotiations of humanitarian protection in war-torn contexts. It seeks to explore the complex space between the humanitarian frameworks and protection outcomes that remain largely unseen. What happens between the official frameworks at one end, and protection outcomes at the other, where there exists a mix of different actors, interests and agendas? What if the key things that affect protection outcomes in contemporary conflicts are not only, or even primarily, the universal laws and principles? In this, my concern is *how* these frameworks operate in contemporary wars where civilian protection and relief are negotiated by a complex network of actors.

To this end, I will focus on the lived experiences of humanitarian workers who routinely grapple with these frameworks in real-world contexts. But first it is important to step back and examine the established understandings of how these international laws and principles work. This chapter will then go on to examine non-state armed actors, whose presence has proved so disruptive to these official frameworks, before outlining a critical perspective of humanitarian laws and protection outcomes in contemporary wars.

Humanitarian protection in war: the official story

The established humanitarian protection philosophy is based on international law and the state system. International humanitarian law (IHL), international refugee law (IRL) and international human rights law (IHRL) form the central pillars of the array of legal frameworks that guide the behaviour of actors during times of war to protect the lives of non-combatants. In simple terms, these laws limit the behaviour of armed actors towards civilians and promote access for neutral and impartial humanitarian relief. At the local level, humanitarians fill a central role, disseminating these laws to ensure they are widely understood, conducting humanitarian advocacy to bring actors into line with these laws and providing neutral, impartial relief to affected communities in line with the provisions of the law. These laws are seen as universal, with the Geneva Conventions commonly cited as being ratified by 196 countries and being applicable to all actors, all the time. Similarly, a growing array of human rights instruments relevant to protection in armed conflict are promoted as universal.

IHL is the most significant body of law relating to civilian protection in war. The four Geneva Conventions of 1949 form the central foundation of these laws, protecting wounded soldiers, the shipwrecked, prisoners of war and civilians, respectively.[1] These four Conventions are supplemented by the two Additional Protocols of 1977 which incorporate non-international armed conflicts and non-state armed actors into the frameworks.[2] They have been gradually complemented by an array of other IHL treaties banning particular weapons and methods of war.[3] These laws are rooted in the universal legal norms of restraint, restricting the means and methods of war by clarifying standards of appropriate conduct. A set of legal principles underpin these efforts, notably distinction, proportionality and precaution. According to the principle of distinction, those engaged in armed conflict must distinguish between legitimate targets (combatants) and those not taking part in the fight (civilians). Proportionality seeks to reduce the risks to civilians by requiring that the means and methods of an attack are proportional to the anticipated military advantage. Precaution requires that combatants take into account the presence of civilians in order to avoid, or at least minimise, harm.[4]

While IHL protects non-combatants in war, IRL focuses more specifically on the protection of refugees, including those displaced by war. Originally a response to the mass displacement in Europe following World War II, refugee law expanded in scope as the problem of displacement spread around the world. The 1951 Refugee Convention and its 1967 Additional Protocol define who is a refugee, articulate the rights of refugees, and assign a set of obligations to states. Under these laws – particularly the underlying principle of non-refoulement – a state cannot force a refugee or asylum seeker to return to the country where they are liable to be persecuted. Furthermore, the convention sets out the minimum standards for the treatment of refugees, including the basic social and economic rights to which they are entitled.

IRL is a subset of IHRL, which lays down the obligations of states towards citizens and others within their jurisdiction. Traditionally, IHRL was seen as distinct from IHL, the former protecting people from abuses of power, the latter regulating the conduct of armed actors during times of war. However, there has increasingly been a recognition that IHRL complements the protections provided by IHL, with the two legal frameworks applying concurrently (see, e.g., Droege,

2007, p. 316). This appears specifically in the growing array of human rights conventions that are pertinent to protection in armed conflict.[5] In addition to this treaty-based international law, the 1948 Universal Declaration of Human Rights includes a number of articles relevant to humanitarian protection, many of which are now considered customary law and hence binding on all states.

In simple terms, this interrelated set of legal and normative frameworks can be understood as an agreement between key actors. They represent a codification of agreed behaviour when interstate politics evolves into armed conflict. First, they recognise that the obligations of states and the rights of individuals outlined in international law also apply in times of armed conflict. Furthermore, under these agreed rules of war, combatants are to show restraint, and civilians are to be left alone, provided they do not take part in the conflict.

A small but significant component of this agreement is the right of humanitarian organisations to promote the protection of civilians and provide assistance. The ethical framework known as the humanitarian principles, in particular the well-known ideas of impartiality, neutrality and independence, represent humanitarianism's side of this agreement.[6] The argument goes that armed actors will honour their side of the agreement and provide access to populations at risk if humanitarians honour the principles of political neutrality and impartiality. That is to say they generate access through "a 'deal' whereby the belligerents agree to respect humanitarian principles, and humanitarians will not interfere in conflicts" (Leader, 2000, p. 2). Essentially, the principles of impartiality, neutrality and independence combine to construct an environment in which humanitarians can operate – a humanitarian space.

Mandated humanitarian agencies and protection

These international laws and humanitarian principles have a direct bearing on how humanitarian agencies carry out protection and underly the general preference for legalistic approaches and arguments. The International Committee of the Red Cross (ICRC) and the United Nations High Commissioner for Refugees (UNHCR) – arguably the two most important humanitarian agencies engaged in protection – have specific mandates that are legally recognised by states. The legal mandate of the ICRC is derived from the Geneva Conventions and Additional Protocol 1, while the legal mandate of the UNHCR is derived from IRL. Furthermore, these laws are not restricted to their "owners", for, as discussed in more detail below, they also guide the protection practices of humanitarian-focused international non-government organisations (INGOs).

Within this protection philosophy it is possible to identify a range of practices aimed at protecting people from violence in armed conflict.[7] The ICRC's core protection work consists of reducing the threat of violence posed by armed actors to civilians and mitigating the consequences of violence through the provision of humanitarian relief. As the ICRC's protection policy states: "Protection relates firstly to the causes of, or the circumstances that lead to, violations – mainly by addressing those responsible for the violations and those who may have influence over the latter – and secondly to their consequences" (ICRC, 2008, p. 752). These efforts to reduce violence against civilians primarily involves changing the behaviour of armed actors, the key instigators of violence. In the immediate context, this focuses on increasing compliance with IHL, which it primarily does through bilateral, confidential dialogue with armed actors (see Bradley, 2016).

Beyond these efforts to change the immediate behaviour of armed groups, the ICRC seeks to change attitudes towards IHL, in particular increasing respect for the laws and related humanitarian principles, and ultimately fostering a broader understanding of what constitutes appropriate behaviour (see, e.g., Bradley, 2016; Ratner, 2011). This emerges in the form of dissemination, an ICRC term that encapsulates efforts to build knowledge of IHL among armed groups in the understanding that this will influence attitudes towards what constitutes appropriate behaviour. Furthermore, as part of its mandate the ICRC works to develop and expand the legal framework to incorporate new actors and contexts. As Bradley explains: "The ICRC emphasizes the development of IHL for the very reason that an agreed legal framework is expected to improve combatant behaviour, and hence to yield more effective protection outcomes for civilians" (p. 93).

While the ICRC seeks primarily to reduce the level of threat posed by armed actors to civilians, the UNHCR sees this as being outside its remit. It focuses instead on reducing vulnerability to violence and to mitigating the consequences of displacement (see Bradley, 2016). Vulnerability to all kinds of threats depends largely on location, thus encouraging and facilitating mobility is one way to reduce civilian vulnerability. In practical terms, this involves efforts to educate individuals about their rights and to persuade states to meet their responsibilities to displaced people. As Bradley goes on to explain in her examination of the two mandated agencies, UNHCR officials invariably prefer legal arguments in their efforts to change state behaviour, turning to relevant international and domestic laws. Like the ICRC, the UNHCR complements these persuasion and education efforts with humanitarian relief, providing material assistance to facilitate movement away from violence and to mitigate the consequences of displacement.

INGOs and protection

To a large extent, INGOs reflect the protection strategies and objectives of the two mandated agencies (see Barnett, 2005; Leader, 2000). Like the ICRC and the UNHCR, these organisations see relief as part of their protection practices, providing material assistance and services such as healthcare to mitigate the immediate consequences of violence. They also follow the UNHCR in its efforts to alleviate the violence, facilitating movement away from the violence and collaborating in camp management. Furthermore, many INGOs have adopted a version of the traditional dissemination and compliance functions of the ICRC and UNHRC, educating people of their rights under international law and reminding states of their responsibilities through the use of immediate and long-term advocacy (see Slim & Bonwick, 2005, pp. 84–87). While the use of more robust forms of advocacy to bring pressure on governments and armed actors clearly differs from the confidential dialogue of the ICRC, the focus on promoting compliance with international law remains consistent.

This is reflected in the widely agreed working definition, which outlines how protection encompasses "all activities aimed at ensuring the full respect for the rights of the individual in accordance with the letter and the spirit of the relevant bodies of law (i.e. human rights law, humanitarian law and refugee law.)" (Caverzasio, 2001, p. 19). Protection-focused INGOs largely embrace this legal understanding in their policies. For the International Rescue Committee (IRC), protection involves all activities aimed at ensuring full respect for the rights of the individual in accordance with international humanitarian law, refugee law and human rights law. For the Norwegian Refugee Council (NRC), protection of refugees and the internally displaced involves "protection of rights pursuant to internationally accepted conventions, principles and standards". For *Médicins Sans Frontières* (MSF), protection is about ensuring freedom from violence, abuse and deliberate neglect in accordance with international law (see O'Callaghan & Pantuliano, 2007, p. 2).

Similarly, while there has been an evolution towards a more open political engagement among some humanitarian actors, it is not as extensive a change as many argue. Rather, this apolitical cover remains an important part of humanitarianism, with most protection-focused agencies signing onto the ground rules outlined in the humanitarian principles. Some may adapt the language. In a more flexible interpretation of the humanitarian principles, MSF maintains the discourse of neutrality, while "bearing witness" to acts of violence against civilians. Others may advocate for change on the global stage, while maintaining the semantics of neutrality and independence as part of their relief operations. As Davey (2012) explains in her historical analysis of the sector, the humanitarian system as it stands today remains heavily influenced by the International Red Cross and Red Crescent Movement. "The core principles of humanitarian action – humanity, impartiality, neutrality and independence – have become a central component of the system's collective identity and are seen as a key to its ability to respond effectively" (p. 2).

Protection and non-state armed actors

To reiterate, the humanitarian protection frameworks are based on a set of rights and responsibilities set out in IHL, IRL and IHRL. Under this global architecture, the state bears primary responsibility to protect all those who reside in its jurisdiction. If a state is unwilling or unable to do so, this responsibility to protect falls to the international community of states as members of the UN and parties to the Geneva Conventions. These laws and conventions also confer a set of protection responsibilities on mandated agencies, such as the ICRC and the UNHCR.

Furthermore, in times of armed conflict all armed parties are bound by IHL and hold legal protection responsibilities for those people within the territory they control (see ICRC, 2009, pp. 29–30). This appears in the Geneva Conventions, which have been gradually extended to incorporate internal conflicts and non-state armed actors. Internal armed conflicts were incorporated into the Geneva Conventions in 1949 through Article 3 of the Third Geneva Convention. In 1977, Additional Protocol I provided that wars of national liberation would be considered as international armed conflicts and Additional Protocol II added further rules and language to incorporate non-state armed groups into the framework. Statements of customary law have also contributed to efforts to incorporate non-state armed actors into the protection frameworks. Like the treaties, the rules of customary IHL address the protection of people who are not part of the fight. A rule is deemed customary, and as such binding on all state and non-state armed actors, if it is based on widespread practice supporting the requirement of the rule. Finally, the increased focus on human rights law has brought multiple new actors into the protection architecture. These rights are promoted as universal, with both state and non-state actors having a responsibility to respect them.

Non-state armed actors and restraint

On one level, there is merit to this understanding of non-state actors behaving like states. Some of the literature on insurgent organisations argues that these entities should be seen as states in all but name or states in waiting. In this insurgent as state-builder model, non-state armed actors do not necessarily set out to challenge the international system, but aspire to become part of it, building political institutions, establishing a level of political order and delivering services to the population (see, e.g., Arjona et al., 2015; Caspersen, 2012). In an apparent sign of the effectiveness of the normative frameworks, rebel movements often sign up to the same international protective mechanisms as states (see Jackson, 2016; Stanton, 2016). The highly disciplined Peshmerga controlling the borders of the autonomous zone of Iraq is but one clear example, having publicly committed to international norms that promote civilian protection (see MERI, 2016).

Armed actors in contemporary conflicts, however, do not necessarily fit neatly into these descriptions. Rather, there are tremendous variations in patterns of behaviour across today's wars, with armed actors identified as much by their variable identities and actions as identifiable consistencies (see Kalyvas, 2006; Staniland, 2012). In the words of Kalyvas (2003), a leading researcher into insurgent violence, "civil wars are not binary conflicts but complex and ambiguous processes that foster an apparently massive, though variable, mix of identities and actions – to such a degree as to be defined by that mix" (p. 475). Returning to our present predicament as a case in point, the Peshmerga, Shia militia and ISIS are vastly different actors in a single conflict space. Furthermore, while there may be some similarities across conflicts, there are also many differences in armed groups fighting around the world today, whether it is anti-government rebels in South America, Christian and Muslim militias facing off in north Africa, or Taliban militants in Afghanistan. Importantly, there is a degree of dissonance between the political, cultural and religious traditions these non-state armed actors assert and the Western-inspired frameworks that guide humanitarian protection.

As a consequence, the established protection frameworks, with their state-based legal tradition, are less relevant in contemporary wars fought by non-state armed actors. These actors selectively accept or transgress these legal frameworks according to the circumstances, sometimes following the established laws, while at other times asserting strategic, political or cultural justifications to target civilians, manipulate relief aid and deny humanitarian access. As research into insurgent violence and rebel governance suggests, these decisions are often driven by underlying logics, calculated to meet insurgents' immediate and long-term goals (see Kalyvas, 2006; Metelits, 2010; Staniland, 2012). For Kalyvas, violence against civilians is the product of rational actions by insurgent organisations and civilians working to fulfil their interests within a given territorial space. Staniland writes of how bargains and tacit understandings influence the level of violence as states and insurgents manoeuvre to achieve tactical goals. He also emphasises that patterns of violence may change over time as a result of interactions with other groups, including enemy organisations and civilian communities.

In this spectrum, restraint, too, has its own underlying logic, designed to advance institutional goals rather than being a direct response to humanitarian norms and principles. On a tactical level, restraint can be part of a reciprocal deal between states and insurgents, where warring parties share or assign territory in order to minimise joint damage. During these times, "violence is deployed along particular boundaries and capped at certain levels as part of a cooperative (though not harmonious) relationship" (Staniland, 2012, p. 250). Reciprocity also emerges as a key driver of restraint towards civilians. As Metelits (2010) explains, there are times when rebel groups seek a more reciprocal relationship with civilians, providing goods and services to host communities in return for resources and support. When not faced with competition from other armed actors, this "contractual" relationship with civilians can prove more efficient over the long term than the use of violence and coercion (Metelits, 2010, pp. 26–27).

Restraint can also be driven by a long-term need for legitimacy and community collaboration. For as insurgents are only too aware, legitimacy can bring support and acknowledgment from the international community, reduce the authority of rival state and non-state actors and, importantly, build and sustain acceptance from the local community they seek to govern and tax. Evidence suggests that those insurgent organisations that deliberately violate or ignore this social contract with the community lack long-term stability and eventually "crumble away after brief periods or stagnate for years" (Schlichte, 2009, p. 16). In fact, rather than violence and coercion, establishing "civilian collaboration is often *the* central immediate concern for the warring sides in a civil war" (Arjona et al., 2015, p. 3, emphasis in the original).

These top-down motivations of reciprocity, legitimacy and community support emerge from the social and political interactions between various institutional actors, particularly insurgents, civilians, state rivals and international organisations. However, armed groups are more than institutions. They are made up of ensembles of independent individuals, social groups and less structured collectives who bring with them norms that are opposed to violence and coercion.

Clearly, the strength of the institution is central to the influence of these norms and can override them if they are only held by a small number of individuals. However, the institution itself may also endorse and reinforce such norms. In fact, no matter how radical a political movement, its practices are embedded in the historically contingent values, norms, beliefs and forms of governance of the community they have emerged from. Thus, they tend to draw on these same community norms and values, and publicly demonstrate their support for them. Indeed, rebel groups that disregard these community norms put their legitimacy and long-term viability at risk since they are likely to lose the necessary community support, intelligence, taxes, supplies and labour (Kalyvas, 2006, pp. 174–176).

Yet in the face of these shifting drivers of violence and restraint, the basic assumptions of international law and humanitarian principles as the universal protection mechanism are rarely questioned by scholars and policy makers. Furthermore, the legal mechanisms which guided the protection practices of the ICRC and the UNHCR in their early years continue to guide their approaches in contemporary wars and engagement with non-state armed actors. As Bradley (2016) explains, "To a great extent both organizations have replicated the means, methods, and understandings of protection from older issue-areas within their mandates to new ones" (pp. 23–24). Adding to this hegemony, conflict focused humanitarian and human rights organisations essentially reflect the protection practices of these two mandated agencies, largely adopting their frameworks, principles and practices. Ultimately humanitarian protection remains heavily influenced by a system designed to regulate international armed conflict and state actors.

Behind the official story

At one level, the consistency of this official approach to humanitarian protection in the face of the changing nature of conflict is the result of the instrumental view that dominates the sector and is pursued by most researchers and policy makers. Theirs is a rational approach, which identifies problems and then returns to the established literature and resources to find solutions (see, e.g., Caverzasio, 2001; Niland & Polastro, 2015; O'Callaghan & Pantuliano, 2007; Slim & Bonwick, 2005). Indeed, the more complex situations become, the more effort goes into nuancing and extending these frameworks. In what Cox (1981) describes as problem solving theory, which he contrasts to critical theory, getting the established frameworks right is seen as the key to addressing failures and improving these frameworks the solution to problems faced in contemporary wars. However, while this problem-solving approach has an important role to play, it does not deal with the structures that underpin the technical problems that are being addressed (see also Christie, 2015, pp. 38–41).

It is the humanitarian equivalent of the policy trap reflected in the work of scholars in related fields. Murray Li (2007) articulates this particularly well in her examination of state bureaucrats and their practice of "rendering technical", or the framing of complex political problems in a way that lends to technical fixes that do not necessarily address root causes. In her examination of state-run development, she describes a cycle of identifying problems through the lens of the available solutions, and then responding with those same established technical mechanisms. Similarly, Mosse (2005) highlights the preoccupation among development agencies and researchers with generating the right policy models to drive development programs at the expense of examining the relationships between these models and complex local practices.

At another level, this consistent response to new contexts is a result of the powerful discourse that the humanitarian frameworks are intimately bound up in, which Dunn (2010) describes as the discourse of "state-ness". In this state discourse, politics revolves around the relations between states, state entities hold the monopoly on the legitimate use of violence and it is international legal frameworks that are the appropriate mechanisms for limiting this violence.[8] The dominance of this discourse limits the field of view of many scholars and policy makers, ensuring they repeatedly return to the established tools when faced with new challenges and problems. Because of this narrow gaze, the end-point of even the best investigations into the seemingly eternal "humanitarian crisis" or of "humanitarianism under attack" almost inevitably call for official frameworks and principles to be bolstered or extended (see, e.g., de Torrente, 2004; Rieff, 2002). As Dunn explains in his comparable research on discourse and international development, the uncritical acceptance of this "universal", "common sense" approach has limited our ability to understand alternative points of authority and conceive relevant strategies.

Ultimately, the strength of the powerful state discourse and the instrumental approach favoured by humanitarian policy makers and researchers has left us with a limited conceptualisation of humanitarian protection. It remains a product of the European state system, invested in international norms and a set of universal principles (see Rostis, 2016). Things beyond the scope of this view are rendered out of bounds. In this partial view, it is the protection frameworks that promote protection outcomes. But there remains the black box between official humanitarian frameworks at one end and the real-life effect of these frameworks at the other, which conceals how these frameworks are implemented in everyday practice.

The relationship between these two, or more specifically how the frameworks actually work to promote humanitarian protection, has received little attention. Importantly, people are also not highlighted in this research space of legal frameworks and universal principles. Individual actors, the people who occupy this space between the protection frameworks at one end and protection outcomes at the other, are granted little agency.[9] It is the legal mechanisms that provide for civilian protection. Humanitarians are supporting characters, envisioned as relatively passive figures implementing and disseminating the rules as they were devised.

While the instrumental view has dominated humanitarian protection scholarship, other areas of study have extended their gaze and examined similar relationships and the roles various actors play, with productive results. In his seminal study, Mosse (2005) upends the common image that policy shapes how development is done. Instead, the image that appears in his book *Cultivating Development* is of development projects driven by a complex network of actors, each endowed with their own agency. Policy, rather than driving development projects, is seen as a form of narrative glue that unifies this complex network of actors, aligning often competing agendas. Development consultants play a central role in sustaining this unifying narrative that mobilises support and maintains the networks that drive a project. Murray Li (2007) follows a similar tradition. Taking a broader, more historic approach than Mosse, her study examines the inherent contradictions and tensions in contemporary development and the multiple interactions that take place in the development encounter at a national level. Her book, *The Will to Improve,* reveals how development structures retain the limitations of the colonial programs they replace and how people creatively and consistently make space for themselves among these structures. My research follows this tradition, setting out to fill a similar research gap in humanitarian protection scholarship, exploring the relationship between the official frameworks that seek to guide the protection of civilians and the way that protection efforts actually take shape in practice.

Methods and concepts

This study follows in the methodological tradition of "new ethnographies of development" (Mosse, 2005, p. 11). This scholarship sees international development as a complex set of interactions at both the global and local level, involving actors of differing status with varying resources and often competing goals. These scholars have revealed these complex relationships by exploring development on multiple fronts. First, they have engaged with development instrumentally, as anthropologist consultants, applied researchers and program evaluators, examining the institutions and policy frameworks that seemingly guide practice. It is a comparable view to that which dominates much of humanitarian protection scholarship today. They have, however, partnered this with a non-instrumental perspective, examining the social process of policy and the informal relationships and real-life situations of development workers (Lewis & Mosse, 2006). These hidden processes in development have been revealed through the insider's perspective provided by ethnographic field research.

The ethnographic perspective

My research applies this ethnographic gaze to humanitarian protection in order to explore the tensions that exist between the official protection frameworks and the real-world context in which they are implemented. It uses the international humanitarian aid worker – who occupies a pivotal place between official frameworks and their local impact – as the primary focus for examining that link. The everyday practices of these actors were revealed through personal observations in the field, made possible through my own professional experiences as an aid worker. This ethnographic fieldwork was carried out in northern Iraq during the battle for Mosul – some two years after our encounter with Shia militia on the road to Sinjar – and then later in Geneva, the so-called home of the humanitarian frameworks. These personal insights and observations were then complemented by interviews with some 40 humanitarian protection workers experienced in other conflicts in order to further explore the wider contextual complexities the humanitarian frameworks are meant to deal with.[10]

With the insider's view provided by participant observation, this research is able to move beyond the question of *whether* the protection frameworks are working – the domain of normative scholarship – to reveal *how* they are interpreted and used by practitioners in the field. By borrowing these research tools from the anthropological discipline, it is able to build an understanding of relationships that were previously obscured or silenced by the fixation on frameworks and then articulate these through real-world examples and detailed narratives.

Theoretical frameworks

Importantly, these new ethnographers of development have taken their investigations beyond "thick description" (Geertz, 1973, p. 3) and detailed narratives. They have combined these revealing traits of ethnographic observation with critical theory analysis. My work continues this amalgamation of critical theory and ethnographic observation, drawing on many of the same theoretical foundations that have guided these ethnographers. At one level these scholars have been informed by the work of Foucault, analysing development as a discourse that limits the description of development and what constitutes appropriate action. Foucault's conceptualisation of discourse and power in relation to the development context is perhaps more clearly articulated through the work of Ferguson (1994), who uses it to argue that development institutions generate their own form of discourse. In a retrograde logic, this "anti-politics" discourse turns a society's complex political realities into technical problems appropriate for a development solution. This Foucauldian view sees development as a historically specific discourse of power, which serves to universalise the Western experience and project it onto the rest of the world (see Lewis & Mosse, 2006).

While providing important critical insights into development, the Foucauldian framework of analysis used by authors such as Ferguson (1994) has been criticised for tending to see development as a homogenising, disciplinary power. It fails to acknowledge that hegemonic power is never total, but is rather an ongoing contest with multiple actors, albeit of different status. For as Murray Li (2007) explains, the "fragmentory experiences, attachments, and embedded cultural ideas" of local populations do not simply disappear in the face of an all-powerful development discourse, but remain as a source of ongoing tension, undertaking a form of resistance to the imposed order (p. 22). These local actors retain a level of agency, which, while not the main concern of most Foucauldian scholars, has been the focus of many anthropologists. Taking a bottom-up perspective provided by fieldwork, these anthropologists and development sociologists have long highlighted the continued significance of individual agency, arguing that actors use their social networks and their discourses as resources to "process information and strategize in their dealings with various local actors as well as with outside institutions and personnel" (Long & van der Ploeg, 1994, p. 64).

Like their predecessors, new ethnographers of development have emphasised individual agency and the relationships between multiple actors. Mosse (2005), a leading advocate of this form of ethnography, places the development actor at the centre of his investigation of policy and practice. The picture he paints in *Cultivating Development* is not the image of the monolithic and all-powerful development industry described by Ferguson (1994), but rather a fragmented, complex affair in which actors at all levels are endowed with agency. However, in introducing agency, Mosse and his ilk have not abandoned the discursive effect of the "anti-politics machine", but instead subject it to a variety of opposing forces (see Lewis & Mosse, 2006). In this view, individuals are not only influenced by the structures in which they work, as Ferguson (1994) suggests, but their actions can also contribute to changing and adapting those same structures. My research, in essence an ethnography of humanitarian protection, takes a similar theoretical position, acknowledging both discursive power and individual agency. In this I join Mosse (2005) in turning to more recent examinations of agency and everyday practice for my theoretical foundations, notably de Certeau (1984) and Scott (1990).[11]

A critical view of humanitarian protection

To reiterate, the question this research seeks to address is *how* protection works in contemporary conflicts. This book challenges the assumption that the official frameworks drive humanitarian protection in today's conflicts in the normative sense. That conceptualisation sees protection as the direct result of international norms, or standards of behaviour defined in terms of specific rights and obligations, for which violation carries a price. These norms are underpinned by a series of rules, the specific application of norms in particular situations (see Boas, 2012). Instead, this book builds an alternative vision of how protection works in a line of argument that consists of four steps. First, humanitarian protection is driven by the relationships that develop among the complex network of actors who occupy the humanitarian arena, including states, their militaries, insurgent organisations, aid organisations and the affected communities themselves, among others. Protection occurs when these actors are able to reach a mutually beneficial consensus on an appropriate behaviour towards civilians. Sustaining this relationship and its benefits, which outweigh other needs and goals, is what drives protection, rather than the legal frameworks in their traditional sense.

This is not to say the frameworks do not matter. Rather, it is not the role that we have long assumed they held, a set of international rules to be followed, or prosecuted if obligations are not met. Instead, the frameworks act as the foundation of this mutually beneficial consensus, presenting a broad agreement on what is appropriate behaviour and thus establishing and sustaining the relationships that drive protection. With this in mind, I reconceptualise these humanitarian frameworks and principles as a *unifying narrative* that enrols different actors into the *protection network*, linking their agendas to that of humanitarian protection.

These actors are tied into the network for different reasons. As critical analysts of policy discourse have argued, a simple, coherent narrative on its own can be a powerful force in creating a level of consensus among disparate actors (see, e.g., Mosse, 2005; Roe, 1994). Like the policy narratives outlined by Mosse and Roe, the protection narrative's strength lies in a simplicity and vagueness that can be accepted by diverse actors, as well as tied in with a dissemination (or advocacy) strategy that recruits and retains new actors. In this we can reflect on the Geneva Conventions and the universal humanitarian principles, which, for all the legal arguments, are relatively easy to explain. With this in mind, in a second step, I argue that humanitarians have long acted as the official disseminators of this official narrative, reifying its norms and principles through constant repetition and performance. Historically, these dissemination efforts, a role recognised in the frameworks themselves, tied state actors to the established narrative. These official dissemination efforts have extended over recent decades in an effort to recruit non-state actors into the narrative.

Yet, this is not the only response to the increasingly complicated mix of actors who are asserting their authority in the so-called "new wars" (Kaldor, 2006). In a third step, I go on to argue that humanitarians have helped to extend the protection network beyond its state-based actors through unofficial practices. Some humanitarian disseminators take up another role, acting as unofficial brokers, who travel throughout the humanitarian network, translating the official frameworks in order for them to align with the often-competing agenda of non-state armed actors. In other words, they take the legal concepts that form the foundation of the protection narrative and translate them to make them more relevant to the diverse actors they encounter in the humanitarian arena. This process seeks to overcome dissent among actors with political and cultural beliefs that are at odds with the state-based protection frameworks, without undermining the frameworks themselves.

Finally, I argue that these unofficial practices have allowed the established humanitarian protection frameworks to be sufficiently successful in contemporary wars to ensure that they remain the focus for state and humanitarian actors. They are in essence an unofficial humanitarian fix to the challenges of transferring these official frameworks to contemporary wars where the traditional institutions of power these frameworks rely on are weak. This notion of a humanitarian fix has both literal and metaphorical significance. In the literal sense, the humanitarian fix resolves the challenges of applying the humanitarian principles in contemporary contexts. In doing so, the unofficial fix does not replace the official frameworks. Rather it resolves these inevitable contextual challenges without undermining the "universal" frameworks and their power in more traditional contexts. Furthermore, like the metaphorical meaning of Harvey's (1982) trademark "spatial fix", from where the terminology has been borrowed, the resolution achieved by the humanitarian fix is temporary and needs to be reapplied in each successive context.[12]

To initially understand the nature of these translations that are part of this fix we can reflect on the thoughts of Faisal, the Shia driver, who sees the militia acting according to an agenda that benefits their community, rather than any legal norms that were at the front of my mind, fresh from Geneva. The militia at the checkpoint are making a reasoned decision, rather than responding to any legal dissemination effort or the universal norms. The immediate results, however, are the same: after a brief conversation about who we are, where we are going and what we are doing, the Shia gunman waves us through the checkpoint and on to Sinjar.

How this story unfolds

In this chapter, I have put forward the reasons why this study is warranted, and established an alternative way of examining humanitarian protection. In building this account, the rest of this book is presented in two parts – the first conceptual, the second ethnographic.

Chapter 2 – the stepping off point for Part I – provides a critical history of humanitarian protection in war, unpacking the established discourse to allow us to proceed from a fresh premise. Here we will see that the concepts of nation state, war and humanitarian protection have long worked together as a Eurocentric package. In other words, the history, sociology and legal philosophy of European nation states at war provide the conceptual apparatus for the study of war and humanitarianism in general and humanitarian protection in particular. It will in part turn to scholars who have engaged with post-colonial theory to explain why these frameworks remain faithful to a Eurocentric way of thinking; their almost universal adoption among humanitarian agencies is the result of a powerful discourse derived from Western experience (see Barkawi, 2016; Megret, 2006; Young, 2001).

Chapter 3 provides the foundations of an alternative way to view the complex world of humanitarian protection. It is a world reflected in the work of many development scholars, who see international development as a complex set of local, national and cross-cultural social interactions (Lewis & Mosse, 2006; Mosse, 2005). This chapter discusses further the works of these development ethnographers, which will form the foundations to move beyond the official narratives of humanitarian protection, examine the agency of humanitarian actors and build an understanding of the role they have in the broader humanitarian network. Drawing from Mosse's (2005) seminal ethnography of development policy and practice and related critical theorists (de Certeau, 1984; Scott, 1990), I build a three-tiered conceptualisation of humanitarian protection. First, humanitarian protection is a category of practice; it is shaped through the interaction among a complex group of actors. Second, the humanitarian frameworks and principles help build a level of consensus and establish relationships to ultimately provide what we know as humanitarian protection to at-risk groups. In other words, they are a unifying narrative. Finally, humanitarians, positioned at the junctures between these different actors, play a central role in sustaining this unifying narrative, modifying its meaning according to the context.

The next three chapters – Part II of the book – are the result of ethnographic fieldwork in Iraq and Geneva and interviews with humanitarian workers from conflicts around the world. Chapter 4 begins this ethnographic journey across Iraq in particular, and humanitarian protection in general, by exploring the official representation of these humanitarians. In this official role, they can be viewed as neutral intermediaries, disseminating the universal laws and principles as they have been laid out. Whether through constant repetition of the message or performance of their prescribed role, these actors work to reify the abstract concept of humanitarian space intended to bring order to international armed conflicts. The chapter then goes on to explore how non-state armed actors – who bring competing strategic, political and cultural agendas to those of the state-based frameworks – have disrupted these efforts, increasingly targeting civilians and denying humanitarian access.

Chapter 5 discusses how humanitarians have responded to this complex mix of actors that selectively transgress the official humanitarian frameworks. Rather than solely acting as the intermediaries of the previous chapter, transporting meaning without transformation, humanitarians also act as brokers or active mediators. These brokers translate the official discourse of the protection frameworks in a way that makes them relevant to the multitude of actors that occupy the humanitarian arena. They do this by turning to comparative reasoned, moral and cultural arguments that represent both the foundations of the normative frameworks and the motivations and belief systems of actors who are not historically part of this Western, legal tradition. They are in essence an unofficial *humanitarian fix* to the challenges of transferring these official frameworks to contemporary wars where the traditional institutions of power these frameworks rely on are weak.

Chapter 6 explores travelling and its functional effects on the humanitarian figure, both as intermediary and broker. It considers this mobility and its established place in the humanitarian endeavour through three interrelated ideas: the international humanitarian traveller; the solidly set local staff they rely upon; and "the field" where they work, which is defined in opposition to "the centre".[13] This travel has significant structural effects, allowing international humanitarians to transfer knowledge across these two spaces, and casting them as the neutral and impartial outsider. However, a state of constant transience is also responsible for some of the most problematic aspects of the humanitarian sector, such as the common phenomenon of international expats imposing outside values and norms on a context they do not fully understand. Furthermore, travel works to sustain the power imbalance between the international humanitarian, expert in the official laws and principles, and local staff, who are cast in a supporting role despite the significance of their local knowledge for implementing the humanitarian fix.

Chapter 7 summarises the main arguments of the book and provides a discussion of the findings before going on to propose applied functions and possibilities for further research.

Notes

1 Originating with the Geneva Convention of 1864, which protected wounded soldiers, the four Conventions were significantly updated in 1949 following World War II.

2 The third Additional Protocol of 2005 relates to the emblems used by National Societies, introducing the red crystal as an alternative to the red cross and the red crescent.

3 These include the Mine Ban Treaty (1997), the Optional Protocol on the Involvement of Children in Armed Conflict (2000) and the Convention on Cluster Munitions (2008).

4 For a useful and concise breakdown of the relevant Articles of the Geneva Conventions and Additional Protocols, see Bradley (2016, pp. 71–72).

5 These instruments include: the Convention on the Prevention and Punishment of Genocide (1948); the Convention Relating to the Status of Refugees (1951); the Convention on the Elimination of All Forms of Discrimination Against Women (1979); the Convention Against Torture and Other Cruel, Inhuman or Degrading Treatment or Punishment (1984); the Convention on the Rights of the Child (1989); and the Rome Statute of the International Criminal Court (1998).

6 The four humanitarian principles are humanity, impartiality, neutrality and independence. The value of humanity represents the goal that humanitarian action sets out to achieve. Impartiality is an expression of the notions of universality and non-discrimination that sit at the heart of humanitarian action and is operationalised through objectivity and a needs-based response. Neutrality and independence in turn serve as practical measures to achieve this goal in the highly politicised environments of armed conflicts. Neutrality implies not favouring one side over the other in an armed conflict. The principle of independence is primarily about resisting the influence of outside forces, including state and international actors. If humanitarians can remain free from the influence of other actors, the argument goes, they can operate in an impartial manner.

7 The protection objectives and strategies referred to here and explored in this book are maximalist approaches, that is they are actively linked to reducing threats of violence, vulnerability to violence or mitigating its consequences. Other studies take a more minimalist approach, also framing protection in terms of efforts to avoid making the situation worse. Often referred to as protection mainstreaming, it is arguable that these minimalist approaches are "simply good assistance programming, and should not be labelled as protection" (see Bradley, 2016, p. 103).

8 I understand discourse as "ensemble[s] of ideas, concepts, and categories through which meaning is given to phenomena" (Gasper & Apthorpe, 1996, p. 2) or as "more or less coherent sets of references that frame the way we understand and act upon the world around us" (Hilhorst, 2003, p.8).

9 Some insightful observational studies have emerged in the broader field of humanitarian scholarship in recent years, including ethnographies of medical humanitarianism (Abramowitz & Panter-Brick, 2015) and Fast's (2014) account of violence against aid workers, based on more than a decade of first-hand experience in the field.

10 At the outset of this research, I focused on staff from the key mandated protection agencies ICRC and UNHCR, and the INGOs MSF and NRC. These were complemented with a few representatives from other protection agencies, notably UNICEF, Geneva Call and IRC to give a broader range of views. The eventual sample of aid workers provided further breadth as most of the field staff interviewed have experience with multiple agencies.

11 De Certeau's (1984) theory of "consumer practices" centres on the idea that people are not merely passive consumers of products imposed by a dominant order, but actively manipulate them through their everyday actions. To explain this power struggle, he makes a distinction between "strategies", the overarching frameworks of ruling

institutions, and "tactics", the individual actions of people operating inside those frameworks. Meanwhile, in his theory of everyday resistance, Scott (1990) thinks in terms of the largely concealed goals of subordinate actors, which exist as "hidden transcripts" alongside official, institutional goals, or "public transcripts".

12 Harvey's (1982) "spatial fix" both literally and metaphorically describes the different forms of spatial reorganisation that serve to temporarily manage crisis-tendencies of over accumulation. As Harvey explains, to fix a problem is to resolve a difficulty. But as in the case of the drug addict, the fix also implies that the resolution is temporary, since the need soon returns.

13 There is a need to explain at the outset that terms such "centre" and "field" are not used un-problematically. For the ease of some readers, I have made the stylistic decision to indicate these problematic terms, in the first instance only, with quotation marks.

References

Abramowitz, S., & Panter-Brick, C. (Eds.). (2015). *Medical humanitarianism: Ethnographies of practice.* University of Pennsylvania Press.

Arjona, A., Kasfir, N., & Mampilly, Z. (Eds.). (2015). *Rebel governance in civil war.* Cambridge University Press.

Barkawi, T. (2016). Decolonising war. *European Journal of International Security*, 1(2), 199–214.

Barnett, M. (2005). Humanitarianism transformed. *Perspectives in Politics*, 3(4), 723–740.

Boas, G. (2012). *Public international law: Contemporary principles and perspectives.* Edward Elgar.

Bradley, M. (2016). *Protecting civilians in war: The ICRC, UNHCR, and their limitations in internal armed conflict.* Oxford University Press.

Caspersen, N. (2012). *Unrecognised states.* Polity Press.

Caverzasio, S. (2001). *Strengthening protection in war.* ICRC.

Christie, R. (2015). Critical readings of humanitarianism. In R. MacGinty & J. Peterson (Eds.), *The Routledge companion to humanitarian action* (pp. 38–48). Routledge.

Cox, R. (1981). Social forces, states and world orders: Beyond international relations theory. *Millennium: Journal of International Studies*, 10(2), 126–155.

Davey, E. (2012). *New players through old lenses: Why history matters when engaging with Southern actors* (No. 48; HPG Policy Brief). Overseas Development Institute.

de Certeau, M. (1984). *The practice of everyday life.* University of California Press.

de Torrente, N. (2004). Humanitarian action under attack: Reflections on the Iraq war. *Harvard Human Rights Journal*, 17, 1–29.

Droege, C. (2007). The interplay between international humanitarian law and international human rights law in situations of armed conflict. *Israel Law Review*, 40(2), 310–355.

Dunn, K. (2010). There is no such thing as the state: Discourse, effect and performativity. *Forum for Development Studies*, 37(1), 79–92.

Fast, L. (2014). *Aid in danger: The perils and promise of humanitarianism.* University of Pennsylvania Press.

Ferguson, J. (1994). *The anti-politics machine: "Development," depoliticization, and bureaucratic power in Lesotho.* Cambridge University Press.

Gasper, D., & Apthorpe, R. (1996). Introduction: Discourse analysis and policy discourse. In R. Apthorpe & D. Gasper (Eds.), *Arguing development policy: Frames and discourses.* Frank Cass.

Geertz, C. (1973). *The interpretation of cultures: Selected essays.* Basic Books.

Harvey, D. (1982). *The limits of capital.* Basil Blackwell.

Hilhorst, D. (2003). *The real world of NGOs: Discourses diversity, and development.* Zed Books.

ICRC (2008). ICRC protection policy: Institutional policy. *International Review of the Red Cross*, 90(871), 751–775.

ICRC (2009). *Professional standards for protection work.* ICRC.

Jackson, A. (2016). *In their words: Perceptions of armed non-state actors on humanitarian action.* Geneva Call.

Kaldor, M. (2006). *New and old wars: Organised violence in a global era.* Stanford University.

Kalyvas, S. (2006). *The logic of violence in civil war.* Cambridge University Press.

Leader, N. (2000). *The politics of principle: The principles of humanitarian action in practice* (No. 2; HPG Report). Overseas Development Institute.

Lewis, D., & Mosse, D. (Eds.). (2006). *Development brokers and translators: The ethnography of aid and agencies.* Kumarian Press.

Long, N., & van der Ploeg, J. (1994). Heterogeneity, actor and structure: Towards a reconstitution of the concept of structure. In D. Booth (Ed.), *Rethinking social development: Theory, research and practice* (pp. 62–89). Longman.

Megret, F. (2006). From "savages" to "unlawful combatants": A postcolonial look at international humanitarian law's "Other." In A. Orford (Ed.), *International law and its others* (pp. 265–317). Cambridge University Press.

MERI (2016). *Compliance of armed forces with international humanitarian law.* Middle East Research Institute.

Metelits, C. (2010). *Inside insurgency: Violence, civilians, and revolutionary group behavior.* New York University Press.

Mosse, D. (2005). *Cultivating development: An ethnography of aid policy and practice.* Pluto Press.

Murray Li, T. (2007). *The will to improve: Governmentality, development and the practice of politics.* Drake University Press.

Niland, N., & Polastro, R. (2015). *Independent whole of system review of protection in the context of humanitarian action.* Inter-Agency Standing Committee.

O'Callaghan, S., & Pantuliano, S. (2007). *Protective action: Incorporating civilian protection into humanitarian response* (No. 29; HPG Policy Brief). Overseas Development Institute.

Ratner, S. (2011). Law promotion beyond law talk: The Red Cross, persuasion, and the laws of war. *European Journal of International Law*, 22(2), 459–506.

Rieff, D. (2002). Humanitarianism in crisis. *Foreign Affairs*, 81(6), 111–121.

Roe, E. (1994). *Narrative policy analysis: Theory and practice.* Duke University Press.

Rostis, A. (2016). *Organising disaster: The construction of humanitarianism.* Emerald Group.

Schlichte, K. (2009). *In the shadow of violence: The politics of armed groups.* Campus Verlag.

Scott, J. (1990). *Domination and the arts of resistance: Hidden transcripts.* Yale University Press.

Slim, H., & Bonwick, A. (2005). *Protection: An ALNAP guide for humanitarian agencies.* Overseas Development Institute.

Staniland, P. (2012). States, insurgents, and wartime political orders. *Perspectives on Politics*, 10(2), 243–264.

Stanton, J. (2016). *Violence and restraint in civil war: Civilian targeting in the shadow of international law.* Cambridge University Press.

Young, R. (2001). *Postcolonialism: An historical introduction.* Blackwell.

Part I

Critical history and theoretical framework

2 A contested history of humanitarian protection

Many contemporary accounts humanitarian protection convey the impression that it began with the Geneva Conventions, providing a relatively unproblematic history of these international laws and related principles. However, to fully understand humanitarian protection today, and to "decentre common sense" (Rostis, 2016, p. 12), it is important to first unpack this accepted history. It is in large part a Western history and a particularly European history rooted in colonialism and imperialism. This is not to say that these perspectives are wrong or misguided, but that they present only a singular view of war and the possible humanitarian responses. This view – originating from a specific place and time – has largely eclipsed all other ways of understanding and practicing protection. Echoing post-colonial scholars, the argument I make here is that humanitarian protection is inevitably understood and acted upon through Western perspectives. It is important that these preconceived understandings are relinquished at the outset of this project in order to advance from a fresh premise, which I take up in the following chapter. With this in mind, this chapter unpacks the accepted history of humanitarian protection in war, revealing how a highly specific protection philosophy became a universal endeavour. In doing so it aims to open the way for re-describing the concepts under scrutiny and, in turn, of rethinking what humanitarians are doing.

The discourse of war and the state

"Warfare is a cosmopolitan experience, a shared bane of humanity" (Barkawi, 2016, p. 199). It has existed throughout history, across cultures and in many different forms. Independent warlords around the world long ruled their fiefdoms by virtue of their capacity to wage war. Pirates, mercenaries and bandits are hardly a novel feature of contemporary wars, having historically fought empires and sustained themselves and their communities through different forms of violence. Pre-colonial Africa, with its highly complex concepts of territory and power, had its own typologies of war before the colonisers arrived with their gunboats. Yet in social and political inquiry today, war is a concept imagined primarily in provincial terms, in particular those of the West and its major wars. "Real war is interstate war between nation-states, fought between regular forces" (Barkawi, 2016, p. 199).

This position that the state claims a monopoly over the legitimate use of organised violence is the product of one of the most powerful discourses in Western society, the discourse of the state. Emanating out of Europe as part of the process of colonisation, this powerful state discourse effectively eclipsed all other ways of understanding the world and its social interactions.[1] In this dominant understanding, international politics revolved around relations between states. In turn, war was a state activity, used in the pursuit of state interests, and states held a monopoly of the legitimate use of violence. Other forms of organised violence that have emerged, or re-emerged, are articulated in ways that sustain this established understanding of war. The civil wars that followed decolonisation were the first to be trimmed to fit this dominant state discourse, understood as political phenomena where non-state armed actors attempted to supplant the recognised state. Today, wars are seen as derivatives of these state or non-state categories, whether new or old civil wars, small wars, insurgencies, interventions or uprisings (see, e.g., Kaldor, 2006; Keen, 2012). Meanwhile, those forms of violence that cannot be manipulated into this discourse are distinguished as criminal, rather than political, phenomena (Kalyvas, 2001).

Humanitarian protection and the state

What does this state discourse and this highly particular understanding of war mean for modern humanitarianism and its response to contemporary wars? As Barkawi (2016) explains, this discourse has informed basic categories and vocabularies of social and political inquiry across a range of disciplines. This includes humanitarian protection. There has been a tendency for humanitarian scholars to focus on the ideological nature of war, which sees insurgents and rebel organisations as proto-states or states-in-the-making, a variation of the recognised entity that they aim to replace. They have a political agenda, enjoy a level of popular support and have an element of control over acts of violence. This has facilitated efforts to fit renegade conflicts into the established state approach to humanitarian protection. As discussed in Chapter 1, the protection frameworks that limit behaviour in war have been gradually extended to encompass internal conflicts and non-state armed actors, while humanitarian organisations have largely carried over existing protection practices to these so-called new wars.

Here I argue that the concepts of nation state, war and humanitarian protection work together as a Eurocentric package. This understanding reflects much of post-colonial theory, which examines the way in which European ideas inform vocabularies and categories used by social and political thought today (see, e.g., Cooper, 2005; Stoler, 1989; Young, 2001). Post-colonial theory suggests that colonialism was such a powerful force that it has spread European practices and discourses over the broad sweep of time. Indeed, "the values of colonialism have seeped much more widely into the general culture … than ever had been assumed" (Young, 2001, p. 6). As part of this process, protection frameworks that date back to 19th-century Europe remain central to modern approaches to humanitarianism broadly, and humanitarian protection in particular, as it is practiced around the world. As Rostis (2016) contends, humanitarianism "largely reflects a primacy of an established Western epistemology and political-economic order" (p. 7). It is presented as a taken-for-granted practice with an unproblematic past. But this is not the case. Rather, the development of humanitarian protection as we know it has been selective, guided by a colonial discourse that excluded other forms of power and violence.

Humanitarian protection in war

Before the Westphalian notions of the state and war reached their ascendency, limits to warfare were highly particular, with different cultures and civilisations turning to their own value systems to limit behaviour in war. These were largely religiously inspired, customary traditions that in part included beliefs on how war should be conducted. For example, in the Orient, Sun Tzu's emphasis on the use of force only as a last resort reflected "Confucian idealism and the political culture it spawned" (Handel, 2001, p. 136). Within this system there was no place for a dichotomy of private and public ("just") violence now so familiar in the West. Individual and state morality were inseparable. The Islamic world had particularly well-developed rules around warfare, in part expressed through *siyar*, a religious and legal system that guided dealings with non-Muslims in peace and war. These laws were defined by their religious dimension, the instinct to comply with them out of a desire to obey God, a lack of consistent codification and the specificity of its context and sources (Al-Dawoody, 2017, pp. 999–1000). To further build this provincial picture, a diverse collection of customs – often relying on oral traditions conveyed through proverbs – guided behaviour in war across Africa (see Provost, 2007, p. 623). Meanwhile, other traditions shunned the basic assumptions behind the regulation of war, and instead produced pacifist traditions. Here Buddhism and notions of "do no harm" come to mind (see Megret, 2015, p. 683).

In Medieval Europe, restraint in war was motivated by the reciprocal expectations of the military elite of the era, guided by notions of what constituted chivalrous and civilised behaviour. Derived from the Christian ethic, this included notions of honour, fair play, mercy and protection of the weak. Seldom if ever realised in full, these ideals

> remained a source of inspiration, pervading the political, social and literary life and filling an important need as the yardstick for the mores of the period. Chivalry in the Middle Ages was thus a mix of reality, poetry and legend.
>
> (Meron, 1998, p. 5)

Customary rather than statutory in nature, this behaviour was in part formalised by Pope Gregory IX, who in the 13th century came up with a list of who should be protected in war. Like many motivations of restraint, there was an element of self interest in Gregory's list, which included priests, monks and friars, but it also included those who he considered "naturally weak" – women, children, widows and orphans. This medieval list set out what was moral behaviour in conflict, distinguishing between the "armed and the unarmed, the potentially harmful and the essentially harmless, the strong and the obviously weak" (Slim, 2007, p. 13). Subsequently, there were also various royal ordinances formalising these Christian customs, including Henry V's early 15th century codification of rules protecting women from rape, and churches and people belonging to the church from assault, robbery or capture (see Meron, 1998, p. 5).

As the modern state system took shape in post-Westphalian Europe, these Christian values were incorporated into a set of secular rules, which laid out appropriate behaviour in the ever-escalating inter-state wars of the time. This codification of the law of war gained traction in the mid-19th century with the 1856 Declaration of Paris, which regulated maritime warfare. In the American Civil War, the so called Lieber Code of 1863 guided the conduct of the Union Army in its war against the South, including the rights of the unarmed enemy population. In balancing an explicit principle of "military necessity" with a corresponding principle to protect the unarmed population, it set the tone for future discussions about the protection of civilians in war (see Slim, 2007, p. 18). Five years after the adoption of the Lieber Code, 16 European states signed the St Petersburg Declaration of 1868, the first formal agreement limiting the use of certain types of weapons in war, including a ban on explosive bullets. Designed "to reconcile the necessity of war with the laws of humanity", it declared that "the progress of civilization should have the effect of alleviating, as much as possible, the calamities of war" (cited in Friedman, 1972, p. 192).

Among the earliest instruments of international law, these treaties laid out what constituted legitimate warfare between states and placed limits on the violence that could be applied. In this, they were a very specific response to a peculiarly Western problem. They were a response to the specific view of war that emerged in the 18th and 19th centuries; a view which was intimately bound up in the emergence of the nation state and notions of "just" public violence. In this particularly European view of war – outlined by Rousseau (1762) and Clausewitz (1832) – war was a state activity used in the pursuit of state interest and states held a monopoly over the legitimate use of violence. Rousseau summed it up as follows: "War is in no way a relationship of man with man but a relationship between states, in which individuals are enemies only by accident. Not as men, nor even as citizens, but as soldiers" (cited in Fresard, 2004, p. 37). Other forms of organised violence – carried out by an assortment of militias, bandits, and independent warlords – were largely ignored by this discourse, leaving the state-based definition dominant.

The emergence of the nation state also militated the establishment of sizeable and at least semi-professional standing armies which became the hallmark of European states, important as both a signifier of statehood and as the means of deploying the legitimate use of international force. History shows that the scale of these armies and the ferocity of interstate violence grew over the 19th century, propelled by the emergence of nationalism and liberalism as political forces, the advent of conscription and the growing industrialisation of warfare (see Barnett, 2005; Megret, 2006).

> These radical developments, largely unknown anywhere else, and extending as they did the theatre of operations to the territories of entire states, announced the total wars of the twentieth century. As such they threatened the very fabric of the nascent international community.
>
> (Megret, 2006, p. 311)

The response to this escalating violence and the decline of communal values emerged from the same state-making process that established war as a specific form of violence practiced by the state. The unfolding rules of war were a direct function of the nascent international community's embrace of positivism, with its emphasis on the state as the sole source of law, and thus as the framework for international law.[2] This was in contrast to many cultures that existed at the time, and even Europe's own traditional emphasis on notions of reciprocity, chivalry and civility. The ultimate effect would be to shift the onus of humanitarian protection – at a formal and explicit level at least – "from the province of moral or chivalrous compulsion to a positive law" (Megret, 2006, p. 283).

The laws of war

The high-water mark of these rules, and arguably the birth of modern humanitarianism, was the original Geneva Convention of 1864, inspired by Henry Dunant's experiences in Solferino. His account of these experiences – *A Memory of Solferino* – described the shocking scenes that followed one of the bloodiest battles of the 19th century. In emotive language, he recounts the events that took place over three days in June 1859 near the small town in northern Italy. "A mere tourist with no part whatever in this great conflict," he describes some 500,000 French and Austrian troops marching into battle, "drums beating and bugles sounding". But then came a "hand-to-hand struggle … sheer butchery; a struggle between savage beasts … the most dreadful sights imaginable" – the sick and wounded of all nations lying side by side "on the flagstone floors of the churches of Castiglione". But along with this desperation and suffering, Dunant also witnessed signs of compassion and restraint. He writes of local women who, at his initiative, came together on the third day of the battle to offer help. He also describes the "humanity of simple troopers" and their "kindness and sympathy towards defeated or captured enemies" (Dunant, 1862, cited in Thurer, 2007, pp. 49–50).

Upon returning home to Switzerland, Dunant drew upon these experiences to campaign for restraint in war and the creation of private societies to aid the wounded. As Barnett (2005) explains, the Red Cross founder envisioned a network of charitable relief societies which would help save lives on the battlefield, stimulate Christian principles of charity and promote ideals of civilised society (p. 78). States, which were concerned by the increasing brutality of war and rising public outrage, saw an opportunity and adopted some of Dunant's ideas to establish the original Geneva Convention protecting wounded soldiers and those caring for them (see Barnett, 2011, pp. 79–80). They voluntarily signed up to these mutually beneficial ground rules that outlined what was agreed behaviour when interstate politics evolved into armed conflict. The idea of distinction, drawing a line between those who were actively part of the fight and those not involved, was central to these new rules of war. Combatants were to show restraint, the wounded were to be treated with compassion, and neutral and impartial humanitarians were to be given access in order to provide protection and medical care.

Here it is worth reiterating that these new rules of war were highly contextual, not only temporally in their links to the emerging state system, but geographically through cultural and religious beliefs. For while the belief that people should be protected from the extremes of war was shared across cultures and civilisations, it was largely guided by local cultural and religious mechanisms. In Europe, the notion of restraint evolved within a profoundly Christian culture. At its most basic level, restraint was linked to moral ideas of mercy and charity, underpinned by a pragmatic commitment to reciprocity, also found in Christian teachings. It also emerged in the "just war" tradition, which established moral restraint on war in part as an effort to justify Christian participation in war (see Kinsella, 2011, pp. 34–35). Dunant's efforts to establish an international law limiting the conduct of war were essentially framed in these same terms. As Dunant's Red Cross co-founder Gustave Moynier explained at the time, international humanitarian law remained the product of a Christian civilisation, but justified on the basis of natural law and international positivism (see Cockayne, 2002, p. 604). Thus, in establishing the original Geneva Convention protecting wounded and sick soldiers, a key achievement was to effectively shift the normative basis of restraint in war from moral codes and the canons of the Christian church to the structures and practices of international law and the state. As Megret (2015) explains, "The Geneva Conventions, as paragons of the modern project of regulation of warfare, fundamentally shift the basis for restraint in warfare to an obligation that lies in positive international law as a result of state consent" (p. 683).

It is indeed striking how central this point in time and the experiences of Dunant and his compatriots are to what would become the international humanitarian system decades later. Indeed, the touchstones of humanity and impartiality emerge from the Christian ethos of the era, notably the European traditions of charity and compassion, with Dunant and others framing their ideas in these exact terms. As Barnett (2011) explains, the Geneva committee that established the first Convention was substantially guided by religious feelings and found inspiration in the Gospels, particularly the parable of the "Good Samaritan" (pp. 78–81; see also Forsythe, 2005, pp. 27–28). Dunant, an evangelical Christian, went so far as to describe himself as "an instrument in the hands of God", while his Calvinist co-founder Moynier "was particularly taken with the possibility that charitable organizations might stimulate (Christian) notions of progress, charity, and humanity" (Barnett, 2011, p. 79). Indeed, this discourse of Christianity remained central to the humanitarian conversation through at least the turn of the century, when the humanitarian movement began to expand around the globe and the language of universal secularism finally eclipsed the Christian notions of charity and compassion. Though even as late as 1945, then ICRC President Max Huber would talk of Christian mercy and compassion and write of the Gospels and the work of Red Cross (see Steinarcher, 2017).

The humanitarian principles of neutrality and independence can also be seen in Dunant's experience, notably how he navigated has way across the battlefield and between the opposing French and Austrian armies. For while humanity and impartiality provide the moral ideal and ethical framework of humanity in war, neutrality and independence represent the means of achieving these ends. As Slim (2015) articulates in his examination of humanitarian ethics, this second pair of principles "serve as practical ethical measures to achieve this goal … in the real conditions of intense political rivalry and competing interests that characterize war" (pp. 65–66). During the battle of Solferino, the Swiss traveller negotiated access using his position as the neutral outsider, and rallied volunteers to assist the wounded and dying from both sides of the battle, free from the influence of the two opposing forces. Later, as a direct result of Dunant's experiences and advocacy, the first three principles of humanity, impartiality and neutrality were enshrined in the 1864 Convention, the first building block of IHL.[3] Thus, at the outset at least, the principles are historically specific, the product of a particular geopolitical context, an interstate conflict with its clear separation of military and civilian in which state sovereignty is inviolable.

This period also saw the emergence of the ICRC, the singular humanitarian agency in the new protection agreement. While it clearly evolved over time, like the laws of war themselves, the humanitarian organisation was predicated on the international state system at a certain point in its evolution. From the outset, it was a European organisation, a product of Western (Judeo-Christian) values, despite presenting itself as a secular and global Good Samaritan (Forsythe, 2005, p. 281). Furthermore, the emergence of the ICRC was not in response to the idea of war in general, but as a reaction to a particular European conflict and a particular notion of war and the state. In the tradition of Dunant's experiences in Solferino, it was created to supplement state action in protecting wounded combatants who were *hors de combat*, or "outside the fight". This operational role as a neutral and impartial actor providing relief to the wounded and sick dovetailed well with the rules of sovereignty and methods of warfare of European powers. Indeed, the ICRC emerged as IHL's principle "norm entrepreneur", persuading states to embrace these international limitations of warfare (see Provost, 2007, p. 642). Devised in 1864, this central role in developing, promoting and interpreting the humanitarian norms would become standard practice for the organisation, eventually to be formalised in the 1949 Geneva Conventions.

Dunant's story and the first Geneva Convention it inspired are just as notable for what they left out. The international laws that emerged from Dunant's experiences and the set-piece battles that played out in 19th-century Europe focused on protecting fighters – first wounded soldiers and then shipwrecked sailors and prisoners of war in the coming decades – while the civilian was largely neglected. This, as Best (1994) explains, was in contrast to ideas of earlier jurists, "who were less concerned with what the fighters did to each other than with what they did to the civilians and the property around them" (p. 60). It was also notably different to what the laws of war would become a century later. The relatively brief focus on the combatant reflects the dominant perception of war in that particular time and place, with the state monopolising the use of force, deploying well organised, semi-professional armies across relatively contained battlefields. The civilian was not clearly visible in this space. Indeed, not until 1949 was the civilian formally introduced into IHL. And not until the Additional Protocols of 1977 was the civilian formally defined, and then only in terms of what it was not – a member of the armed forces – creating the binary distinction on which modern humanitarian law rests.

Universality

International humanitarian law is seen as universal, applying to all armed actors, regardless of their specific religious, cultural or political belief systems. The fact that all states in the international community have ratified the 1949 Conventions is often cited as evidence of this universality. It is argued that this universal ratification is one of the best guarantees of their implementation, consolidating their conventional authority (see Megret, 2015). In the broader sense, universality also implies that IHL represents a common belief system that exists across different civilisations and cultures. As Megret (2015) goes on to explain:

> The expression of these basic emotional impulses may vary according to culture and be tainted by a degree of idiosyncrasy, but all ultimately and inevitably converge to create the need for some form of restraint that respects, say, the fundamental dignity of human beings, or at least the sacredness of life.
> (p. 681)

This more nuanced understanding of universality – expressed through customary law – works to counter the challenges that cultural and religious differences can bring to a global humanitarian regime.

However, universality itself is geographically and historically situated. As argued earlier, the Geneva Conventions emerged out of a purely European experience and a particular vision of legitimate warfare as a state activity. The non-European "other" living beyond the boundaries of the state-making project was at the time irrelevant to these emerging laws and principles. Indeed, there was no real attempt to articulate a universal vision of humanitarian protection during the 19th century, even as Europe asserted its control over large parts of what would become the Global South. As Megret (2006) explains, this "land-grabbing process" was not seen as war at all but bringing Western civilisation to "savage peoples" (p. 270). Once the conquest was complete, colonising powers successfully claimed that they were maintaining order, rather than engaging in actual armed conflict. In other words, they were police actions and so escaped the problematic trappings of the nascent humanitarian laws and principles. Thus, colonialism effectively limited early notions of universality by ensuring non-European people remained beyond the margins of international law. For while there were undoubtedly humanitarians arguing for the applications of the laws of war and humanitarian principles in colonial wars, Dunant among them, they largely went unheeded.[4]

This limited universalism continued beyond World War II, when there was a major redrafting of the Geneva Conventions. It was then, following the experiences of the two world wars, that the civilian was recognised through the fourth Geneva Convention. That these European wars provided the background for this re-drafting exercise may have further reinforced the Western focus of the Conventions, at the expense of the colonial other. Indeed, just as the world beyond Europe was not part of the initial conversation a century earlier, they were effectively excluded from the agreements of 1949. For example, of the 59 states invited to the conference in Geneva, only Egypt and Ethiopia were from the African continent. As Megret (2015) explains:

> The absence of what was not quite yet the Third World was barely noticed, a sign perhaps of how disconnected the 1949 exercise was from some of the passions that had long begun brewing at the periphery of the Second World War's theatre.
>
> (p. 679)

In a sign of issues to come, the lack of representation from large swathes of Africa, as well as Asia and the Middle East, was in part the result of the Conventions' state focus. These people were not yet directly represented in the international community of states that were at the heart of the laws of war.

It was ultimately the process of decolonisation and the post-colonial state making process that brought about a universalisation of the humanitarian instruments. Treaty-based law and humanitarian principles were slowly exported from Europe as the surface of the earth was partitioned into territorially differentiated sovereign states, ultimately including the former colonies. These new states were quick to ratify the Conventions as part of a package of international laws that came with statehood. As Megret (2005; 2016) explains, in doing so they were largely driven by the benefits of statehood rather than any underlying belief in the norms outlined in the Geneva Conventions or that they matched local understandings of war and protection. In fact:

> One might argue that the adherence to the laws of war as incarnated by the Geneva Conventions is ultimately more a manifestation of accession to a historically located grammar of statehood than the manifestation of an intemporal and truly universal aspiration.
>
> (Megret, 2015, p. 688)

Invested in being part of the international community, these emerging states were highly unlikely to question the Conventions and subsequent state-focused protection mechanisms, even if there was some scepticism over their European origins and focus on international conflict. When they eventually did make their presence felt, emerging states did so in the language of international law rather than by challenging them. Additional Protocol I – which effectively upgraded the wars of national liberation to international wars – can be seen as a response to these efforts. Similarly, Additional Protocol II recognised the different kinds of war unfolding beyond the boundaries of Europe by incorporating non-state armed groups into the frameworks. Other emerging protection mechanisms, notably the Refugee Convention of 1951, followed this same arc. The 1967 Protocol removed the Convention's temporal and geographic restrictions so that it extended beyond post-war Europe to apply universally.[5] Rather than acknowledging the specificity of these wars and armed actors, contemporary wars were instead incorporated into an international regulatory regime. In effect this post-World War II period of state expansion produced a particular kind of universalism, one operating between states but effectively detached from the local context.

This is not to say this approach was misguided, for the state-centric idea of humanitarian protection held up pretty well in the relatively stable post-colonial world where the threat of interstate conflict was front of mind. This was in part sustained by Cold War rivalries, as the world divided into the East, West and non-aligned. Selected states were supported and provided with aid to ensure their ongoing viability and potentially destabilising conflicts were mediated through inter-state relations. Also, the need to manage the Cold War threats of inter-state conflict continued to relegate the importance of the post-colonial world and its internal conflicts to the sidelines (see Duffield, 2007). As history shows, however, this changed following the end of the Cold War, when the erosion of the established order saw a weakening of state-centred notions of power and more diffuse forms of authority (see Duffield, 1998).[6]

As Duffield (1998) articulates, new political projects emerged in this geopolitical vacuum, often associated with religious fundamentalism and ethnic separatism. This included a resurgence of non-state armed actors, many asserting religious and cultural traditions at odds with the Western legal frameworks. The so-called "new wars" they waged were often about identity politics, rather than the geopolitical or ideological goals of earlier wars (Kaldor, 2006, p. 7). Some of these actors could even be seen as a form of resistance against the very same colonial expansion that had brought the European view of the world to "the rest" (Barkawi, 2004, p. 22). The irony, of course, is that by this time emerging states had substantively committed to a set of Western norms which often proved ineffective in Kaldor's (2006) new wars, which directed their fury "not against opposing sides, but against civilian populations" (p. 53). Moreover, these contemporary laws of war had effectively displaced existing, locally situated traditions that had historically promoted civilian protection. In their new-found focus, emerging states had largely turned to ideas of humanity, sovereignty and positivism at the expense of any indigenous vocabulary of restraint in war, be it divine command, chivalry or ritual (Megret, 2015, p. 687).

The broad response to this emerging localisation has been to lean into the universality argument. At one level, this has been done through the language of international legal positivism, continuing to proclaim that the laws are applicable to all state and non-state actors. It is an argument best supported by the overwhelming ratification of the Geneva Conventions and the apparent willingness of many non-state armed actors to sign up to the same international protection mechanisms (see Chapter 1). The authority of the laws of war are no doubt enhanced by this state function, given the authority of the international system of states. Indeed, this wide embrace may indicate that at least in some cases the international norms have effectively displaced the local, "such is arguably the power of norms backed by formidable symbolic power" (Megret, 2015, p. 687).

In a related effort, scholars and IHL advocates increasingly highlight how the principles of humanitarian law are a reflection of the traditional values of many non-Western cultures and civilisations. In his examination of Asian values, Boll (2001) argues that "the principles which led to the establishment of these laws emanate from a perception of warfare which has been common to mankind through the ages" (p. 55). In his examination of the Indian approach to humanitarian law, Mani (2001) explains how *Manu-smriti*, a hybrid ethical and normative framework from 200BC, is reflected in many of the basic principles of humanitarian law. These ancient texts emphasised that civilians near the battlefield should not be harmed, banned weapons that caused unnecessary suffering and dictated that surrendering warriors were to be captured and treated with dignity. Perhaps the most substantive body of this work compares the traditions, customs and laws of warfare in Islam to IHL (see Al-Dawoody, 2017; Cockayne, 2002, p. 597). To sum up, the broader argument is to the effect that the Geneva Conventions merely codified an aspiration or a set of rules common to all civilisations, so are a representation of more broadly held beliefs.

A critique of universality

As discussed earlier, it is true that many cultures and civilisations have previously come up with indigenous traditions of restraint, limiting the means and methods of war and protecting civilians and others who are outside the fight. However, when reflecting on this research, several general points warrant consideration. First, these explorations are retrospective. There is a tendency to begin with universality as an established premise and then focus efforts on fitting alternative traditions into the contemporary frameworks. Or as Cockayne (2002) succinctly articulates in his examination of IHL and Islamic Law, "These comparative analyses tend to exhibit a subtle orientalism, taking the Western system as a yardstick against which the adequacy or compatibility of the oriental Islamic 'other' is measured" (p. 597). Second, as Cockayne goes on to explain, there is a tendency to reduce different protection traditions to "static, monolithic constructs", ignoring the fact that they are complex traditions, "both dynamic (varying over time) and plural (made up of varying sub-traditions)" (p. 597). The effort to substantiate universality fails to take into account the complexity of how war is understood and articulated in different cultures, often thinking of it through the singular lens of religion, rather than a mosaic of evolving and regularly contested moral, social and political ideas (see also Megret, 2015, p. 682).

Finally, as Megret (2015) adds, "the devil is in the detail", and "whilst a broad historical brush may depict all societies as having had some sort of notion of restraint in warfare, it is also clear that not all have emphasized the same ideas or adopted the same institutions" (p. 683). For example, while many cultures have identified groups of people who should be protected in war, these vary considerably, whether in response to local traditions, community structures or simple self-interest. Similarly, while different cultures and civilisations have limited the means and methods of warfare, on closer examination these can vary considerably depending on distinct traditions and local histories. Perhaps most importantly, humanitarian law represents a fundamental shift from cultural and religious mechanisms to a regulatory system embedded in positive law and state authority. "In doing this, the Conventions place much of the onus on respecting IHL on states, even as statehood, or at least a certain European understanding of it, may not be the most widely shared form internationally" (Megret, 2015, p. 683).

When this critical exercise is carried out, the humanitarian protection frameworks can be seen as being universal if understood as referring to the international state system from which they emerged. Supporting this are the more technical arguments about their customary character, with substantive research showing that the Conventions reflect non-Western laws and customs of war. This widely shared sentiment of their universal character undoubtedly enhances both their legal and moral authority and is perhaps one of the best guarantees that they are respected beyond international conflicts. However, while the protection frameworks may be widely ratified, that does not mean they are universally accepted across cultures and civilisations. In fact, as Megret (2015) explains:

> The "statism" of the Geneva Conventions may discredit them in the eyes of certain non-state actors that will not be formally party to them, will not have participated in their adoption, and may even think that the Conventions, steeped as they are in inter-state reality, do not reflect their peculiar needs and constraints in warfare.
>
> (p. 684)

Furthermore, while some aspects of the humanitarian frameworks are consonant with indigenous traditions and customs, as customary law implies, there is also some degree of dissonance. This indicates the existence of indigenous protection practices and beliefs that have been effectively eclipsed by the universalisation of a Western, state model "that exercises a monopoly over our imaginations about state violence and what can be done about it" (Megret, 2006, p. 312).

Conclusion: protection in contemporary wars

Where it once resided in the ordered world of sovereign states, humanitarianism now occupies the complex arena of contemporary wars, where civilian protection and relief are negotiated and shaped by a network of actors. Non-state armed actors have re-emerged as some of the most influential actors in the arena, challenging the state's monopoly of violence. This is particularly the case in parts of Africa and the Middle East where a combination of state fragility, conflict and instability has enhanced the military, political and social importance of non-state armed actors. As discussed in Chapter 1, these actors defy the simplistic state versus non-state categories we are used to. Instead, both in their use of armed force and their relationship with communities, they are characterised by multilayered identities and strategies that defy labelling. Their behaviour is often defined by indiscriminate violence against communities. However, as recent research into insurgent organisations has revealed, they can also be providers of a level of governance and community services that blur the line between state and non-state actors. In this way, their ambiguity is a fundamental part of their identity.

Ironically, these non-state actors have come to the fore after the Western model of humanitarian protection had been successfully exported throughout the world along with the state system. This Eurocentric typology was part of a sovereign-state package in which the basic unit was the nation state, international politics involved relations between nation states, war was a state activity and state militaries held a monopoly of violence. In this protection philosophy, states agreed to abide by a set of rules restraining their behaviour and provide access to neutral and impartial humanitarians. This system stood up reasonably well in the relatively stable post-colonial world, when Cold War rivalries helped sustain the modern state and warfare model. The end of the Cold War and the subsequent process of globalisation eroded the state system, creating more diffuse forms of authority. Thus, with the decline of the state, there is a greater reliance on other means of social mobilisation such as religion and ethnicity, taken to its brutal extremes in places like Rwanda and Bosnia. For other non-state armed actors, it is the struggle against globalisation or the West that is the mobilising force, a form of colonial resistance borne out most recently in the violence emanating from the Middle East.

The response has in part been to increase efforts to squeeze these so-called new actors into the state/non-state protection discourse, with the overriding assumption that they will want to comply with the international protection norms. To this effect, the original rules of war have been extended to incorporate non-state entities, notably through the Additional Protocols and a growing list of human rights treaties relevant to protection in armed conflict. This effort has proven partially successful, as these new actors sometimes mimic their state counterparts. However, ongoing violence against communities and selective disregard for humanitarian norms clearly shows that they do not consistently fit into these "Western patterns of allegiance and discourse" (Kalyvas, 2001, p. 104).

Parallel to this have been concerted efforts to convince these new actors that the international frameworks are indeed universal in the broader sense. Often framed through the lens of customary law, this scholarship has rediscovered the variety of indigenous humanitarian traditions that historically promoted restraint in war, showing how compatible they are to international laws and humanitarian principles. While making important links, much of this scholarship has avoided the issues of cultural particularism, instead beginning from the established universal premise. Here, again, we can see the power of the Eurocentric protection discourse, which "is presented as a universal, common sense approach to suffering caused by disaster and war" (Rostis, 2016, p. 101).

This has left us with a limited conceptualisation of humanitarian protection, which largely remains a product of the European state system and its laws. These established protection leavers have struggled in contemporary wars, where non-state armed actors selectively transgress the universal frameworks agreed to by state and humanitarian actors. While efforts have been made to address this problematic Eurocentric history, extending the protection frameworks to account for emerging non-state armed actors, the underlying paradigm remains intact. Protection remains a legal mechanism, significantly invested in notions of the state, despite the emerging authority of non-state armed actors.

As I have argued here, drawing on post-colonial scholarship, this legal/state approach to protection has been sustained by a powerful discourse, which works to constrain knowledge, limiting our ability to understand alternative points of authority and conceive relevant strategies. This chapter summons us to rethink how protection works, seeking a vantage point that is not vested in the established logic of Eurocentric laws and principles, but acknowledging the diverse network of actors and interactions that humanitarian protection entails. Chapter 3 takes this further, reconceptualising humanitarian protection in a way that allows us to better understand this complex network and how humanitarian actors navigate its unpredictable realities to protect at-risk communities.

Notes

1 While the state may have emerged as the pre-eminent social structure in Europe, and ultimately emerged as the "universal" international system, it was in reality just one of a number of regional systems that existed at the time. Before colonisers arrived and asserted their specific laws and institutions, East Asia had its own Sino-centric normative order, while the Islamic world turned to its own normative system known as siyar (Mälksoo, 2019). In pre-colonial Africa concepts of territory and power were highly complex. "Political space was conceived as a multilayered structure of concentric circles of diminishing control, radiating from the various sources" (Dunn, 2009, p. 226).

2 Henkin et al. (1993) provide a useful summary and a historical account of the emergence of positivism. "The rise of positivism in Western political and legal theory, especially from the latter part of the 18th century to the early part of the 20th century, corresponds to the steady rise of the national state and its increasingly absolute claims to legal and political supremacy" (Henkin et al., 1993, p. xxv).

3 For example, Article 6 maps out early notions of non-discrimination while Article 5 stated: "Generals of the belligerent Powers shall make it their duty to notify the

inhabitants of the appeal made to their humanity, and of the neutrality which humane conduct will confer".

4 Henry Dunant, in his later years, largely reversed his initial pro-colonisation stance and condemned the way war had been waged against some non-European nations, specifically regretting the asphyxiating by smoke of Arab insurgents in 1845 by French troops (see Megret, 2006).

5 As a history of humanitarian protection, this chapter focuses largely on IHL, though much of the discussion about the central role of the state applies to the more recent International Refugee Law, which emerged as a protection mechanism in 1951 in response to the mass displacement in Europe. As discussed in Chapter 1, IRL is a state-centric solution to the inevitable fact that states are sometimes unwilling or unable to protect their own citizens.

6 As Duffield (1998) explains, globalisation eroded the authority of the nation state, producing more diffuse and less hierarchical forms of authority – a shift from "government to *governance*" (p. 69, emphasis in the original).

References

Al-Dawoody, A. (2017). Islamic law and international humanitarian law: An introduction to the main principles. *International Review of the Red Cross*, 99(3), 995–1018.

Barkawi, T. (2004). On the pedagogy of "small wars". *International Affairs*, 80(1), 19–37.

Barkawi, T. (2016). Decolonising war. *European Journal of International Security*, 1(2), 199–214.

Barnett, M. (2005). Humanitarianism transformed. *Perspectives in Politics*, 3(4), 723–740.

Barnett, M. (2011). *Empire of humanity: A history of humanitarianism*. Cornell University Press.

Best, G. (1994). *War and law since 1945*. Oxford University Press.

Boll, A. (2001). The Asian values debate and its relevance to international humanitarian law. *International Review of the Red Cross*, 84(841), 45–58.

Cockayne, J. (2002). Islam and international humanitarian law: From a clash to a conversation between civilizations. *International Review of the Red Cross*, 84(847), 597–626.

Cooper, F. (2005). *Colonialism in question: Theory, knowledge, history*. University of California Press.

Davey, E. (2012). *New players through old lenses: Why history matters when engaging with Southern actors* (No. 48; HPG Policy Brief). Overseas Development Institute.

Duffield, M. (1998). Post-modern conflict: Warlords, post-adjustment states and private protection. *Civil Wars*, 1(1), 65–102.

Duffield, M. (2007). *Development, security and unending war: Governing the world of peoples*. Polity Press.

Dunn, K. (2009). Environmental security and spatial preservation in central Africa. In D. Howland & L. White (Eds.), *The state of sovereignty: Territories, laws, populations* (pp. 222–242). Indiana University Press.

Forsythe, D. (2005). *The humanitarians: The International Committee of the Red Cross*. Cambridge University Press.

Fresard, J.-J. (2004). *The roots of behaviour in war: A survey of the literature*. ICRC.

Friedman, L. (1972). *The law of war: A documentary history*. Random House.

Handel, M. (2001). *Masters of war: Classical strategic thought* (3rd edition). Routledge.

Henkin, L., Pugh, R., Schachter, O., & Smit, H. (1993). *International law: Cases and materials* (3rd edition). West Publishing.

Kaldor, M. (2006). *New and old wars: Organised violence in a global era*. Stanford University Press.

Kalyvas, S. (2001). "New" and "old" civil wars: A valid distinction? *World Politics*, 54(1), 99–118.

Keen, D. (2012). Greed and grievance in civil war. *International Affairs*, 88(4), 757–777.

Kinsella, H. (2011). *The image before the weapon: A critical history of the distinction between combatant and civilian*. Cornell University Press.

Mälksoo, L. (2019). Civilizational diversity as challenge to the (false) universality of international law. *Asian Journal of International Law*, 9(1), 155–164.

Mani, V. (2001). International humanitarian law: An Indo-Asian perspective. *International Review of the Red Cross*, 83(841), 59–75.

Megret, F. (2006). From "savages" to "unlawful combatants": A postcolonial look at international humanitarian law's "Other". In A. Orford (Ed.), *International law and its others* (pp. 265–317). Cambridge University Press.

Megret, F. (2015). The universality of the Geneva Conventions. In A. Clapham, P. Gaeta, & M. Sassòli (Eds.), *The 1949 Geneva Conventions: A commentary* (pp. 669–688). Oxford University Press.

Meron, T. (1998). *Bloody constraint: War and chivalry in Shakespeare*. Oxford University Press.

Provost, R. (2007). The International Committee of the Red Widget? The diversity debate and international humanitarian law. *Israel Law Review*, 30, 614–647.

Rostis, A. (2016). *Organising disaster: The construction of humanitarianism*. Emerald Group.

Slim, H. (2007). *Killing civilians: Method, madness, and morality in war*. Columbia University Press.

Slim, H. (2015). *Humanitarian ethics: A guide to the morality of aid in war and disaster*. Oxford University Press.

Steinacher, G. (2017). *Humanitarians at war: The Red Cross in the shadow of the holocaust*. Oxford University Press.

Stoler, A. (1989). Rethinking colonial categories: European communities and the boundaries of rule. *Comparative Studies in Society and History*, 31(1), 134–161.

Thurer, D. (2007). Dunant's pyramid: Thoughts on the "humanitarian space". *International Review of the Red Cross*, 89(865), 47–61.

Young, R. (2001). *Postcolonialism: An historical introduction*. Blackwell.

3 Reframing humanitarian protection

Introduction: protection through the lens of anthropology

In recent years, humanitarian scholarship has moved away from the definition of a neutral humanitarian space, with its clean boundaries and pre-ordained actors. Instead, Hilhorst (2010) and her followers have called for a broader definition that acknowledges that humanitarians occupy a complex political, military and legal arena where aid is negotiated and shaped by a range of actors. As Allie (2011) points out:

> [Humanitarian space] is a space for negotiation, power games and interest-seeking between aid actors and authorities.... It is the product of repeated transactions with local and international political and military forces. Its scope depends largely on the organisation's ambitions, the diplomatic and political support it can rely on and the interest taken in its action by those in power.
>
> (p. 3)

It is a somewhat unremarkable revelation that had previously been embraced by development scholarship, which sees international development as a complex set of local, national and cross-cultural social interactions. As two of the leaders in this field explain: "It is no longer possible to isolate interactions in the realm of development from those related to state apparatus, civil society, or wider national or international political, economic, and administrative practices" (Mosse & Lewis, 2005, p. 1). Instead, development involves a great number of interactions between actors of different status, with varying resources and dissimilar goals, "for whom development constitutes a resource, a profession, a market, a stake or a strategy" (de Sardan, 2005, p. 11).

Appreciating that these interactions exist is one thing; consciously building on this initial insight in order to reveal how these interactions work is another thing entirely. The multiplicity of interactions experienced in development have been revealed through anthropology, which has focused attention on the social processes and negotiations of meaning and identity in heterogeneous social arenas in a way that challenges narrow, instrumental approaches. As Lewis and Mosse

(2006) explain, anthropologists have engaged with development from multiple fronts. First, they have engaged with development *instrumentally*, examining these institutions as applied researchers, consultants, managers or bureaucrats. Similar to researchers of humanitarian protection, these development anthropologists-cum-consultants have often been compelled to adopt the instrumental "means-ends" rationality that characterises these policy worlds, "paying their way with knowledge products that are normative/prescriptive and usable in enhancing development effectivness" (Lewis & Mosse, 2006, p. 3).

Some anthropologists have also adopted *non-instrumental, non-normative perspectives*, paying "equal attention to the social processes of policy and the informal relationships and real-life situations of development workers" (Lewis & Mosse, 2006, p. 3). This has included various participatory approaches, which first drew on the local and then have more recently extended to the macro level of research to develop more sophisticated conceptions of local-global relations (see, e.g., Lewis & Mosse, 2006). Through an insider's perspective, these "new ethnographies of development" (Mosse, 2005, p. 11) have provided powerful commentary on hidden processes, multiple perspectives or regional interests behind official policy discourse. Through multi-positioned analyses, they have examined the relationship between the rhetoric of policy and politics, and the world as understood and experienced by development actors.

An emphasis on understanding personal, individual agency and relationships between multiple actors is also a strong feature of this research. Mosse (2005), a leading advocate of these new ethnographies, places the development actor at the centre of his seminal examination of policy and practice. The picture he paints in *Cultivating Development* is not the common image of the monolithic and all-powerful development industry, but rather a fragmented, complex affair in which actors at all levels are endowed with agency. Backstage, development staff and consultants play a central role in developing and sustaining a common narrative that mobilises support and maintains the networks that drive a project. Furthermore, this new ethnography does more than produce thick description and write detailed narratives, also substantively incorporating critical theory into the methodical approach. Combining critical theory analysis with ethnographic observations of development professionals, it has produced fine analyses of the actual practice of every day aid work and the intended and unintended effects these have.

While development scholars have unpacked this complex network, their humanitarian counterparts have largely left the humanitarian arena in general, and humanitarian protection in particular, unexplored and ill defined. Instead – with some emerging exceptions (see, e.g., Fast, 2014; Smirl, 2015) – the focus has continued to be on examining the normative protection frameworks in purely instrumental terms.[1] As a result, humanitarian researchers setting out to explore this complex network routinely begin their journey at a place dominated by the state-legal humanitarian discourse, often building their argument on little more than a collection of powerful quotes saying that a complex humanitarian network exists. This chapter takes the next step, moving beyond the established discourse to methodically build a new, three-tiered conceptualisation of humanitarian protection through which to guide further discussion and research. It does this by turning to the new ethnographies of development – in particular Mosse's seminal study – for its theoretical and methodological foundations.

The first component of this conceptual triad, outlined in detail below, sees humanitarian protection shaped through the interaction of a complex group of actors. These humanitarian actors have varying resource, differing statuses and dissimilar, often competing, motivations. Second, the humanitarian norms and principles help build a level of consensus among these disparate actors, which facilitates the relationships that ultimately provide what we know as humanitarian protection to at-risk groups. As will be explained, those norms and principles are a unifying protection narrative. However, these actors do not display consistent behaviour in every situation, but act according to their own priorities at the time and the significance of their relationships with others, rather than in line with the unifying narrative. This then leads to the third conceptual component. Humanitarian field workers, positioned at the junctures between these different actors, work behind the scenes to counter these fractures, modifying the unifying narrative to suit the context.

Framing development ethnographies theoretically

Much of the work of the new ethnographers of development has been informed primarily by the work of Foucault. It analyses development as a discourse – "a system of knowledge, practices, technologies and power relationships that orders and limits description and action within its field" (Lewis & Mosse, 2006, p. 4). In this orientation, development is seen as a historically specific discourse of power of the West over the developing world. This approach is most clearly illustrated by Escobar (1995), who analyses the "systems or relations" that determines what can be said about development (p. 40). He argues that the social relations and the texts created through them constitute the "hegemonic worldview of development" (p. 17). This institutionalisation and professionalisation of international development "brings the Third World into the politics of expert knowledge and western science in general" (p. 45). Foucault's conceptualisation of discourse and power also emerges in the ethnographic work of Ferguson (1994), who argues that development institutions generate their own form of discourse. As Ferguson explains, this discourse constructs the target society as a fantasy that bears little relation to the realities on the ground, but is suitable for the technical solutions development agencies can offer, rather than political ones they cannot intervene in.

While providing important critical insights into development, this deconstructive anthropological orientation has been criticised for tending to see development as monolithic and controlled from the top. Such a view overlooks the collaboration and complicity of marginal actors in development, such as beneficiaries "who understand and manipulate the rhetorics, rules, and rewards of aid delivery" (Lewis & Mosse, 2006, p. 5). Moreover, this Foucauldian model effectively demotes agency and negotiation, instead describing a powerful "development machine" that works to deliver specific outcomes "behind the backs or against the wills of even the most powerful actors" (Ferguson, 1994, p. 18). In other words, this deconstructive orientation fails to examine the relationship between policy and politics, and the world as understood and experienced within the lives of development actors (Lewis & Mosse, 2006, p. 5).

Agency and negotiation

More recent ethnography of development has begun to move beyond the discourse and power conceptualisations favoured by anthropologists in the past. This ethnography is "distinctly uncomfortable with the monolithic notions of dominance, resistance, and hegemonic relations" which leave little space for agency and negotiation (Mosse, 2005, p. 6). Nor do they turn to the more populist position that privileges the local by describing "every diversion or side-tracking of development as a popular resistance arising from the presumed autonomy of the subaltern" (Lewis & Mosse, 2006, p. 4). Instead they have turned to more recent examinations of agency and everyday practice for their theoretical foundation, such as de Certeau (1984) and Scott (1990). De Certeau (1984) has added nuance to the understanding of agency by revealing the "devious, dispersed and subversive 'consumer practices', which are not manifest through [their] own products, but rather through [their] ways of using the products imposed by a dominant economic order" (p. xiii). In other words, while beneficiaries or development workers may consent to dominant models – using the authorised scripts given them by projects – they make of them something quite different. Scott (1990) writes about the "hidden transcripts" that exist alongside the "public transcripts" of development policy. "The hidden transcript is produced for a different audience and under different constraints of power than the public transcript" (Scott, 1990, p. 5).[2]

This critical theory adds substantial weight to ethnographies of development, which similarly argue that people do not just adapt to or resist development, but have much more complicated strategies and reactions. This is reflected in the work of Long and Long (1992), who introduced an actor-oriented approach to development that "recognises the 'multiple realities' and the diverse social practices of various actors" (p. 5). Similarly, it can be seen in the work of more recent ethnographers who have extended the scope of development research from those at the receiving end of aid to include development professionals and their relationship with the organisations they work for (see Fechter & Hindman, 2011; Mosse, 2011).

Actor-oriented approach

The actor-oriented approach is based on the idea that social change can only be understood by analysing the relationship between social structures and human agency. It follows Foucault in his notion that all actors have access to power, even those actors occupying subordinate positions. Yet while Foucault emphasises the power of discursive regimes, the actor-oriented approach stresses the power of social actors to influence and transform these regimes by employing alternative ways of formulating their objectives and deploying specific modes of action (Long & Long, 1992, p. 25).

Applied in the field of development research, an actor-oriented approach requires "a full analysis of the ways in which different social actors manage and interpret new elements in their life worlds, an understanding of the organizing, strategic and interpretive elements involved, and a deconstruction of conventional notions of planned intervention" (Long & Long, 1992, p. 9). In this view, development interventions are not the simple outcome of a value-free and linear planning process, but rather the changing and negotiated manifestation of diverse and sometimes competing interests.

Multiple narratives

Since they are not constrained to privilege authorised (instrumental) interpretations, ethnographies of development have also looked beyond policy language. They have revealed how the official development narratives work to "enrol supporters ... forge political connections, and create common realities from heterogeneous networks" (Lewis & Mosse, 2006, pp. 15–16). According to Mosse (2005), policy is this narrative, designed to mobilise and maintain political support in order to legitimise development activities (p. 14). A successful policy, therefore, is one that utilises sufficiently ambiguous terminology so that it is able to achieve a high degree of convergence of disparate interests (Mosse, 2005, p. 46).

Furthermore, ethnographies of development have gone beyond this unifying narrative, or what Roe (1994) calls a metanarrative, to examine the largely concealed counter narratives. Development ethnographers such as Mosse (2005) first explored these multi-layered narratives theoretically. Returning to Scott (1990), the backstage counter narratives are "hidden transcripts", which exist alongside official narratives, or "public transcripts". In *The Practice of Everyday Life*, de Certeau (1984) makes a distinction between "strategies" as the tools used by institutions, enterprises and governments to enforce their will over a particular space, and "tactics" as opportunistic acts that take place within a social space dominated by strategies. The conceptualisation of multi-layered narratives described by these critical theorists is then complemented with thick descriptions, collected from the inside through participatory observation (see Mosse & Lewis, 2005). This approach to understanding development aid and policy reform has uncovered what Mosse and Lewis term "the hidden processes and multiple perspectives or regional interests" behind official policy discourses (p. 1).

Development actors and their unifying narrative

Mosse's *Cultivating Development* (2005) is the path-breaking contribution that inspired what he titled "the new ethnography of development" (p. 11). His methodology and highly original argument open up plenty of space for further discussion and research. The subject of the study is the Indo-British Rainfed Farming Project (IBRFP), a participatory project geared towards bringing agricultural technologies and innovations to tribal communities in rural India. During the mid-1990s the DFID-funded project was considered "absolutely cutting edge" and "the jewel in the crown" of British aid (Mosse, 2005, p. 183), even though it had little to show for itself in reality. Only a few years later, when some positive dynamics were starting to appear, DFID's policy model had moved on and the project began to be regarded as a failure.

Mosse (2005) was able to gain his insights through multi-positioned and multi-sited analysis, and his eight-year involvement as the project's consultant anthropologist. During this time, he routinely visited the project, spending time with project staff at office meetings and workshops, in their homes, or on the long journeys to the scattered villages that were participating in the project. His observations as a participant-insider – complemented by document analysis and interviews with project staff – sit at the core of his research and provide the first-hand accounts that make this an engaging, stimulating study.

Mosse's (2005) central concern in this study is not whether, but rather *how* development works (p. 2). In this regard, Mosse focuses particularly on the complex relationship between policy and practice, stressing the discontinuities between the two. He asks:

> What if development practice is not driven by policy? What if the things that make for good policy are quite different from those that make it implementable? … What if, instead of policy producing practice, practices produce policy, in the sense that actors in development devote their energies to maintaining coherent representations regardless of events?
>
> (p. 2)

From the study, it becomes evident that the dynamic between policy and practice is deeply important to the project, but not for the reasons one would think. The picture that appears is of an intervention driven by the relationships between a network of actors – including donors, local and federal governments, corporations and farmers – rather than by policy. Meanwhile policy, rather than being an instrumental tool that shapes how development is done, is a unifying narrative that preserves and validates this network of actors. As Mosse (2005) explains, policy is not primarily concerned with orientating practice, but rather is designed to mobilise and maintain political support in order to legitimise development activities (p. 14). On the ground there is profound disjuncture between what policy-makers say should happen and the logics that actually shape project practice (pp. 232–236).

As a platform for my own research, I have taken this ethnographic picture as a starting point and developed a conceptual triad of how development works. This is a reconceptualisation of the original five propositions outlined by Mosse (2005),[3] but one that provides a more useful platform for further research. In the first component of this conceptual triad, development is shaped by the interaction between a complex *network of actors* rather than by policy. Second, policy helps build a level of consensus and establishes relationships among these disparate actors. In other words, it is a *unifying narrative*. Finally, using concepts Mosse extended in a later collaboration (Lewis & Mosse, 2006), *development brokers* actively recruit and maintain these actors.

Networks of actors

Anyone who has experience in international development will know that it involves multiple interactions between actors of differing status, varying levels of resources and dissimilar, often competing goals. Policy brings together these "diverse, even incompatible interests, for example those of national governments, implementing agencies, collaborating NGOs, research institutions, or donor advisers of different hues" (Mosse, 2005, p. 15). In the process it builds a level of consensus and establishes alliances – or relationships – that work to bring a project into existence. In other words, development policy ideas are important less for what they say than for whom they bring together – "what alliances, coalitions and consensuses they allow" (Mosse, 2005, p. 15).

However, policy models that effectively mobilise and maintain political support in order to legitimize development activities do not necessarily provide good guides to action (Mosse, 2005, p. 16). Instead, what drives action is the immediate needs of these organisations balanced against the need to maintain these relationships. Mosse (2005) argues that discourses become the end, rather than the means of development because a simple, coherent narrative creates a far better framework for maintaining relationships than contradictory development realities.

Policy as unifying narrative

As critical analysts of policy discourse have explained, the operational control that bureaucracies have over events and practices is quite limited. In the case of development projects and NGOs, policy makers, donor staff, consultants or senior managers are often marginal actors who are able at most to shape codes and rules to guide the behaviour of others with wills and motivations of their own. What usually has more impact is control over the interpretation of events – the narratives that maintain an organisation's definition of the problem and the relevance of the solutions proposed.

Partly this comes through good marketing, successfully selling a concept to the audience of actors involved. Partly it comes through the ambiguity of the narrative. A successful policy, therefore, is one that utilises sufficiently ambiguous terminology so that it is able "to achieve a high degree of convergence of disparate interests" (Mosse, 2005, p. 46). Finally, and most importantly, it is the development of a narrative powerful enough to effectively cover over complex, real-world realities and the contradictory practices that make up a development project.

Mosse (2005) offers participation as a clear example of this. According to Mosse, there is a profound disjuncture between the clean official narrative of participatory development that works to unify disparate actors, and the logic and actions that actually shape project practice. Rather than being participatory, the project delivery system given as a case study relies on strong vertical control for its success. Here it is useful to return to Scott's (1990) hidden and public transcripts. Development outputs are brought about by a complex set of practical improvisations, and institutional and political relations – informed by hidden transcripts. Meanwhile the project was compelled to promote the consensus view that these activities were the result of the implementation of official participatory development policy – its public transcripts.

Development brokers

A considerable amount of effort has to go into first enrolling the range of supportive actors required to establish a development project and then sustaining the unifying narrative that allows these often-disparate actors to work together. In a practical sense this takes the form of model building and reporting, field visits and review missions, public events, and promotional literature or publicity and marketing. In other words:

> Project models and their interpretations, upon which project success and survival depends, have to be secured and stabalised socially, not only by winning the compliance of beneficiaries, but also through actively recruiting and enrolling other supporting actors who tie their interests to the representations of the established project order.
>
> (Mosse, 2004, p. 657)

This work falls on development brokers – advocates, managers, consultants and fieldworkers – who translate the meaning of the project into the many different institutional languages of its stakeholder supporters (Mosse, 2005, p. 8; see also Latour, 1996, p. 78). In other words, these actors develop and sustain the common narrative that mobilises support and maintains the networks that drive a project.

A new development framework

Here we can see that the picture Mosse (2005) paints is not the established image of the monolithic, all-powerful development industry, but a site of struggle between competing interests, conflicting agendas and diverging conceptions. It is a complex network of government bureaucracies, corporate donors, development agencies and beneficiaries, all with diverse, even incompatible interests: "An arena in which people with different responsibilities, tasks and different constructions of reality competed for power" (Mosse, 2005, p. 104). Similarly, Mosse's description of how these contradictions are lived and resolved does not reflect the rational-instrumental understanding of development as the execution of international policy. Instead, it is a complex affair in which policy is not concerned with orientating practice, but rather is designed to build consensus and establish the relationships that drive development activities. In this, Mosse provides a provocative and fresh understanding of development that has stimulated much rethinking about policy discourse, and the interactions and practises they are assumed to drive.

From development to humanitarianism, policy to legal frameworks

As ethnographers have unpacked this complex relationship between development actors, scholars have largely ignored the interplay between political, military and humanitarian actors in the humanitarian arena. We are largely left with an instrumentalist interpretation of how they interact, with humanitarian handbooks calling for sustained engagement with the normative frameworks and repeated calls to respect the humanitarian principles. In doing so they have largely missed the non-instrumentalist, non-normative view that ethnography has taken in the related field of development. This position pays little attention to the relationship between formal frameworks and protection outcomes, and largely ignores the social processes between actors in the humanitarian arena. What follows is an effort to develop a new view of humanitarian protection, which draws on the concepts of networks, narratives and brokers that have been introduced in recent ethnographies of development.

In drawing on how the ethnography of development literature rethinks the relationship between policy and practice, and gives agency to different actors, it is first important to acknowledge that I am making two conceptual moves: first from development to humanitarianism and second from policy to legal frameworks. There are obviously some important differences here.

The divide between the systems of development and humanitarianism has been there since the beginning, each emerging at different times and evolving at different speeds. "They were born on different planets," says Barnett, the author of *Empire of Humanity* (2011).

> Humanitarian aid – whose modern roots can be traced back to the 19th century – was born largely out of emergency situations – natural and human based. A lot of the work then was on symptoms or keeping people alive. The development world was born out of colonialism, beginning pre-World War II, and morphed into modern development assistance after [the war]. These monies tended to go for technical assistance, education, health, jobs training, agriculture … the focus was livelihoods, growth and getting people out of poverty.
>
> (As cited in Anyangwe, 2015)

Conceived to address different problems, they traditionally draw resources from different funding pools, are coordinated separately and have vastly different implementation timeframes. Development work is funded in three- to five-year time frames, while humanitarian aid comes with conditions that require money to be spent in six to eighteen months. Importantly, humanitarianism defines itself as largely apolitical. "It offers to save individuals, but not to eliminate the underlying causes that place them at risk" (Barnett, 2005, p. 724). Development meanwhile, aspiring to restructure underlying social relations, is inherently political (Barnett, 2005).

Certainly, after the Cold War the lines between humanitarianism and development have become blurred. INGOs operating along the development-rights-relief continuum have disturbed the traditional divisions, embracing the idea that they might try to eliminate the root causes of conflicts that place people at risk. As well as providing humanitarian assistance, they have remained long-term to tackle inequality and poverty through human rights and development programs (see Barnett, 2005). However, while the lines are blurred, the divide between the two systems – the development projects of Mosse's work and humanitarian protection of this study – by and large remains.

Similarly, my study does not directly reflect Mosse's (2005) examination of policy discourses. His is a world where white papers, mission statements, strategic plans and policy forums attempt to create coherence in development policy at a global level, while strategies, models and designs occupy the local level. For Mosse, policy ranges from the wider policies of international donors, such as the paradigms of "participatory" development and "poverty focused" development, to policy models such as "sustainable rural livelihoods". He envisions policy as quite a loose term, broader than the purely instrumental view that policies are rational and problem solving, directly shaping the way that development is done.[4]

Humanitarian protection, on the other hand, is guided by legal frameworks rather than by policy. At the global level, these encompass a growing array of legal instruments, including international humanitarian law, refugee law and human rights law. Underneath these, a series of soft laws – professional standards, principles and codes of conduct that have evolved from these international frameworks – guide how protection is done in practice. In this way, while Mosse (2005) follows in the tradition of a group of scholars who have taken to describing policy as discourse (see Bacchi, 2010, p. 45), this study is linked to a related body of literature which describes laws as discourse (see McCann, 1993, p. 6). As Galanter (1983) explains, law should be understood broadly "as a system of culture and symbolic meanings (more) than as a set of operative controls. It affects us primarily through communication of symbols – by providing threats, promises, models, persuasion, legitimacy, stigma, and so on" (p. 127, as cited in McCann, 1993, p. 6).

Nevertheless, while there are some important differences between the two studies, the basic analytical angle is preserved and the essence of Mosse's (2005) work is carried over to this research. First, humanitarian protection, like development, is shaped through the interaction of a network of actors, which includes states, their militaries, insurgents, aid worker and affected communities. Second, the protection frameworks, like Mosse's development policies, can be viewed as narratives: simple interpretations of complex, real-world realities and relevant solutions that can be accepted by a heterogeneous network of actors. Lastly, like development projects, humanitarianism has interpretative communities who provide reasons for its heterogeneous network of actors to participate in this established order (see Sayer, 1994, p. 374).

Humanitarian protection as a network of actors

Humanitarianism and its guiding principles are often confused with the universal ethic. Instead, these terms represent the institutions through which this humanitarian ethic is expressed and the frameworks that guide them. Humanitarian agencies are only one part of this network of actors – which also includes states and their militaries among its commonly recognised actors. Others, including civil society, non-state armed actors and even affected communities, while only recently recognised, have also long been part of this network. Humanitarian protection, I argue here, is shaped through the interaction between these multifaceted political and military actors.

This network of actors has been part of modern humanitarian protection since its inception in the mid-19th century, when states, their militaries and humanitarians signed on to the first Geneva Convention. These mutually beneficial rules were in essence a formal humanitarian agreement between key actors of the day, outlining how they should interact with each other. States agreed that their combatants should show restraint towards each other, specific groups of "innocents" were to be left alone, provided they did not take part in the conflict, and humanitarian actors were to be provided space to operate, on the condition that they met certain conditions of non-interference. Clearly, this initial network of actors represents the European, state-centred discourse of the era, which failed to recognise other actors of the day and their multiple, sometimes conflicting, agendas. Civilians remained passive recipients of aid, while the other centres of power that existed at the time – be they warlords, rebels, bandits or embryonic states – were largely ignored.

A more detailed picture of this humanitarian protection network has emerged in recent years as the dominant framework of the humanitarian space has been replaced by an alternative paradigm through which to view aid delivery and humanitarian protection. In this new humanitarian arena, aid is negotiated and its outcomes are shaped by the interaction between multiple actors. Aid in this perspective is the outcome "of the messy interaction of social actors struggling, negotiating and at times guessing to further their own interests" (Bakewell, 2000, pp. 108–109). In this arena approach, the kind of actors considered to be humanitarian are not predetermined by the humanitarian discourse, but are shaped in practice.

Through this lens it becomes clear that humanitarian aid and protection encompass many more actors than the original discourse recognised. This includes UN agencies and the International Red Cross and Red Crescent Movement, multiple NGOs, various state organisations, religious affiliated groups and commercial suppliers from the private sector. State military contingents have long been an important part of this network, providing aid in inaccessible areas or protecting its delivery by other actors. In the same way, non-state armed actors have been revealed as key players, providing protection and facilitating or restricting the delivery of aid to communities under their control according to their own motivations. Last, but not least, aid recipients have agency in this complex humanitarian arena rather than being passive recipients or victims, as is commonly portrayed. They do not passively hang about until aid arrives, but are active actors, working to reach agencies to access aid or rebuild and fortify their communities.

Different actors, different motivations

Humanitarian protection involves a complex network of actors with varying resources, differing statuses and dissimilar, often competing goals. Importantly, these actors do not display a consistent behaviour in every situation. Instead, their practices are driven by different motivations; decisions are taken in response to the needs of the situation, their own priorities at the time and the significance of their relationship with other actors in this network. From this perspective, the protection frameworks are not a universal set of rules and principles, but are socially negotiated and acquire meaning in practice. They are constantly reinterpreted and renegotiated by different actors, changing over time as the nature of conflict changes, as motivations change and as ideas of what is acceptable behaviour changes (Leader, 2000). In other words, they are contextual and imbued with different meanings by different actors at different times (Hilhorst & Schmiemann, 2002).

Here it is useful to briefly return to the actor-oriented approach, which is able to recognise the multiple realities and diverse social practices of various actors. Language and discourse play an important part in facilitating this. As Long and Long (1992) point out, there are always multiple discourses at work:

> Since social life is never so unitary as to be built upon one single type of discourse, it follows that, however restricted their choice, actors always face some alternative ways of formulating their objectives, deploying modes of action and giving reasons for their behaviour.
>
> (p. 25)

In other words, different actors in the network advance or legitimise their respective interests by strategically and tactically using the language of humanitarian protection. The humanitarian norms are not simply used for their official purpose, but to achieve a range of goals and political needs.

Actors base their humanitarian decisions on a range of driving forces besides the often cited "humanitarian desire" to reduce the impact of war and "alleviate human suffering wherever it may be found". Political motivations, for example, at least partly inspire a range of these actors. Following the end of the Cold War, states increasingly used humanitarianism as a strategy for political containment, using relief as a response to human security problems. As Barnett (2011) puts it, "the willingness of states to become more involved in the organisation and delivery of relief owed not only to a newfound passion for compassion but also to a belief that their political, economic and strategic interests were at stake" (p. 107). This has only increased following September 11, 2001, as many states began to see counterterrorism and humanitarianism as "crime-fighting partners" (Barnett, 2005, p. 726).

Aid agencies, one of the original network partners, have multiple motivations beyond the desire to alleviate human suffering. Humanitarian protection can be motivated by organisational politics – the desire to continue operations and retain staff – or as a form of legitimisation politics – showing the public that an agency is doing good work (Hilhorst & Jansen, 2010). The need for funding is also a well-known driving force for humanitarian action, reflected in the size of humanitarian operations in the Western sphere of concern while forgotten crisis are left under staffed and under resourced. Similarly, the focus on short-term relief is driven by the demand of major donors for immediate and measurable results (Bookstein, 2003).

Non-state armed actors, while not necessarily fully invested in the legal frameworks, are part of this network of actors and respond to its driving forces. As outlined in Chapter 1, they practice pro-civilian restraint and provide services, especially protection, for reasons of international acceptance, community support and reciprocity. They also embrace humanitarian relief, which, while often from a contradictory position to the humanitarian ethic, is not far removed from the political reasoning of state actors.

Humanitarian aid – delivered or redirected by insurgent organisations – has the potential to build community support and influence the power balance between rival organisations, reflecting the reasoning of state-sponsored humanitarian efforts in places like Afghanistan. The provision of humanitarian assistance also contributes to the legitimisation of insurgent organisations by allowing them to fulfil their social and material obligations to the communities they purport to represent with minimal effort or cost (see Anderson, 1999; Terry, 2002). Terry (2002) extends this argument further by suggesting that negotiations with faction leaders by aid agencies to gain access and security guarantees "implicitly recognised those groups' authority over a territory or population" (p. 44). This in turn boosts their local and international legitimacy. As such: "Humanitarian aid, viewed through this lens, can be imagined as a conduit between places and people, facilitating relief and reconstruction assistance as well as political legitimacy and, hence, the political and economic stability of a place" (Kleinfeld, 2007, p. 170). This network extends to include private actors motivated by commerce, religious organisations with a religious mandate, and even the affected communities themselves, who manipulate humanitarian relief to suit their specific purposes.

It is also important to remember that each actor in this arena can simultaneously deploy different interpretations of these humanitarian principles at the same time. For example, an armed faction can protect the rights of communities in areas it controls, while simultaneously restricting the delivery of aid to the enemy in areas it does not control. A state can provide both impartial humanitarian aid *and* work to win the hearts and minds of insurgent supporters in the very same space. An external power can use humanitarian intervention to end the human-rights abuses of a state, while working to strengthen the state's capacity to protect it citizens.

Here we start to see a picture of the broad network of actors that operate in the humanitarian arena and the complex mix of motivations that drive them. Importantly, these actors do not display the same behaviour in every situation, but are driven by different guiding motives at different times. Their decisions are made in response to their interpretation of the political and humanitarian needs of the situation, and how these decisions will impact their relationships with other actors. Mutually beneficial deals are continually made as different actors seek political advantage, community support, acceptance and legitimacy; behaviour is modified to sustain these arrangements, often to the benefit of humanitarianism and affected communities. For in the humanitarian arena of today's civil wars and complex emergencies, humanitarian protection comes through the interactions between these multiple actors, rather than any overriding commitment to the normative frameworks and humanitarian principles.

The unifying protection narrative

This is not to say the normative frameworks do not play a key role in humanitarian protection, for they are clearly significant, just not in the traditional sense of rules to be followed or prosecuted. The lack of prosecution for breaches of these rules is an indicator that their influence lies elsewhere. Instead, I posit that it is more useful to view these humanitarian frameworks and principles as part of a unifying narrative that first helps enrol these different actors into the protection network, linking their agendas to that of humanitarian protection. This network is not a coordinated partnership or formal collaboration, but an ongoing negotiation between disparate actors with their often-competing agendas. This narrative then helps to sustain a level of agreement among this diverse network, balancing their immediate needs and objectives against the need to maintain the relationships, which in turn drives humanitarian protection.

Foundations of the unifying protection narrative

As critical analysts of policy discourse have argued, power lies in the narratives that maintain an organisation's particular interpretation of the problem. Roe (1994) has tackled policy controversies demonstrating how conflicting policy "stories" can be brought together under a unifying "meta-narrative" to promote a level of consensus. According to Roe, these narratives are "strategic simplifications" that generate consensus around major policies and make political action possible. In other words, this narrative is able to unify different actors by allowing different positions to be relevant at the same time. As discussed earlier, Mosse

(2005) makes a valuable contribution to this conceptualisation in his examination of development policy narratives. The development anthropologist views policies not as measures for gaining results on the ground, but more as tools for co-opting different, shifting interests. He argues that successful policies employ abstract and ambiguous concepts "which mediate or translate between divergent interests" in order to "achieve a high degree of convergence of disparate interests" (p. 46). Indeed, the success or failure of a development project depends on establishing this "wider networks of support and validation" (p. 18).

Transferring this concept to humanitarianism, I posit that protection depends on the stabilisation of a particular interpretation of events that is able to embrace the often-competing positions of the different actors. The protection frameworks are in essence this unifying interpretation, or unifying narrative, bringing together key actors. Historically this has included states, their militaries and humanitarians, but more recently these frameworks have been tasked with uniting a more complex arena of actors. Like the policy narratives outlined by Roe (1994) and Mosse (2005), the protection narrative's strength lies in a simplicity and vagueness that can be accepted by this disparate network of actors as well as a marketing strategy that recruits and retains actors.

This simplicity can be seen through an examination of the Geneva Conventions, which form the original foundation of the protection frameworks, or the protection narrative. With some common sense and a minimum of good will, it is possible to build an understanding of these rules of war without the need of a law degree. In fact, to simplify them to the extreme, the rules were summed up by one international lawyer through four concepts: "Do not attack non-combatants, do not attack combatants anyhow, treat persons in your power humanely, protect the victims" (David, 2008, pp. 1039–1040). To revisit Mosse's (2005) conceptualisation, such a simple, coherent narrative creates a far better framework for maintaining relationships among different actors than contradictory protection realities.

Similar to the development narrative described by Mosse (2005), the protection narrative rests on metaphors whose "vagueness, ambiguity, and lack of conceptual precision is *required* to conceal ideological differences" and "to allow compromise and the enrolment of different interests" (p. 230, emphasis in the original). The civilian, for example, remains an indeterminate figure in this humanitarian narrative, recognised by what it is not – a combatant – rather than for what it is, thus leaving room for interpretation. Similarly, the concepts of neutrality and impartiality are so open to interpretation that the ICRC, INGOs, UN agencies and even governments have been able to employ them.

Finally, the effectiveness of this humanitarian narrative has been reinforced over the decades by good marketing, repeatedly selling the concepts to the audience of actors the narrative seeks to encompass. In this way, actors are continually recruited into the network and reminded how it is important to them and their own interests. Or, as Slim (2003) explains in "Marketing humanitarian space": "If those who hold economic, social, political and military power in a war can be persuaded to 'buy' the humanitarian norms and principles of international humanitarian law (IHL) then civilians are more likely to be protected than killed" (p. 3).

Here we can start to envision a quite powerful narrative, which has proved effective in uniting the state, military and humanitarian actors that formed the original network. The 19th century laws of war – borrowing from Mosse's (2005) development policy language – brought together these "diverse and incompatible interests", providing a "level of consensus" on what was appropriate behaviour. The benefits of maintaining these relationships – limits to the scale and impact of industrialised warfare – provide the motivation to put aside competing needs in order to sustain the network. Clearly, different actors have stepped outside this network with devastating humanitarian consequences, but this original humanitarian network's resilience over time is testament to the strength of the unifying narrative.

It is, however, a network based on a 19th century European concept of war, where states held the monopoly of the legitimate use of violence. This vision of what was real war excluded forms of violence beyond the borders of the continent, whether the brutal land-grab that would soon be underway in Africa or the conflicts that had always existed locally in other parts of the world. The colonial other was not part of this European concept of humanitarianism or the original humanitarian protection network. As discussed previously, this Eurocentric conceptualisation of war and humanitarian protection remain highly relevant and applicable today, for they are part of a powerful colonial discourse that has left its residue across modern social and political life (see Rostis, 2016; Young, 2001). As a result, the original humanitarian narrative remains central to modern approaches to humanitarianism broadly and humanitarian protection more specifically. It can be seen in the formal protection frameworks that guide practice across the humanitarian spectrum. What has changed, in the meantime, is the nature of the wars in which humanitarians are involved; in these so-called new wars humanitarians now need to engage with a much wider array of actors, with diverse motivations that are not necessarily encapsulated by the long-established humanitarian narrative.

The unifying narrative and new wars

Over recent decades, an increasing number of actors have made their presence felt in the humanitarian arena. INGOs, local civil society, non-state armed actors, private corporations and even affected communities have appeared alongside the original state, military and humanitarian actors. Among these new actors, non-state armed actors have done the most to unsettle the established narratives of conflict and protection. In response, there have been concerted efforts to recruit these new actors into the protection network.

Narrative policy theorists have identified two ways to recruit new actors into a network (see Roe, 1994). Broadly speaking, there is the possibility of engaging new narratives, which come from a different position to the existing narrative and are more relevant to these actors. Alternatively, and the path taken with the humanitarian protection narrative, it is possible to extend the established narrative to incorporate new actors. In instrumental terms, it has meant adding to the original normative frameworks – international humanitarian law. While IHL traditionally focused on states and international armed conflict, modern IHL has gradually been extended in an attempt to govern the actions of organised non-state armed actors.[5] Statements of customary law have also contributed to recent efforts to extend IHL and make it more relevant to non-state armed actors who do not have an historical allegiance to state and European-centric laws. Like the treaties, the rules of customary IHL address the protection of people who are not part of the fight. They are seen to be more relevant in non-international armed conflict, where treaty law has been found wanting. A rule is deemed customary, and as such binding on all state and non-state armed actors, if it is based on widespread practice supporting the requirement of the rule.[6]

The protection narrative has been further extended through the incorporation of IRL and an array of human rights conventions pertinent to protecting people from violence during armed conflict (see Chapter 1). This state-legal discourse of rights has worked to help integrate multiple new actors into the protection network, with both state and non-state armed actors having a responsibility to respect these international laws. Civilians too have been absorbed by this new discourse, for they are no longer passive beneficiaries, but active rights holders in this network of actors (see Slim & Bonwick, 2005). Furthermore, extending the protection narrative to include human rights law has worked to incorporate the INGOs that arrived in the conflict space after the Cold War. It does this through a broader understanding of protection that accommodates the different approaches of these new humanitarian actors. As the accepted definition discussed in Chapter 1 explains, protection now encompasses "all activities aimed at ensuring the full respect for the rights of the individual in accordance with the letter and the spirit of the relevant bodies of law" (Caverzasio, 2001, p. 19). Whether they are advocacy groups campaigning for the rights of affected communities, or relief agencies providing neutral and impartial humanitarian assistance, they can align their different approaches with this new, broader protection narrative. Ultimately, we now have a spectrum of legal frameworks that form an extension of the original protection narrative that has worked for decades to unite disparate actors behind a specific definition of the problem and the way to mitigate it.

Maintaining the network

To reiterate, power lies in the narratives that maintain an organisation's interpretation of an event (see Roe, 1991, 1994). Transferring this to humanitarian protection, success has depended on the stabilisation of the normative legal frameworks and universal principles as the accepted definition of the problem, its cause and the way to solve it.[7] This state-centric approach evolved out of a European understanding of war as an extension of state politics with the frameworks working to unify the key actors of the day – states, their militaries and humanitarians – into a common interpretation of humanitarian protection.[8] As our conceptualisation of war has slowly expanded over the past 150 years, so too have the frameworks and the actors they have attempted to unite. In the complex arena of the so-called new wars this has included efforts to encapsulate new humanitarians and non-state armed actors. Ultimately, the more interests recruited into this particular interpretation of events, the more dominant these humanitarian frameworks become and the more effective they are. This is an extension of Latour's (1996) argument that project success is not inherently attributable to its technical design. Rather, it is a consequence of the projects "ability to continue recruiting support and so impose … [their] growing coherence on those who argue about them or oppose them" (p. 78).

There is potentially, however, an ironic twist to these efforts to extend the protection frameworks – or the humanitarian narrative – to cover more actors in the complex and strained environment of contemporary wars. While at one level extending the narrative helps to recruit more actors, it raises the spectre of two negative consequences introduced by Roe (1991) in narrative analysis and Mosse (2005) in development anthropology. The first comes through the approach used to recruit new actors. As outlined above, by extending the narrative, it has become more complicated, undermining the simplicity and ambiguity that sits at the heart of a successful unifying narrative. Does this increasing complexity mitigate against the humanitarian narrative's success in complex, contemporary wars? Research in narrative theory and development policy/practice analysis would indicate that it does.

Second, the broader the network and more disparate the interests, the more difficult it is to unify all actors under a single narrative. As discussed earlier, this common humanitarian narrative is supported for different reasons and serves an increasing diversity of actors. The international community has used it to rescue its self-image as civilised and humane, states to justify intervention, and militaries to reduce the lethality of modern war and protect their own. Humanitarian agencies use it for different purposes, its simplicity and ambiguity allowing them to justify their presence and approach. Insurgents have somewhat selectively adopted notions of humanitarian restraint as a strategy to garner community support and promote their international legitimacy. To repeat the question, is this diversity mitigating against the narrative's success in complex, contemporary wars? As Mosse (2004) explains in the field of development, diversity destabilises and militates against coherence: "The greater the number of people who are invited to the party the more energy is expended attending their needs, and the more their needs shape the project" (p. 647).

It is here we start to see the increasing role of humanitarians, not for their ability to deliver relief or protect the rights of at-risk communities, which is quite limited, but for their unofficial role in recruiting new actors and maintaining the narrative that holds them together. As Mosse (2004) goes on to explain, this recruitment and maintenance of diverse actors is the task of skilled brokers who translate the meaning of the unifying narrative into the different institutional languages of its stakeholders (p. 647). In other words, linking this to protection, brokers interpret the official frameworks so that they reflect the practical interests of different actors, giving them a reason to participate in the established order.

Humanitarian brokers, translators and travellers

In the earlier humanitarian network, the responsibility and the capacity to protect lay firmly with states and their militaries. On their own, the original humanitarians had quite limited levels of influence over events. They relied on states and their militaries to provide the space to work. What they did have, however, was influence over the interpretation of events through their mandate to disseminate the laws of war and the humanitarian principles. Dissemination is a rather sterile word that does not fully encapsulate this central role, which the ICRC has filled as both guardian and promoter of the original humanitarian norms. In this conceptualisation, the ICRC and its field delegates were intermediaries, spreading the message about humanitarian principles and normative frameworks to the actors of the day. It is a role they continue to fill in the modern humanitarian space.

Today, humanitarian actors have increasingly gone beyond this role as intermediaries to become active mediators. As Latour (1993) explains, the intermediary makes no difference to the transaction, while the mediator is "endowed with the capacity to translate what they transport, to redefine it, redeploy it" (p. 81). These humanitarian mediators have emerged in response to the fragmented political authority of today's wars, where power is spread across multiple actors, including warlords, criminal networks and rebel movements. These network specialists have extended the role of the original intermediary or disseminator in an effort to make the protection narrative relevant to this wider network of actors. They follow in the tradition of brokers, who have emerged in response to other complex political environments in recent decades.

Who is the broker?

Brokers are network specialists whose ability to straddle multiple knowledge systems and life-worlds enables them to act as gatekeepers across various social synapses or choke points. This classic figure in the anthropological literature first appeared in the context of de-colonialisation and mobilisation theory of the 1950s and 1960s. In this historical era, Wolf (1956) defined brokers as "groups of people who mediate between community-oriented groups in communities and nation-oriented groups which operate primarily within national institutions" (p. 1075). These brokers were "Janus-like", turned in two directions at once and came to "stand guard over the crucial junctures or synapses of relationships which connect the local system to the larger whole" (Wolf, 1956, pp. 1075–1077). With the rise of the nation state, new forms of trans-local relations evolved, as did new brokers. As Geertz (1960) phrased it, while before the broker was a "scholar, curer, and mystic teacher, he is now a politician," albeit "an amateur one" (p. 247). There were explicit disciplinary concerns in the rise of the broker as well. For Geertz, the focus on the broker was an attempt to find a space between the predominance of community-based studies in anthropology and political science's concern with elites.

By the late 1970s, the broker largely vanished from view as local-level political analysis ceded ground to the rise of structuralist models. These structuralist (particularly Marxist) models of political analysis positioned the post-colonial state as the primary source of power and domination in the "global South". For the next two decades, the focus was broadly placed on how power disciplined and shaped individual subjectivities, and questions concerning agency were effectively sidelined. In this world, the local-level broker appeared increasingly insignificant.

The return of the broker

In the last decade there has been a renewed interest in the broker within anthropology as state-centred models of power and sovereignty have been increasingly problematised. In this context, the broker has emerged as an actor positioned along these fault-lines. But the broker is not simply a figure who stands between powerless people and the imposed power of the modern state. Instead, the broker "activates the continuing interplay between apparently irreconcilable discourses and practices" (James, 2011, p. 335). This conceptualisation is seen in works ranging from popular culture, where brokerage is celebrated for its creativity and inventiveness (Barber, 1987), to that of scholars in development studies, who celebrate its capacity to translate across divergent networks (Lewis & Mosse, 2006; Mosse, 2005).

The global rise of NGOs in the context of the development aid industry and transnational activism has led scholars to consider the role of broker in these processes. Of particular interest in the emerging literature of development brokers is *Brokers and Translators* (Lewis & Mosse, 2006) which combines the actor-oriented approach rooted in the Manchester school of anthropology with a Latourian concern with translation in actor network theory.[9] Rather than considering brokers as strictly mediating between aid donors and recipients, these authors ask how unpredictable development projects are actually implemented through the translation of interests, concepts and practices, and how particular forms of meaning are established in the process.

Brokers of humanitarianism

Particular types of individuals – often multilingual and comfortable in multiple settings – have emerged as ethnographic exemplars of the broker: the African chief, the traditional healer engaged with Western medicine, the local religious leader translating the teachings of Rome or Mecca. As noted above, these brokers have emerged as anthropological informants when fault lines appear in concepts of the state, whether it is the shifting forms of political authority in the post-colonial era or the more recent fractures in state-models of power. James (2011) notes as much in relation to transitional settings in post-apartheid South Africa, where "state, market, and patrimonial/patriarchal-style political authority intersect" (p. 318). She sees the re-emergence of brokers who can mediate between these spheres, in her case in the context of land reform. Bierschenk, Chauveau and de Sardan (2002) locate their development broker within the fragmented politics of the post-colonial state, where power is exercised both by state structures and through a diverse range of supra-local associations and networks, in which there is a host of intermediate actors and networks.

With this in mind, it is timely to return to the humanitarian worker, positioned within the fragmented politics of contemporary war. Historically positioned as intermediary between the different actors in armed conflict, these so-called guardians of humanitarian law were officially tasked with disseminating the humanitarian laws and principles. This paper argues that they are no longer just intermediaries, simply following normative scripts, but important mediators. Here it is important to return to Latour (2005), who makes a critical distinction between intermediaries and mediators. The intermediary "transports meaning without transformation", while mediators "transform, translate, distort, and modify the meaning of elements they are supposed to carry" (p. 39). Drawing from the history of research into brokers and brokerage, in particular the ethnographies of development – which deal with a similar group of actors – it is possible to develop a picture of whom these brokers of humanitarianism are, the space they occupy and the roles they play.

Travellers

In previous research it was quite clear who the broker was mediating between and the space they occupied – the village and the national capital, community and the state. In this conceptualisation they formed the link between two systems (see Geertz, 1960; Wolf, 1956). This picture has become more complex in contemporary research, which incorporates multiple actors. Development brokers connected development institutions with partner organisations, donors and communities (see, e.g., Lewis and Mosse, 2006). The space that humanitarian brokers work in is ever more complicated. They are dealing with multiple actors: state and non-state armed actors, allied and competing humanitarian agencies, communities, donors. They are travelling across multiple borders/junctures to do so. To borrow from Clifford (1992), they are a "travelling culture", identified as much by the borders they cross and the groups they encounter as the spaces they inhabit.

Translators

Humanitarian brokers also play a key role in sustaining the unifying narrative that brings multiple actors into line with the legal, state-centred approach to protection. Following the thinking of Latour (1996) and Mosse (2005), this concept of humanitarianism has become real through the work of generating and translating interests, creating context by tying in supporters and so sustaining interpretations. It is here that the act of translation becomes important. It is this process that overcomes fragmentation and dissent, enrolling heterogeneous actors and consolidating their interests behind the unifying narrative. As Lewis and Mosse (2006) explain:

> The overall system can be stabilized only when actors are able to reconstruct the network of interactions through the creation of coherent representations, which they do through a process of "translation" that permits the negotiation of common meanings and definitions and the mutual enrollment and cooptation into individual and collective objectives and activities.
>
> (p. 14)

These roles fall on skilled brokers who translate the meaning of a project – or framework, principle, code of conduct – in order for it to align with the different motivations of multiple actors and then back again to fit the dominant narrative. While from the perspective of actor network theory there exists an endless number of mediators – and thereby brokers – it is humanitarians who are ideally positioned to fill this role of translating the official protection frameworks and in doing so providing a temporary fix to the problems faced in contemporary wars.

Conclusion: Towards an ethnography of humanitarian protection

Mosse's (2005) highly original research and the new ethnographies of development it inspired (see, e.g., Fechter & Hindman, 2011; Mosse, 2011) have opened up space to reframe humanitarian protection. His examination of development policy and practice provides the foundation for an innovative lens through which to take a fresh look at humanitarian protection. The three-tiered view of humanitarian protection developed in this chapter first allows us to analyse and describe the complex *network of actors* who shape and drive humanitarian protection. Importantly, it takes us beyond simply acknowledging the complex make-up of the humanitarian arena to incorporating the multiple interactions that drive humanitarian protection. Second, it steps away from the dominant state-legal discourse to re-imagine the protection frameworks as a *unifying narrative* that establishes relationships and builds a level of consensus among these disparate actors. For it is this consensus, rather than the legal frameworks, that drives protection. Finally, it places the *humanitarian broker* at the centre of this network. These humanitarian brokers travel throughout the network, translating the meaning of the protection frameworks in order for them to align with the often-competing agendas of different actors. These brokers are also a central analytical tool for this study, for it is the broker who interacts with the multiple actors in the arena; it is through this central actor that we can develop a story explaining how humanitarian protection works. It is these actors I turn to now, providing an account of their everyday practice under the three themes of intermediaries, brokers and travellers.

Notes

1 Smirl's (2015) examination of the spaces and objects of aid using critical theory and personal observation, and Fast's (2014) first-hand account of violence against aid workers are two examples of how some humanitarian scholars have started moving beyond the instrumental perspective, using ethnographic methods to grapple with some of humanitarianism's complex interactions.

2 What is of interest here is less the relationship between dominance and resistance, but the relationship between hidden and public transcripts, between the dominant development policy models and the scattered, informal practices surviving below.

3 Mosse (2005) centres his study around five propositions in order to answer his initial question, "How does development work?" First, Mosse argues that development policy primarily functions to "mobilise and maintain political support", that is to "legitimize rather than to orientate practice". Second, development interventions are "not driven by policy, but by the exigencies of organisations and the need to maintain relationships". Proposition three is that "development projects work to maintain themselves as coherent policy ideas or systems of representations". Mosse's fourth proposition holds that projects "do not fail" but "are failed by wider networks of support and validation". This makes success and failure "policy-oriented judgments that obscure project effects", which is proposition five (pp. 14–19).

4 Mosse's (2005) justification for adopting such a broad conception of policy is the strong inter-connection that exists between project designs (causal theories, e.g., summarised in logical frameworks), policy models (frameworks and approaches, e.g., sustainable rural livelihoods) and the wider policy of a donor agency (e.g., participatory and poverty focused development). This research adopts a similarly broad conception, incorporating international laws and humanitarian principles, as well as the frameworks, principles and handbooks that guide action at the local level.

5 As mentioned previously, internal armed conflicts were incorporated into the Geneva Conventions in 1949 through Article 3 of the Third Geneva Convention. In 1977, Additional Protocol I provided that wars of national liberation would be considered as international armed conflicts and Additional Protocol II added further rules and language to incorporate non-state armed groups into the framework.

6 The ICRC has identified 161 rules of customary IHL, which have been published in what they describe as a "user friendly", "easily accessible", two-volume guide, to complement the established treaty laws (Henckaerts & Doswald-Beck, 2005b, 2005a)

7 These make up the narrative's beginning, middle and end as described by Roe (1991).

8 Some would argue Dunant recruited states into his vision for humanitarianism, but states were equally active, co-opting Dunant's principles to suit their own agenda, thus recruiting humanitarians into their framework.

9 In the early 1950s, a group of scholars at the University of Manchester's school of anthropology developed a distinctive approach which focused on the role of conflict in society, acknowledged the importance of the wider context (particularly the impact of colonialism), shed light on the issue of multiple identities through their studies of urban and rural communities and advanced a new analytical model known as social network analysis.

References

Allie, M.-P. (2011). Introduction: Acting at any price? In C. Magone, M. Nueman, & F. Weissman (Eds.), *Humanitarian negotiations revealed: The MSF experience*. Hurst & Co.

Anderson, M. (1999). *Do no harm: How aid can support peace—or war*. Lynne Rienner.

Anyangwe, E. (2015, December 4). Is it time to rethink the divide between humanitarian and development funding? *The Guardian*.

Bacchi, C. (2010). Policy as discourse: What does it mean? Where does it get us? *Discourse: Studies in the Cultural Politics of Education*, 21(1), 45–57.

Bakewell, O. (2000). Uncovering local perspectives on humanitarian assistance and its outcomes. *Disasters*, 24(2), 103–116.

Barber, K. (1987). Popular arts in Africa. *African Studies Review*, 30(3), 1–78.

Barnett, M. (2005). Humanitarianism transformed. *Perspectives in Politics*, 3(4), 723–740.

Barnett, M. (2011). *Empire of humanity: A history of humanitarianism*. Cornell University Press.

Bierschenk, T., Chauveau, J.-P., & de Sardan, J.-P. (2002). *Local development brokers in Africa: The rise of a new social category* (Working Paper No. 13). Institute for Ethnography and African Studies.

Bookstein, A. (2003). *Beyond the headlines: An agenda for action to protect civilians in neglected conflicts*. Oxfam International.

Caverzasio, S. (2001). *Strengthening protection in war*. ICRC.

Clifford, J. (1992). Travelling cultures. In L. Grossberg, C. Nelson, & P. Treichler (Eds.), *Cultural studies* (pp. 96–116). Routledge.

David, E. (2008). *Princepes de droit des conflicts armes* [Principles of law of armed conflict] (4th edition). Bruylant.

de Certeau, M. (1984). *The practice of everyday life*. University of California Press.

de Sardan, J.-P. (2005). *Anthropology and development: Understanding contemporary social change*. Zed Books.

Escobar, A. (1995). *Encountering development: The making and unmaking of the Third World*. Princeton University Press.

Fast, L. (2014). *Aid in danger: The perils and promise of humanitarianism*. University of Pennsylvania Press.

Fechter, A.-M., & Hindman, H. (Eds.) (2011). *Inside the everyday lives of development workers: The challenges and futures of Aidland*. Kumarian Press.

Ferguson, J. (1994). *The anti-politics machine: "Development," depoliticization, and bureaucratic power in Lesotho*. Cambridge University Press.

Galanter, M. (1983). The radiating effects of courts. In K. Boyum & L. Mather (Eds.), *Empirical theories about courts* (pp. 117–142). Longman.

Geertz, C. (1960). The Javanese kijaji: The changing role of a cultural broker. *Comparative Studies in Society and History*, 2(2), 228–249.

Henckaerts, J.-M., & Doswald-Beck, L. (2005a). *Customary international humanitarian law: Vol. 2: Practice*. ICRC.

Henckaerts, J.-M., & Doswald-Beck, L. (2005b). *Customary international humanitarian law: Vol. 1: Rules*. ICRC.

Hilhorst, D., & Jansen, B. (2010). Humanitarian space as arena: A perspective on the everyday politics of aid. *Development and Change*, 41(6), 1117–1139.

Hilhorst, D., & Schmiemann, N. (2002). Humanitarian principles and organisational culture: Everyday practice in Médecins Sans Frontiéres-Holland. *Development in Practice*, 12(3/4),490–500.

James, D. (2011). The return of the broker: Consensus, hierarchy, and choice in South African land reform. *Journal of the Royal Anthropological Institute*, 17(2), 318–338.

Kleinfeld, M. (2007). Misreading the post-tsunami political landscape in Sri Lanka: The myth of humanitarian space. *Space and Polity*, 11(2), 169–184.

Latour, B. (1993). *We have never been modern* (C. Porter, Trans.). Harvard University Press.

Latour, B. (1996). *Aramis, or the love of technology* (C.Porter, Trans.). Harvard University Press.

Latour, B. (2005). *Reassembling the social: An introduction to actor-network theory* (R. Crease, Trans.). Oxford University Press.

Leader, N. (2000). *The politics of principle: The principles of humanitarian action in practice* (No.2; HPG Report). Overseas Development Institute.

Lewis, D., & Mosse, D. (Eds.). (2006). *Development brokers and translators: The ethnography of aid and agencies*. Kumarian Press.

Long, N., & Long, A. (Eds.) (1992). *Development sociology: Actor perspectives*. Routledge.

McCann, M. (1993). *Rights at work: Pay equity reform and the politics of legal mobilization*. University of Chicago Press.

Mosse, D. (2004). Is good policy unimplementable? Reflections on the ethnography of aid policy and practice. *Development and Change*, 35(4), 639–671.

Mosse, D. (2005). *Cultivating development: An ethnography of aid policy and practice*. Pluto Press.

Mosse, D. (Ed.) (2011). *Adventures in Aidland: The anthropology of professionals in international development*. Berghahn Books.

Mosse, D., & Lewis, D. (Eds.) (2005). *The aid effect: Giving and government in international development*. Pluto Press.

Roe, E. (1991). Development narratives, or making the best of blueprint development. *World Development*, 19(4), 287–300.

Roe, E. (1994). *Narrative policy analysis: Theory and practice*. Duke University Press.

Rostis, A. (2016). *Organising disaster: The construction of humanitarianism*. Emerald Group.

Sayer, D. (1994). Everyday forms of state formation: Some dissident remarks on "hegemony." In J. Gilbert & D. Nugent (Eds.), *Everyday forms of state formation: Revolution and the negotiation of rule in modern Mexico* (pp. 367–377). Duke University Press.

Scott, J. (1990). *Domination and the arts of resistance: Hidden transcripts*. Yale University Press.

Slim, H. (2003). *Marketing humanitarian space: Argument and method in humanitarian persuasion*. Centre for Humanitarian Dialogue.

Slim, H., & Bonwick, A. (2005). *Protection: An ALNAP guide for humanitarian agencies*. Overseas Development Institute.

Smirl, L. (2015). *Spaces of aid: How cars, compounds and hotels shape humanitarianism*. Zed Books.

Terry, F. (2002). *Condemned to repeat? The paradox of humanitarian action*. Cornell University Press.

Wolf, E. (1956). Aspects of group relations in a complex society: Mexico. *American Anthropologist*, 58(6), 1065–1078.

Young, R. (2001). *Postcolonialism: An historical introduction*. Blackwell.

Part II

An ethnography of humanitarian protection

4 Intermediaries and the humanitarian network

Introduction

A small red cross emblem clipped to his shirt, the ICRC delegate runs through the well-rehearsed presentation, outlining the laws of war to another cohort of soldiers. Today the presentation is being carried out in the Kurdish zone of northern Iraq, some 100 kilometres from where a fierce battle for the control of Mosul will soon take place. The audience are junior officers of the Peshmerga, the military forces of the autonomous region of Iraqi Kurdistan. Dressed in US-style desert camouflage, the young officers sit in neat rows in the conference room, listening attentively to a presentation that countless other soldiers have heard. In its simplest form, the delegate's message can be caricatured as "you shouldn't target civilians because it is against the law". It is almost identical to what I heard more than 20 years ago, as an Australian Army recruit sitting among another group of young men in desert camouflage. I remember it as a welcome break from the gruelling repetition of rifle drills and cleaning equipment. Then, as now, a neatly dressed ICRC dissemination officer introduced us to the legal concepts of proportionality and restraint, the need to avoid unacceptable human suffering and the protective significance of the red cross emblem. In fact, with incremental updates this message has remained consistent since the laws were conceived some 150 years ago in Europe.

Having been exported around the world, this doctrine remains remarkably consistent irrespective of where it is articulated and by whom. Whether it is addressed to soldiers in Iraq, armed militias in central Africa or teenage recruits in the Australian desert, the language may change but the message is the same. "It's a universal set of rules that determine what can and cannot be done during armed conflict; they apply to state and non-state actors alike, whether in deserts, jungles or cities," Pascal, the ICRC delegate leading the dissemination team, explains to me following the presentation in Iraq.[1] The message is the same some 4,000 kilometres away at the Swiss headquarters of the 150-year-old humanitarian organisation where these and other ICRC protection delegates have learnt the intricacies of these normative frameworks.

While the Swiss-based organisation has made extensive efforts to internationalise in recent years, almost half of its staff are Swiss nationals. Water engineers, logisticians, military advisers, communications specialists, translators and accountants join the stereotypical health professional in the regular recruiting rounds. Protection remains a core component of the organisation, attracting graduates of law and international relations who are fluent in the ICRC's working languages of French and English. They are inducted into the institution at Ecogia, the ICRC's training facility just outside of Geneva. There they are taught how to navigate minefields, talk their way through checkpoints and respond to kidnappings. It is made clear to them that they must remain neutral and impartial, and that their security depends on the authority of the red cross and red crescent emblems. From Geneva they are deployed to some 80 countries around the world where the humanitarian organisation is helping people affected by armed conflict and violence. There they join the mix of United Nations and international NGO staff with similar backgrounds and training, who ply the same trade, providing humanitarian relief to those affected by conflict and promoting the mosaic of legal frameworks that work to protect civilians.

These are the aid workers that occupy the official world of humanitarianism introduced in Chapter 1, where normative frameworks curb the behaviour of armed actors and humanitarians are guided by a set of principles. The first of three empirical chapters, this chapter aims to understand these "official" humanitarians, and their relationships with the normative frameworks and the armed actors these frameworks seek to influence. As this chapter will explain, it is their work spreading the word about these frameworks and principles through dissemination and everyday practice that creates and reinforces the imagery of the neutral humanitarian space.

In this official role, humanitarians can be viewed as neutral intermediaries, moving freely between the different actors who occupy humanitarian space and disseminating the universal laws and principles as they have been laid out. This chapter begins by examining these humanitarian intermediaries, and how their work has been effective to some extent in creating humanitarian space and limiting the behaviour of armed actors. However, as this chapter goes on to reveal, a complex network occupies this space, made up of multiple, shifting actors who do not always conform to the universal humanitarian norms. Sometimes they simply behave as a state or state-in-waiting, accepting the letter of the law as signed by every nation in the world. Alternatively, they will abide by these frameworks because they align with their own motivations and agendas, whether it is for securing international legitimacy, community support or military advantage. Increasingly, armed actors will selectively reject these legal frameworks, asserting strategic, political or even cultural justifications to target civilians and deny humanitarian access.

This chapter then examines the official response to these digressions. In the face of these shifting realities, many aid workers and policy makers remain literalists, holding firm to the protection frameworks and finding ways to sustain their relevance to these complex realities. They remain the intermediaries introduced in this chapter, working to bolster the official narrative that still brings a level of order to the network of actors that occupy the complex humanitarian arena of contemporary wars. A few reject these frameworks, engaging in politics if only briefly and for convenience, risking undermining the official narrative. Meanwhile, some attempt to underpin the official frameworks by finding ways to fix their contextual shortcomings. As the following two empirical chapters of this book will go on to explore, travelling between different actors they modify the official frameworks to suit the context, thus providing an unofficial humanitarian fix.

Humanitarians as intermediaries and disseminators

Humanitarians can be viewed as intermediaries, a go-between or messenger who does not affect the final transaction. This is most apparent in their capacity to move freely around the humanitarian arena, accessing affected communities on the grounds that they remain neutral and impartial. As discussed in more detail below, this mobility is also an end in itself as it allows them to promote the official frameworks across the network of actors that occupy this arena, which in turn helps secure ongoing access. In doing this they do not modify or distort the message, but maintain consistency that encourages the universal application of the frameworks and minimises uncertainty. "Everyone has the same obligations, everyone is held to the same standard, so the essential message is the same," explains Pascal, who has spent the past six years sharing the same message with combatants across the Middle East, Afghanistan and northern Africa. Whether Muslim rebels, Christian militias, Taliban insurgents, Afghan government forces or the state-like Peshmerga, for the Swiss humanitarian worker the context has changed substantially, but the official script has remained the central component of these engagements. It is a fixed code, not open to interpretation or adaption by any actors, let alone those responsible for its dissemination.

Many humanitarians, both in the field and in headquarters, assert a similar consistent position that rests on stable, universal laws. To distort this message, they argue, is to undermine these universal norms and their position as neutral messengers. It is a political action that would change them from intermediaries – who make no difference to the transaction – to active mediators, which is essentially a political process. As Latour (2005) explains in his own analysis of various actors and networks, an intermediary "transports meaning without transformation", unlike mediators who "transform, translate, distort, and modify meaning or the elements they are supposed to carry" (p. 39).

As will become clear, these ideal type distinctions between the humanitarian intermediary and mediator are difficult to sustain, particularly in the ever-changing landscape of contemporary conflicts. Spending time with Pascal and other aid workers slowly reveals nuances to how they interpret the official script as they navigate the humanitarian arena. Sometimes holding strictly to the official message does not ensure access or guide the behaviour of armed actors. Rather, humanitarian protection is a product of the dynamic interplay between competing interests, institutions and processes. Yet, to initially frame the humanitarian as an intermediary provides a useful insight into these "neutral" actors and the significant role they fill in this capacity.

To fully understand this role and its significance it is worth briefly revisiting the past, for while the term may be new to humanitarian scholarship, this humanitarian intermediary has long been a central component of the humanitarian system. This history remains a source or rationalisation of present structures. I posit that the original humanitarian frameworks built a level of consensus between competing states and their militaries on what was appropriate behaviour during times of war. Phrased slightly differently, it was an agreed narrative that unified these competing actors when it came to their behaviour towards specific at-risk groups. The humanitarians of the day were positioned at junctures of this interaction between warring states. Under this arrangement, humanitarians were provided access to warring parties, war-torn spaces, no-go areas and at-risk communities, provided they gave assurances that their relief efforts would not jeopardise strategic interests or state sovereignty (see Collinson & Elhawary, 2012; Leader, 2000). Their operational role follows logically from this intermediary position, providing neutral and impartial relief, speaking on behalf of at-risk communities, and as disseminators of the humanitarian norms and protection frameworks.

Relief and access

It is in the relief component of this tripartite of humanitarian protection that the neutral go-between is most clearly seen in action. Classical emergency humanitarianism labours to remain separate from politics – to make no difference to the political transaction that sits at the heart of conflict. They attempt to remain neutral intermediaries in both words and actions. This position is succinctly outlined in a seminal speech by former MSF president Christophe Fournier to the United Nations.

> Our purpose is not to bring war to an end. Nor is it humanitarian to build state and government legitimacy or to strengthen governmental structures. It's not to promote democracy or capitalism or women's rights. Not to defend human rights or save the environment. Nor does humanitarian action involve the work of economic development, post-conflict reconstruction, or the establishment of functioning health systems. Again, it is about saving lives and alleviating suffering in the immediate term.
>
> (as cited in Barnett, 2011, pp. 37–38)

This neutral position in turn increases the freedom of movement needed to deliver assistance in politically volatile and sensitive environments. Only by honouring the principles of political neutrality and impartiality, the argument goes, will armed actors honour their side of the deal and provide access to populations at risk. In this sense, "neutrality is a pragmatic position that helps ensure access," says Francis, an MSF delegate who helped establish health clinics in Afghanistan's Helmand province. "It's our neutrality and impartiality that allows us to operate here. The example we have set is enabling possible expansions into other disputed parts of the country," he goes on to explain to me from Kabul.

In negotiating this freedom of movement, humanitarian intermediaries are selective in the tools and language they turn to. This is not the traditional political negotiation involving interest seeking, transactions and power games between different political players. Rather it is a conversation within pre-determined parameters, with the humanitarian intermediary turning to the agreed legal frameworks and their humanitarian mandate to secure access. For Francis, who is now in regular conversations with warring parties to establish clinics in war-ravaged Kunduz province, this involves focusing on MSF's humanitarian imperative to help those most in need as well as the principles of neutrality and impartiality that separate them from Western and Afghani governments. "The conversation is about agreed principles, not politics; If politics comes into it, it's to explain how we are not part of that world," he says of his negotiations with the government, tribal leaders and armed militias alike. These principles of treating the sick and the correlating protection of medical personnel and facilities have been at the core of the modern humanitarian frameworks since their inception 150 years ago. These are the same parameters that were taught to the Peshmerga officers at the beginning of this chapter and countless other combatants in conflicts around the world. It is about presenting these norms as the case for providing access, rather than engaging in a political argument over the rights and wrongs of different parties.

As another humanitarian access adviser explains, after more than a decade working in conflicts around the world with UN agencies, the ICRC and the NRC

> IHL remains a strong foundation on which to discuss key humanitarian issues with both state and non-state actors, whether it's access to affected communities, or the limitations on the means and methodologies of war. It's a conversation with agreed parameters.

The laws and principles can hold in the most complex and protracted of conflicts. In Afghanistan, after decades of war, even relatively junior commanders, whether from the government or militias, can have a rudimentary understanding and respect for the laws of war and the humanitarian principles. "If you are held up at a checkpoint, you don't want to get into a debate about why you should be allowed access," says an NRC access and protection adviser operating out of Kandahar. "Sometimes it's a matter of mentioning international law, that you are there only to provide relief and reminding them that their superiors have agreed to allow access under these rules," he explains to me from Afghanistan. In this way the intermediary who carries the message is able to make the case for humanitarian protection while remaining separate from the murky world of political negotiations.

Less frequently, these humanitarian intermediaries act as a third party to create the conditions for access, facilitating conversations between different actors. "In that case we are simply conveying the message between different parties," explains an NRC delegate after two years working in the Central African Republic (CAR), where he facilitated talks between warring Muslim and Christian groups. "We are not getting into the substance and the content; that is the responsibility of the parties that are involved in the conversation that we are facilitating." Another veteran aid worker explains, also referring to facilitating negotiations between Muslim and Christian rebel groups, "It's like carrying a letter, sometimes literally, between the different sides in an effort to reach a humanitarian outcome." In these conversations, "the role of the international delegate is to be absolutely neutral and not representing through perception or otherwise the views, beliefs, goals or ambitions of one side to the party or the other," says an ICRC delegate. In the tradition of Lindquist's (2015) "go-betweens", these humanitarian actors provide essential, discreet channels of communication between warring parties, holding a position of trust that promotes dialogue while remaining separate from the politics.

For readers now scribbling in the margins that these humanitarian go-betweens clearly practice politics, if only a particular meaning of politics, this ideal type of humanitarian intermediary should not be discounted. Whether reality or an effective representation, there are benefits in being seen as the neutral intermediary. For those aid workers navigating the complexities of contemporary wars, this consistent representation of humanitarian laws and universal principles brings ongoing value. "The power of these principles and frameworks is that they apply to all actors during conflicts," explains an ICRC protection delegate working in central Africa, reflecting the words of Pascal some 3,500 kilometres away in northern Iraq. "It's important to maintain a consistent message across different actors to ensure the universality of these norms remains clear." As another ICRC delegate travelling among the ever-shifting warring parties of the Niger Delta says, maintaining a consistent, apolitical message is central to maintaining access. "If you take different positions with different groups, they will find out; any trust you've built will be gone, along with your access," she explains.

The significance of this position of neutral go-between is also reflected in the words of armed actors themselves, perhaps most succinctly in an anecdote shared with me by two ICRC delegates working in Afghanistan. When veteran ICRC delegate Jacques de Maio asked an anti-government tribal leader – whom he first met in the mountains of Afghanistan 20 years previously – whether the ICRC could travel safely in the areas under his control, he received the following reply:

> Today, like 20 years ago, a government and its international allies are trying to impose a model of society, with all the modernization, reconstruction, development and Western values that go with it. Today, like 20 years ago, I disagree and we all shed blood. Today, like 20 years ago, you come here to try and make sure prisoners are well treated, wounded taken care of, our families not bombed, or starved, or humiliated. We respect that. Now, be warned: just as we do not expect you to support our religious, social, political views and actions, so we expect you not to support – in any way – our enemies'. Know when so-called humanitarian action becomes a sword, or a poison – and stop there.
>
> (As cited in Terry, 2011, p. 188)

Here we can see that the apolitical go-between – whether real or an effective representation – can resonate with those in power, even among non-state armed actors who may not see themselves as bound by the formal humanitarian frameworks.

Dissemination and promotion

The significance of having physical access across the network goes beyond being able to reach those in need. In an interlinked relationship, this ability to move freely between actors is both a means to an end – the provision of relief – and an end in itself – the promotion of humanitarian space across the network of actors. From the very outset of modern-day humanitarianism it was realised that the humanitarian laws and principles must be known and understood by all actors involved, and that there needed to be a proactive approach towards making these laws known. As early as 1869, Red Cross co-founder Gustave Moynier wrote: "If the convention is to be implemented, its spirit must be introduced into the customs of soldiers and of the population as a whole. Its principles must be popularised through extensive propaganda" (as cited in Bernard, 2014, p. 691). Hence, states themselves are required to promote the consensus they have reached among their own armed forces and broader communities, with the Geneva Conventions containing a general obligation for states to "disseminate the text as widely as possible" and to "include the study thereof in their programs of military instruction".[2]

The ICRC, positioned as a neutral intermediary between these state actors, is also tasked with promoting the application of these frameworks and maintaining a consistent message to minimise uncertainty.[3] The various roles this entails today are not easy to discern and delineate, but in an effort to simplify it comes down to maintaining the integrity of the frameworks, protecting them from being undermined and reminding actors of the obligations they have signed up to. This appears most clearly in the humanitarian organisation's dissemination work, which provides some context for the humanitarian actors who emerge in the following chapters.

Dissemination is the ICRC's term for their work spreading the message about humanitarian law and principles among relevant actors. In a sense, everything the ICRC does is a form of dissemination, with all their humanitarian efforts intended to spread the word as widely as possible. For dissemination staff like Pascal, this unglamorous process involves a constant retelling of the norms and principles to soldiers, university lecturers, INGOs and various civil society groups. During ten years with the Red Cross, I have seen this message projected everywhere from the multi-media screens of sandstone universities, to a bed sheet tacked to the outside wall of a remote hut on the Weather Coast in the Solomon Islands, a diesel generator spluttering in the darkness. With senior officers and military lawyers, it can involve an intricate conversation about proportionality when targeting enemy combatants. With students, it can involve advanced video games where players need to make decisions on who they can target. In the field, it can be about using language simple enough for a poorly educated rural teenager armed with an assault rifle to understand. As one dissemination delegate working in Africa explains, "It's about breaking the law down to basic, understandable components: Don't attack or otherwise mistreat civilians, don't abuse enemy combatants who are not part of the fight, don't attack medical personal and installations."

In recent decades these protection frameworks have been supplemented by another body of law, that of human rights. Rather than disrupting the common message, the dual function of helping victims of war and promoting respect for the law has been adopted by rights-based agencies. INGOs and UN agencies have adopted the traditional dissemination function, providing relevant workshops and training to communities based on the understanding that people need to know their legal rights if they are to hold the authorities accountable to them (see, e.g., IASC, 2002; Slim & Bonwick, 2005). On the other side of the ledger, they engage with administration officials and local military units to highlight their responsibilities under the Geneva Conventions and international human rights law. As one UNHCR protection delegate working in South Sudan explains, "Conversations with local authorities will often start with reminding, or explaining to them, the rights of affected communities and what their responsibilities are; from there we work to find ways to help them meet these responsibilities." For her and many others, dissemination of the relevant legal frameworks is a necessary starting point from which to ensure that the underlying responsibilities are then met. Even human rights NGOs advocating on behalf of those in need can be seen as following this dual approach. As one humanitarian lawyer explains, rights NGOs "typically operate by invoking the facts and law to violators and galvanizing attention, all for the sake of both helping the victims and promoting respect for the law" (Ratner, 2011, p. 460).

Here we can see that concepts of the intermediary and the go-between offer another way to view the traditional neutral humanitarian. Whether it is Pascal's somewhat formal lesson in the humanitarian norms, everyday discussions with political actors or advocacy efforts designed to promote the official frameworks, the message spread by humanitarian workers is relatively consistent. By remaining faithful to the frameworks these particular humanitarians can be seen as neutral intermediaries when it comes to the message they share. By promoting this constant message as widely as possible, these intermediaries reinforce the frameworks as the universally accepted norm, which in turn allows them access to provide relief, and further disseminate this message of restraint and humanitarian access. In effect, their consistent messaging helps create a metaphorical humanitarian space where a multitude of actors behave according to these agreed norms.

Humanitarian space

The six-lane freeway to Mosul ends abruptly at the Zab River, where the twin bridges that once carried traffic along the freeway towards the city now lie in ruins on the riverbed, destroyed by ISIS as they retreated west. A temporary, single lane army bridge, with the Kurdish flag flying overhead, allows military traffic and aid convoys to continue; everyone else is turned back by a young Peshmerga officer. Dressed in familiar desert camouflage, handgun at his hip, he directs traffic with the relaxed authority of a man backed up by a heavily armed platoon. The routine life of Erbil and the Kurdish autonomous zone ends here; across the river are the war and the humanitarian response. The Peshmerga have stopped traffic in both directions and moments later two ambulances, emblazoned with the red crescent, rush across the bridge, heading towards the field hospital we passed two kilometres back.[4] It is a reminder of the earlier dissemination session with the young officers in Erbil; ambulances are protected under IHL and should not be unnecessarily delayed at checkpoints.

As we wait in the bottleneck of traffic, Murshid, my travelling companion for this stage of the journey, hops out of the white Land Cruiser with its distinctive red cross, and wanders around the tight cluster of vehicles waiting to cross, smoking and quietly chatting to the soldiers. The ICRC delegate pauses briefly to talk to an officer in a green pickup, nods to the soldiers on guard at the bridge and shares a cigarette with another. There is no clear purpose, he seems simply to be passing the time, but you can see people know the quietly spoken American, or at least the organisation he represents. Suddenly we are moving again, as the young officer signals for the pick-ups ahead of us move aside and waves us forward. Murshid jumps in as we pass by, touching his cap to the officer as we cross the Peshmerga's bridge. "We are here because they have invited us in," he says without any further explanation. "It is their world and we are guests."

The passing comment is a reflection on the reality of who is in charge once we cross the bridge. That neutral and impartial humanitarians are allowed to work free of interference is not a given, but is something provided by armed actors who hold much of the power.[5] It is their decision to follow the normative frameworks that creates a space for humanitarians to work. What humanitarians are able to do is promote these frameworks to those in power, helping to create and sustain this space. In effect, the dissemination efforts of the humanitarian intermediaries introduced in the previous section creates this space that Murshid and I are now traveling in.

Representations of humanitarian space

Humanitarian space is a relatively new addition to the humanitarian discourse. The phrase was first used to describe the limitations imposed on the operating environment of humanitarian agencies working in the highly politicised context of Cold War Central America (Collinson & Elhawary, 2012). The term helped establish metaphorical boundaries in Central American insurgencies that lacked the clean, often physical lines of the conventional conflicts modern humanitarianism had been born into. Since then the term has slowly gained widespread use as part of ongoing efforts to delineate humanitarianism from politics. This effort seems to have begun in the early 1990s when then MSF President Rony Brauman used the phrase "*espace humanitaire*" to describe an environment in which humanitarian agencies could operate independently from political agendas (Brassard-Boudreau & Hubert, 2010). By the late 1990s the term was in widespread use by the ICRC, MSF and other humanitarian organisations and is now firmly established in policy documents and the protection discourse.

For the ICRC, the concept is synonymous with IHL, which allows access to neutral and impartial humanitarian actors. INGOs and UN agencies adopt a similar understanding, which focuses on the independence of humanitarian action from politics. For example, MSF sees it as a space where aid agencies "are free to evaluate needs, free to monitor the delivery and use of assistance, free to have a dialogue with people". UNOCHA refers to the humanitarian space as an "operating environment" in which agencies can adhere to the principles of neutrality and impartiality, and maintain a clear distinction between their roles and functions and those of military and political actors. For UNHCR, humanitarian space is rooted in international refugee law and is essentially about the quality of "protection space" enjoyed by refugees and other civilians (as cited in Collinson & Elhawary, 2012, pp. 1–2).

In their understanding of humanitarian space, these policies focus on the practical, even physical, space in which humanitarian action can take place. This can be conceived narrowly as being in opposition to military or political space, such as refugee camps, humanitarian corridors, hospitals and "safe areas". As a case in point, my journey with Murshid brings us to the gates of a relief camp some 15 kilometres beyond the destroyed bridges. "Khazer Camp" is one of seven camps set up around Mosul, separated from the fight by the front line of this surprisingly linear battle and distance. Established before the attack on the city began, on slightly undulating ground away from major towns, it is an example of the basic protection standards. The Kurdish military may guard the gate, but inside the chain-link fence it is a purely humanitarian operation, where families who have recently escaped from Mosul are provided the basics of life – neat rows of white tents provide accommodation, water tanks and taps are set up at the end of the accommodation rows, power lines link street lights for security at night, Red Crescent volunteers provide hot meals and fresh bread to a long line of people, children play outside the tent-school operated by UNICEF and the NRC, while local government authorities have set up a tent hospital; all just over the horizon from Mosul. It is a humanitarian space in the physical sense.

More commonly, humanitarian space is synonymous with parties to the conflict accepting the role of humanitarian actors and allowing them the metaphorical space to work without fear of attack or interference. In this it reflects back to the Geneva Conventions and other legal frameworks such as international refugee law, which oblige states to provide for the basic needs of civilian populations affected by conflict or to allow and facilitate impartial humanitarian relief.

This metaphorical space is not a physical space apart, set aside for humanitarian activity. Rather, as humanitarian field workers are acutely aware, it is a shared space, occupied by multiple political actors. As Murshid explains, giving me a lesson in the protection frameworks while we wait outside the relief camp for an aid convoy to arrive, the space humanitarians work in is made up of a diverse mix of actors. "Look around you," Murshid says, sweeping his arm to indicate the helicopter gunships on the horizon, a military convoy passing by, two bulletproof SUVs carrying security consultants following behind, tractors and trucks arriving from the other direction carrying people who have escaped Mosul, military police controlling the entrance to the camp behind us, and the flags of the INGOs, local government agencies and civil society organisations who together operate the camp. "This is clearly not, and never has been, some separate space for humanitarians; we have always occupied it with other actors; we are part of this political world," the ICRC delegate explains. In this metaphorical vision, humanitarian space can be described as a complex, permeable *arena* (see Hilhorst & Jansen, 2010; Hilhorst & Serrano, 2010) where a multitude of actors shape the everyday realities of humanitarian action. Thus,

> A more comprehensive and grounded concept of humanitarian space can be derived from a recognition that most of the important aspects of humanitarian space are determined by the interplay of interests among a variety of political, military, economic and other actors, organisations and institutions, in addition to humanitarian agencies and affected populations.
>
> (Collinson & Elhawary, 2012, p. 4)

This is not necessarily a total reconceptualisation of humanitarian space as lived by front-line agencies and field workers. Rather, the two metaphors of humanitarian *space* and *arena* sit easily alongside each other. While promoting the humanitarian space in their dissemination work, the ICRC has always acknowledged that a range of actors occupy the space they work in. Many other front line agencies have long incorporated principles and practices that fit the complex arena depiction of humanitarian space, routinely engaging with multiple actors to shape humanitarian space and arrange access and relief activities. In other words, it is principles and practices such as neutrality and impartiality that create humanitarian space in a complex arena. Aid workers, too, position multiple actors in their vision of humanitarian space and incorporate the official frameworks in their understanding of how it is formed. As my desert teacher explains:

> We have always shared it with other actors. It's about how all these different actors behave in this space, which is where humanitarian law comes in. The normative frameworks bring a level of order to your complex arena, helping create an environment where we can work without interference – a humanitarian space.

In this, humanitarians perhaps unwittingly reflect the ideas of de Certeau (1984) in that space is created by description, symbols and official policy. The French philosopher, whose concepts of agency and everyday practice were discussed in Chapter 3, argues that space is discursively mapped. In his influential chapter "Walking the city", de Certeau asserts that the city is created by the strategies of governments, urban planners and other official agents which seek to influence how residents navigate the city. Similarly, humanitarian space is created and structured by the official humanitarian frameworks, which seek to guide the behaviour of the different actors that occupy it. These frameworks – or "strategies", to borrow de Certeau's terminology – dictate that civilians are to be protected and humanitarians are to be left alone to carry out their life-saving work. They are further supported by symbols and descriptions in the same way that signs, maps and publicity campaigns help guide residents through the streets of de Certeau's cities.

The humanitarian disseminators and intermediaries introduced in the previous section are central in developing and sustaining this representation of space. By continually discussing and promoting the normative frameworks and humanitarian principles they help to ensure that actors in this humanitarian space know the rules and behave accordingly. As one ICRC aid worker in Iraq explains: "If those with power can be educated, persuaded or pressured to abide by the norms and principles of international humanitarian law, then people are more likely to be protected than targeted." A protection adviser from the International Rescue Committee working in the Central African Republic has a similar argument: "The humanitarian space remains relevant when we all acknowledge its boundaries and believe in its ability to protect civilians."

This extends beyond the more formal dissemination practices of humanitarian organisations to other parts of humanitarian work. In a sense, everything humanitarians do is a form of dissemination, with all their humanitarian efforts intended to spread the word as widely as possible. In this way, an aid delivery to affected communities is also a public performance that reinforces the role of humanitarian agencies. The aid convoy that arrives at Khazer Camp is newly painted in the traditional white of aid convoys, with red crescents emblazoned on the vehicles, and the truck drivers wear freshly minted red crescent vests; the local media has been invited to publicise the performance of the familiar white boxes with the red cross on the side being unloaded and distributed to families. Similarly, the ICRC's public insistence that their convoys travel without armed escort sends a message that they are separate from the fight – their windows bearing "no weapons" signs. The state militaries also disseminate this message through everyday practice, limiting the military capacity of their medical personnel and vehicles bearing the red cross or red crescent. These two protective emblems are perhaps the most potent symbols of this public performance, symbolically protecting the wounded, the sick and those who provide neutral and impartial assistance. Whether emblazoned on the side of ambulances or on flags flying above hospitals, they symbolically define how these actors are to behave and be treated in times of war.

Thus, the normative frameworks guide the behaviour of actors, creating a relatively structured arena in which the state, their militaries, non-state armed actors, humanitarians and the affected population interact. Humanitarians, whether through dissemination or the day-to-day performance of humanitarian relief, play a central role in bringing structure to this complex environment and its network of actors.

The humanitarian network

In the northern Iraq desert, Murshid builds a picture of the network of actors in the humanitarian space as he has grown to understand it in over 10 years working in conflict zones around the world, his resume listing Somalia, Afghanistan and Iraq. Drawing a circle around some stones in the sand with a stick, he explains that the humanitarian frameworks guide all actors in this space, bringing a level of order to the conflict by limiting the behaviour of armed actors and allowing humanitarians access that protects civilians.

> It has always been a place of multiple actors, but they are all normatively inside the framework, so are guided by its rules. There are now more and more parties operating in this space than ever before, often with very complex military goals, but that doesn't change the fact they are part of the normative framework. For them it's a question of respecting [these rules], and while you can obviously cite examples when this doesn't happen, it also does prove effective in bringing a level of humanity to conflict.

The picture he describes and that appears around us is not the messy, undisciplined space where actors behave according to their own needs and motivations, as the term arena implies; or as Bakewell (2000) asserts, a multitude of actors "struggling, negotiating and at times guessing in order to further their own interests" (pp. 108–109). Instead, the frameworks bring a level of structure to the interactions of a multitude of actors that navigate conflicts. These frameworks reflect the official consensus of what is the accepted behaviour of actors in armed conflicts, providing a set of rules to guide how they should act in certain situations. A product of the international state system, they facilitate a coordinated approach among different actors that provides for the protection of affected communities and access for humanitarians.

The strength of these strategies also extends beyond traditional state actors who are formally invested in these legal frameworks. While it is common practice to criticise the effectiveness of the humanitarian frameworks in asymmetrical wars, there are numerous examples of how they guide the behaviour of non-state armed groups as intended, particularly when it comes to the protection of civilians. The non-state Kurdish Peshmerga, which function almost entirely independently from the Iraqi Federal Government, are widely recognised as among the most disciplined troops in the region. With a high degree of exposure to the international community, their commanders are able to make detailed references to distinction, proportionality and the prohibition of targeting medical personnel as laid out in the international frameworks. In northern Iraq, they have a constructive relationship with humanitarian organisations, routinely providing access to humanitarian workers and aid convoys, and widely seen by aid workers as "making every effort to follow the humanitarian norms and principles".

This acceptance of the frameworks as legitimate norms goes beyond state-like entities such as the Peshmerga. Geneva Call, an INGO that promotes the respect for international humanitarian norms and the protection of civilians among non-state armed actors, has engaged with more than 100 armed groups, exploring their attitudes towards IHL and the humanitarian principles. Some 60 of them have made commitments to respect these international frameworks. This was true even among those with only a notional understanding of the rules of war and humanitarian principles, and a documented history of violating these norms. As a member of the Karen National Union told Geneva Call field staff: "Although I don't know all the rules, I do think we should take part and fulfil our responsibility" (Jackson, 2016, p. 12). The Islam Army in Syria calls them "good and important rules" (Jackson, 2016, p. 12). After extensive talks, the Taliban leadership issued a clear commitment not to misuse health facilities and ambulances as a means of war. "Even within the more extreme groups, there may be those members or local commanders that recognise the rationale behind having laws in war," one Geneva Call analyst explains to me at the organisation's headquarters in Switzerland.

There are similar attitudes towards the humanitarian principles and issues of access. In the same way the Peshmerga in northern Iraq facilitated access for aid workers around Mosul, other armed actors have demonstrated an acceptance of the humanitarian principles and at least a rudimentary understanding of the deal that allows access to neutral and impartial humanitarianism. When Geneva Call asked non-state armed actors about neutrality, impartiality and independence, they expressed positive views about these principles. The Sudanese People's Liberation Movement states that "operating on a political, religious and racial" basis is the only reason they would deny access to areas under their control (Jackson, 2016, p. 11). Similarly, the People's Protection Units in Syria explicitly recognise the importance of humanitarian organisations working on all sides in the conflict (Jackson, 2016, p. 11). In a reflection of the original deal between states and humanitarianism discussed in Chapter 2, neutrality and impartiality are a provision of access for these non-state armed actors. For example, the Sudanese Liberation Movement considers neutrality and impartiality to be a basic requirement for access. So too does the Free Syrian Army First Brigade, which fought the Syrian Army east of Damascus, stating that humanitarians need to stand "the same distance from everyone and serving everyone regardless of the political orientation, race or religion" (Jackson, 2016, p. 11).

Why do these non-state actors respect these state-based, legal frameworks? Why do they respect IHL and the humanitarian principles? The critics say that rather than an acceptance of the international frameworks as universal norms, this is a public relations exercise, or an effort to garner public support and international legitimacy. "Some armed groups care very much about being perceived as following the law, [although] they may not care about the law itself, but care about the perception," explains one human rights advocate (TNH, 2012). It is an argument that sees some non-state actors behaving according to international rules and humanitarian principles for motivations other than the legal demands. According to these critics, their motivation is the legitimacy that comes with being part of these international frameworks. There is certainly an element of truth to this. There is also a slightly different argument that goes on to link this quest for legitimacy to aspirations of governance and even statehood. As explained in Chapter 1, many armed actors are more than short-term opportunists. Many are interested in establishing governance and acknowledging the normative frameworks is part of this.

Returning to the Peshmerga in northern Iraq, at one level they abide by the letter of the law, ensuring neutral and impartial humanitarian access to the parts of Mosul they control. However, they also come with their own political agenda. On the international stage, there is a push for the Kurdish autonomous zone in northern Iraq to become an independent state; publicly following international norms will clearly benefit this cause. Similar arguments can be put for the other examples above, whether they are separatist rebels like the Sudanese Liberation Movement and the Karen National Union seeking to create a new state, or insurgents seeking to replace the recognised government, as is the case in Syria.

Other, alternative, reasons to respect IHL and the humanitarian principles are more operational. For the Peshmerga, providing access to humanitarian groups was part of a coordinated strategy to extend their borders to incorporate important regional cities such as Mosul. As one UN security adviser argues, beyond facilitating humanitarian access to the outer suburbs of Mosul, the Peshmerga were buttressing their hold over parts of the city by ensuring "their" communities received relief. "This is not simply about providing humanitarian access to communities under their security blanket; it's part of a military tactic to extend the Kurdish state and maintain their support in the city."

While the unifying narrative of the official frameworks guides the behaviour of actors in the humanitarian network, it is clear that they also come with their own agenda and motivation. Here we return to strategies and their inevitable counterpart, tactics, as described by de Certeau (1984). In his theory of everyday practice, de Certeau explains how institutions deploy strategies to create space. Meanwhile, people deploy unofficial tactics to redefine this space as they move through it. According to de Certeau, any strategy necessarily entails the appearance of tactics that will be deployed by those whom the strategy is intended to control. These tactics are inseparable from any strategy and will arise wherever one is imposed.

Thus, in the humanitarian arena there is an inevitable tension between the humanitarian frameworks that guide behaviour, and the agenda and motivations of a variety of actors that occupy this space alongside humanitarian agencies and affected populations. The international norms are effective when powerful actors accept these institutional strategies to benefit humanitarian access and affected communities. This is most clearly seen in the behaviour of state actors, who are themselves invested in the humanitarian norms. This is the normative frameworks at work in their purest form, as explained and promoted by policy realists. While it is unspoken, these norms and principles are also seen as effective when there is an alignment with the agenda and motivations of different actors in a way that promotes the protection of affected communities. The Peshmerga's quest for international legitimacy and support for their own communities is just one example of this, but it extends to other armed actors. It is a common agenda across conflicts and among different armed actors who seek to become part of the international system, whether the Peshmerga in Iraq, the Sudanese People's Liberation Movement or the Free Syrian Army.

In a small example, this quest for legitimacy plays out in Geneva Call's rather stately 19th century Geneva headquarters, where they hold formal meetings with non-state armed actors, often after lengthy negotiations in the field. The INGO engages with non-state armed actors through what it calls an "inclusive approach", whereby these rebel groups have the opportunity to express their adherence to international humanitarian norms and take ownership of these rules by signing "Deeds of Commitment". These actors are generally precluded from becoming parties to relevant state treaties and from participating in the norm-making process. To date, more than 100 such deeds have been signed by non-state actors, committing to protecting children in armed conflict, banning land mines and prohibiting sexual violence, in formal occasions at Geneva Calls head office or important civic buildings.

I watched the Free Syrian Army sign one such deed in the Geneva Town Hall, formally committing to protect children in armed conflict and prohibit sexual violence. Free Syrian Army commanders joined representatives of the Government of the Geneva Canton and members of the humanitarian community in the historic Alabama Room. The room remains virtually unchanged since the original Geneva Convention was signed there some 150 years ago, with its 19th century red velvet chairs, gilt-framed paintings, ornate cornices and elegant ceiling lamps. Other than a single hijab breaking up the dark suits, today's scene is strikingly similar to Armand-Dumaresq's painting of the signing of the first Geneva Convention by major European powers in 1864. Speeches are made confirming "the duty to respect civilians, children and women", the norms first signed in this room so long ago are reaffirmed, and official red seals are imprinted on formal looking documents. The 2017 event with its pomp and ceremony, captured by the official photographer and invited media, transfers a form of the original legitimacy onto these non-state actors. Undoubtedly, these formal deeds work to some extent to guide the behaviour of non-state armed actors. Yet they are not internationally recognised legal documents. Their effectiveness seems to be the entry point into the international community they offer, and the state-like legitimacy they infer through official ceremonies and acknowledgement. This quest for legitimacy by armed actors overlaps, at least partially, with any commitment to humanitarian norms.

Competing agendas and emerging cultures

Clearly, however, the motivations of an increasingly disparate group of actors that operate throughout the humanitarian arena do not necessarily always align with the normative protection frameworks. As one ICRC delegate in Iraq explains:

> The interests and structures of non-state armed actors are not static; they are iterative and evolve over time in response to various internal and external

> factors. At times this can be supportive of humanitarian actors; at other times we become targets.

When refugee camps become militarised, safe havens overrun and hospitals are hit, aid workers are witnessing first-hand the inevitable tension between institutional strategies of the normative frameworks and the competing tactics of the multitude of actors in the humanitarian arena who come with their own agendas. At times, this sees the humanitarian frameworks ignored, with state and non-state actors prioritising their own motivations and agenda over abiding by the frameworks and the benefits this provides. "These norms and conventions are being challenged every day, everywhere, by a whole range of armed actors," explains one MSF protection adviser with more than a decade's experience in conflicts around the world. "We have states who have signed these conventions burning down hospitals, forcing communities from their homes, because it suits their own agenda at the time." Another aid worker, recently returned from Myanmar, talks of armed actors well versed in humanitarian law and human rights law, who had previously expressed support for these frameworks, later "disregarding them completely to suit some national agenda."

These tensions have increased in recent decades as different actors with diverse agendas have begun to make their presence felt in the humanitarian arena. One protection delegate reflects on the ever-increasing number of actors he has needed to negotiate with over the past decade working with the ICRC in Afghanistan and the Middle East. "There are an unbelievable number of parties in Syria, in Yemen, in Iraq, in Afghanistan. Their military goals are very complex, ever changing, and sometimes at odds with humanitarian solutions," he explains. As his experience engaging with Muslim militants indicates, many of these actors come from cultures and religions outside of the Western tradition (see also Chapter 2). As multiple aid workers explained during my interviews, the strength of the normative frameworks is their historic legacy, particularly the four Conventions that have been ratified by all states. "The weakness is that from a perception point of view, they can be viewed as a Western framework," says another ICRC veteran, talking about the changing nature of armed actors in recent years.

> Ten years ago it was hard for me to bump into actors or interlocutors for whom IHL would be taboo. Whereas in the last four or five years I've mostly been in stations where we're dealing with people for whom IHL is either off the table or just utterly rejected because it seems a Western or foreign construct to them.

For many humanitarians, armed actors increasingly rejecting the very notion of Western legal frameworks has proven to be one of the greatest challenges for humanitarian protection. One of the most extreme examples of this is playing out in Mosul some 20 kilometres from where I stand with Murshid. As the aid convoy departs the camp, a pillar of smoke rises up on the horizon after another coalition bombing run on the city's western half, which would ultimately be totally destroyed by these airstrikes and Iraqi artillery. Those who have escaped the city talk of the horrific treatment they experienced at the hands of ISIS during the two years of occupation. When they took the city, the radical Sunni group expelled Christians and massacred Shia and other minorities – torture, rape, summary executions and the deprivation of even the most basic human rights continued throughout their occupation. Any talk of humanitarian space and access ends at the city limits.[6]

Even outside the city, the influence of the humanitarian norms are not as clear as some try and project. To the west of the city lies the uncertain terrain of the various Shia militias. With shifting political allegiances, they are accused of discrimination, religious persecution and targeted killings. Leaving the Kurdish flags behind during my journey across northern Iraq, checkpoints become tense. A militia flag with the image of a sword dripping blood flutters over another bridge where vehicles are being stopped and searched. Attempting to travel to one of the larger relief camps the UN is operating in the area, we are turned back by Shia militia members wearing black balaclavas and skull masks.

Protection frameworks and the official response

On a Geneva hillside with spectacular views of the French Alps, some 4,000 kilometres from the ruins of Mosul, sits the ICRC's headquarters. Scaffolding lines the exterior of the 140-year-old building, which is in the middle of a major renovation. Once the Carlton Hotel, the building was donated to the ICRC in the wake of World War II. Annexes have been added to the complex somewhat haphazardly over the years as the need arose, while the Carlton remains the centrepiece. On the upper floors are the ICRC's heavy hitters, including the Director General and heads of region, while their policy teams occupy the basement. Teams of lawyers, protection advisers and security experts occupy the surrounding annexes.

These lawyers and policymakers are in ongoing efforts to find answers to the protection challenges of armed actors selectively using, or disregarding completely, the normative frameworks. The main response to this has been to continue efforts to buttress these frameworks, whether through legal mechanisms, public advocacy or increasingly nuanced forms of dissemination. "This isn't about [replacing] the normative frameworks, it's about compliance with these laws," explains one senior ICRC lawyer during an interview in his cramped office surrounded by well-thumbed journals and legal texts. "What we need is for the international community to get serious about ensuring that timely prosecutions are undertaken." Some truly believe that this is the way forward. Others privately acknowledge the "aspirational, almost mythical quality of these rules" and the need to constantly reiterate them.

This message is reiterated in the sprawling UN compound across the road from the Carlton. "If prosecution isn't one of the options on the table, then it means you are constantly tolerating violations over and over again; in a sense you are permitting them to happen," says one UNHCR protection adviser. "It's still relevant, it's still strong," argues another. "I think where the problem lies is adherence to the law, respect for the law, and a culture of impunity in a lot of countries." Meanwhile, a short tram ride away, an NRC policy officer extends a similar line:

> For whatever reason, sometimes they ignore those rules. We need to do everything we can to ensure they follow them by making sure the rules are widely known and by speaking out when they break them. The international community needs to play its part too, by prosecuting those who digress.

After spending more time in the corridors of these lead protection agencies, the efforts to bolster the frameworks appear more nuanced. As one ICRC lawyer explains: "You increasingly find that in particular cultures or settings, actors simply don't agree with the norm. Then we have to find ways of upholding the norm, while at the same time trying to find entry points to convince the parties." Further down the narrow corridor lined with tiny office spaces, another agrees: "We need to try and bridge the gap between the language we speak and the language that others speak."

How best to bridge this gap remains the dilemma for the "whole army of policy makers, analysts and lawyers who are waking up every day thinking about and working on ways to make the legal frameworks more effective," explains an ICRC protection adviser in Geneva. For the ICRC, research into customary law and incorporating it into their dissemination efforts has been one of the central approaches. An extension of this has been the embrace of comparative legal studies, which attempt to find commonalities between the normative frameworks and other legal traditions. "While it's true that a lot of the international law discourse, including that of IHL, is largely centred around the West, it's not strictly speaking a Western law. There are equivalent positions in other bodies of law," says one ICRC lawyer. Originally focusing on Afghanistan, this comparative research has spread to other regions where there is a tradition of Islamic law.

A similar approach sees the ICRC explore the codes of conduct of various non-state actors to find overlaps with IHL. "All armed groups have codes of conduct of some form, whether written or unwritten, formal or informal. The idea is to find common ground between these codes of conduct and the normative frameworks," explains another ICRC lawyer with extensive experience in Afghanistan and the Middle East, supporting field delegates' efforts to disseminate the laws among different cultures and religions. These efforts are in line with the ICRC's belief that coherent interpretation of the law enhances respect for it. Thus, their efforts aim to bolster IHL by finding commonalties with other norms and codes, rather than promoting or disseminating competing frameworks (see ICRC, 2016). These legal efforts do not stand alone but work in conjunction with the ICRC's dissemination efforts in the field, providing other avenues to promote the international frameworks and universal principles among actors from different cultural traditions.

Back across Avenue de la Paix, the response at the UN headquarters to these challenges also focuses on nuancing the established normative frameworks.

Often cited is the "Human Rights up Front" initiative (UN Secretary-General, 2014), a reaction to the UN's failures during the war in Sri Lanka. In the tradition of providing policy solutions to protection challenges, the report provides six actions to effectively protect human rights during UN operations. Similarly, the "Whole of System Review" (Niland & Polastro, 2015) makes practical suggestions on how humanitarian protection can be addressed. Another initiative by the Inter-Agency Standing Committee introduced in previous chapters, the review assesses the present protection system of the UN and INGOs, identifying multiple challenges faced over recent years: the system is "of the North" not "of the World"; multiple actors "are occupying spaces that used to be the preserve of the North"; "NGOs have grown and diversified beyond recognition" (Niland & Polastro, 2015, p. 17). An extensive piece of research, it produces detailed recommendations on how the protection frameworks can be bolstered through a "major overhaul of humanitarian coordination machinery", "enhanced monitoring and evaluation" and "strengthened accountability". While extremely nuanced and informed by field research, in its language and findings it matches what has come before, a progression of the normative frameworks. The official response remains focused on the Western norms across the humanitarian spectrum, despite the continual evolution of actors in the humanitarian space and new actors from outside this Western tradition increasingly asserting their authority.

Conclusion

This chapter provides a picture of the official humanitarian protection paradigm and how it has responded to the challenges of contemporary conflicts. First, humanitarian protection is about the law. International humanitarian law, refugee law and human rights law form the central pillars of a raft of legal frameworks that guide the behaviour of actors during times of war in order to protect people from violence. In simple terms, these laws work to limit the behaviour of armed actors and provide for neutral and impartial relief to affected populations. States sign onto these laws, committing to abide by them and prosecute breaches according to the letter of the law. On a slightly more abstract level, they work as a normative power, mapping out what behaviour is desirable and permissible and what is undesirable or not permitted.

Second, protection is non-transactional, involving the linear communication of ideas and messages between people and groups without transformation or modification. Humanitarians are central actors in this effort, helping to disseminate humanitarian laws and principles that promote restraint towards certain groups and provide for neutral, impartial access. By promoting these laws and related principles as widely as possible, humanitarians reinforce the frameworks as the universally accepted norm. In doing so, they do not modify the message, instead maintaining a level of consistency that promotes a universal understanding and application of the laws.

Third, extending from the first two points, humanitarian space is established through discourse. Humanitarian laws are a central component of this discourse, part of a collection of representations which help create a coherent framework of what can be said and done. Humanitarians help establish and maintain this discourse through their dissemination efforts. This extends beyond the more formal dissemination practices, with almost everything humanitarians do becoming part of the discourse that creates humanitarian space, from the neutral and impartial delivery of aid, to flying the familiar red and white flag. In other words, through their dissemination efforts and everyday practice, humanitarians help create a coherent set of references that frame how actors behave and perceive the space around them.

This discourse, underpinned by international law and the dissemination and performance of a range of humanitarian actors, has proved somewhat effective in guiding the behaviour of powerful actors in armed conflict, notably states and their militaries. These actors are invested in international law, which was established to guide the relationships between states, so they readily accept its related space-making discourse. However, tensions have started to arise in recent decades as various non-state actors have emerged, asserting cultural and religious traditions that are often at odds with dominant Western legal frameworks. Furthermore, as they are not part of the state-based normative frameworks, they selectively accept, reject or adapt the dominant narrative to suit their own agenda. Returning to the critical theory of de Certeau (1984), they use "popular tactics" to resist the "imposed strategies", turning the "actual order of things … to their own ends" (p. 26).

As this chapter explains, the official effort to counter this resistance is to bolster the established approaches to protection outlined above; or in de Certeau's (1984) terms, they return to the official strategies. The law remains central to protection, with efforts focusing on adding further legal mechanisms and ensuring perpetrators are prosecuted. The official transaction between humanitarians and these new actors also remains the same, with the increasingly nuanced dissemination efforts remaining faithful to the legal tradition and in turn the established discourse that creates the humanitarian space. Yet, as de Certeau explains, those whom the strategy is intended to control will inevitably deploy further tactics. In other words, there is an inexorable tension between the official humanitarian frameworks that guide behaviour, and the agenda and motivations of various actors who occupy the complex space of contemporary wars. In light of the inevitable tensions between the state-based frameworks and cultural, religious and political insurgents, the humanitarian intermediary of this chapter can only go so far.

How do field workers respond to these tensions? Like all other actors in this humanitarian network, they bring their own agency. In other words, they are more than the intermediaries introduced at the beginning of this chapter, disseminating the official frameworks. As the following chapter will explore, they become active mediators who modify the message they carry in order to make it relevant to different actors. In so doing, they provide a humanitarian fix to the official frameworks when they struggle to achieve the purpose they were originally designed for.

Notes

1 The humanitarian workers interviewed for this research have had identifying details changed to ensure a level of confidentiality and their capacity to speak freely. To achieve this, changing the names of fieldworkers to pseudonyms was standard practice, which still allowed for descriptive detail. Sometimes, however, it was necessary to go further, blurring details (e.g. time, place, position) in order to provide a level of anonymity.

2 See Article 126 of Geneva Convention III.

3 To provide detail for the legal reader, Article 5 of the Statutes of the International Red Cross Movement states that the ICRC is tasked to "work for the faithful application of international humanitarian law applicable in armed conflicts and to take cognizance of any complaints based on alleged breaches of that law" (Article 5.2c) and also "to work for the understanding and dissemination of knowledge of international humanitarian law applicable in armed conflicts and to prepare any development thereof" (Article 5.2g).

4 The red crescent and the red cross are equivalent emblems, both providing protection for military medical services and relief workers in armed conflicts.

5 There is a legal requirement for the ICRC to gain state permission to respond in internal conflicts. In practice, consent is also required from non-state armed groups for matters of safety.

6 Complicating this division further, humanitarian assistance is often seen as being from the West, and part of a Western intervention into the Muslim world (see, e.g., Donini et al., 2004). In a self-fulfilling prophecy, this was reinforced in Iraq by humanitarian agencies operating on the geographic side of the coalition for security and logistical reasons.

References

Bakewell, O. (2000). Uncovering local perspectives on humanitarian assistance and its outcomes. *Disasters*, 24(2), 103–116.

Barnett, M. (2011). *Empire of humanity: A history of humanitarianism*. Cornell University Press.

Bernard, V. (2014). Time to take prevention seriously. *International Review of the Red Cross*, 96(895/897), 689–696.

Brassard-Boudreau, C., & Hubert, D. (2010, November). Shrinking humanitarian space? Trends and prospects on security and access. *The Journal of Humanitarian Assistance*.

Collinson, S., & Elhawary, S. (2012). *Humanitarian space: A review of trends and issues* (No. 32; HPG Report). Overseas Development Institute.

de Certeau, M. (1984). *The practice of everyday life*. University of California Press.

Donini, A., Minear, L., & Walker, P. (2004). Iraq and the crisis of humanitarian action. *Humanitarian Exchange*, 26, 37–40.

Hilhorst, D., & Jansen, B. (2010). Humanitarian space as arena: A perspective on the everyday politics of aid. *Development and Change*, 41(6), 1117–1139.

Hilhorst, D., & Serrano, M. (2010). The humanitarian arena in Angola, 1975–2008. *Disasters*, 34(2), 183–201.

IASC (2002). *Growing the sheltering tree: Protecting rights through humanitarian action*. Inter-Agency Standing Committee.

ICRC (2016, March 12). *ICRC launches new guidance bolstering relevance of Geneva Conventions* [Press release].

Jackson, A. (2016). *In their words: Perceptions of armed non-state actors on humanitarian action*. Geneva Call.

Latour, B. (2005). *Reassembling the social: An introduction to actor network theory*. Oxford University Press.

Leader, N. (2000). *The politics of principle: The principles of humanitarian action in practice* (No. 2; HPG Report). Overseas Development Institute.

Lindquist, J. (2015). Brokers and brokerage, Anthropology of. In J. Wright (Ed.), *International encyclopedia of social and behavioral science* (Vol. 2, pp. 870–874). Elsevier.

Niland, N., & Polastro, R. (2015). *Independent whole of system review of protection in the context of humanitarian action.* Inter-Agency Standing Committee.

Ratner, S. (2011). Law promotion beyond law talk: The Red Cross, persuasion, and the laws of war. *European Journal of International Law*, 22(2), 459–506.

TNH (2012, August 15). *Armed groups should not be a law unto themselves.*

Slim, H., & Bonwick, A. (2005). *Protection: An ALNAP guide for humanitarian agencies.* Overseas Development Institute.

Terry, F. (2011). The International Committee of the Red Cross in Afghanistan: Reasserting the neutrality of humanitarian action. *International Review of the Red Cross*, 93(881), 173–188.

UN Secretary-General (2014). *Human rights up front.* United Nations.

5 Humanitarian brokers and translators

Introduction

The Peshmerga command post has been set up in one of the few remaining houses in the village. Almost every other building lies in ruins, roofs collapsed, walls shattered, destroyed by ISIS as they retreated towards the nearby city of Mosul. Soldiers in their distinctive desert camouflage sit in the shade of the house, talking, sleeping, smoking, waiting for the next move. I pass the time with them, leaning against the doorframe, while inside, four men sit around a table – three in camouflage, the fourth in khaki pants, worn desert boots and a faded shirt with sleeves rolled up, revealing tattooed forearms. An impermanent figure, he is not a soldier, but he is also not a civilian, with his closely shaved head and a military posture. The origin of his faultless English is unidentifiable; maybe from somewhere in the middle of the Atlantic Ocean, with his occasional Australian and American turn of phrase. He is not from these parts, but it is hard to tell where he is from; possibly somewhere in Asia; Muslim or Christian? It is not clear. He is comfortable at the table, with a sense of the military about him, yet does not quite belong. Instead, my colleague Vito comes from the impermanent world of humanitarianism. With a resume that lists responses in Iraq, Yemen, South Sudan and Afghanistan, he has spent more than 15 years moving between the network of actors that occupy conflict zones, growing to understand them, engage with them and build relationships with them, while still standing slightly apart. He is back in Iraq working with the Refugee Council providing relief to people displaced by the latest fighting.

They've been talking for almost an hour now, while drinking tea and smoking cigarettes. The conversation is about home and their families. The Filipino pulls out a photo of his two children; two of the soldiers respond with their own, passing the photos around like proud parents everywhere. The conversation naturally moves on to the families who are slowly escaping Mosul, 20 kilometres away and making their way to the Peshmerga's lines. There is a sense of empathy from these young men who, like Vito, are away from their families. Yet, without enough food for themselves, they can do little to help, they say apologetically. Nor can they transport them away from the front line, focusing on the advance towards Mosul. "We can help you with that," explains Vito. Before we leave

20 minutes later, Vito and the soldiers agree to work together to provide immediate relief to the families who arrive at the unit's lines and then transport them back to the camps some 20 kilometres away. The soldiers simply need to call Vito on the phone when civilians arrive and facilitate access for his teams. At no point is it a conversation about mandates, laws or principles. Instead it is a conversation that focuses on building a relationship with the soldiers, and developing an understanding of their needs and how these needs coincide with the humanitarian's.

In this, Vito represents an alternative mode of humanitarian practice to that practiced by the humanitarian intermediary introduced in the previous chapter. This approach sees humanitarian workers exposed to the fluid and multi-layered network of actors in the humanitarian arena reacting with an equally fluid and multi-layered response. It has emerged over recent decades in response to the increasing complexity of contemporary wars. As discussed earlier, political authority has fragmented in these so-called new wars due to the weakening of state-centred notions of power and the resurgence of non-state armed actors. These non-state armed actors are increasingly asserting their own cultural or religious authority, and act according to their own institutional agendas, often at odds with the official protection frameworks that guide behaviour in war. These non-state armed actors inevitably deploy their own tactics in the humanitarian arena, at times following the official frameworks, or strategies, but at other times selectively reinterpreting or circumventing them to suit their own agenda (see Chapter 4).

Faced with this, humanitarian workers like Vito do not remain passive, but counter with their own unofficial response. Rather than solely acting as the intermediaries described in the previous chapter, transporting meaning without transformation, they act as mediators, modifying, transforming and translating the meaning of the messages they carry. In this, they are a reshaped version of the broker, political mediators who have appeared throughout history in response to complex political environments. The original colonial era broker mediated between the European powers and the local leaders of the land they occupied, providing a bridge between different cultures and political systems (see Bierschenk et al., 2002). As discussed elsewhere, these earlier brokers faded from view as the state system spread across the global South. There was no need for brokers in this framework, with states as the primary source of power sharing a common language of universal laws and norms. More recently, we have seen the exploration of development brokers, originally referring to local actors who mediate between local communities and the development sector (Bierschenk et al., 2002). Later, Lewis and Mosse (2006) explicated the development professional as the broker, negotiating a complex network of actors with different statuses, varying resources and dissimilar goals (notably donors, partner agencies, community groups and employing agencies).

The humanitarian broker follows this tradition, mediating between the official protection frameworks and the complex array of actors that are asserting their authority in contemporary wars. In doing so they attempt to address the challenges of transferring the protection frameworks, which are intrinsically linked to the imagery of the international state system and its European antecedents, to the complex world of contemporary wars, occupied by an array of non-state actors from different cultural, religious and political traditions. They are, I go on to argue, providing a humanitarian fix to the official frameworks, allowing them to transfer more effectively to contemporary wars where the traditional institutions of power these frameworks rely on are relatively weak.

This terminology is borrowed from Harvey's (1982) trademark notion of "spatial fix", both a literal and metaphorical term used to describe the different forms of spatial reorganisation that serve to temporarily manage crisis-tendencies inherent in the accumulation of capital.[1] While my work is of a different tradition, Harvey's term makes for a useful adaption. Just as the spatial fix addresses crisis tendencies in capitalism, the humanitarian fix addresses underlying crises that have arisen in humanitarianism. And like the metaphorical meaning of the spatial fix, the resolution achieved by the humanitarian fix is temporary rather than permanent, so needs to be continually applied.[2]

This chapter seeks to understand the nature of these humanitarian brokers and through them build a detailed picture of the practical humanitarian fix they apply in complex humanitarian crises, as well as how this unofficial fix relates to the official frameworks. These humanitarians are able to deploy this alternative approach by using different practices to that of the traditional humanitarian intermediary in the previous chapter. First, they are relationship driven, seeing the world primarily as *relationships* rather than pre-formed entities or institutions that are the focus of the normative vision of humanitarian protection. Importantly, as the chapter goes on to explain, this relational approach allows them to find common ground among diverse actors with different worldviews, forming messy partnerships that promote pro-civilian behaviour. Second, they strategically develop and share different kinds of *knowledge*, notably formal knowledge of global frameworks and an informal knowledge of the local context, in order to engage a diverse spectrum of actors. Furthermore, unlike the official figure of the humanitarian intermediary, they employ this dual knowledge to actively *translate* the meaning of the normative frameworks to make them more relevant to the different actors that occupy the humanitarian network.

Relational actors

The UN compound in northern Iraq is the size of a large city block. Surrounded by a six-metre concrete wall, it sits next to one of the ring roads that circle Erbil, the city's international airport conveniently located to its back in case an evacuation is ever called for. White 4WDs routinely weave around the concrete barriers on the road leading up to the gate, with its dragon's teeth rising up out of the pavement. They are briefly lowered for each vehicle, after assault-rifle-toting guards check identification cards and wave vehicles through. Beyond the first wall, mirrors peer under vehicles and dogs sniff for explosives before each vehicle is allowed to continue to a building entrance, and the second tier of individual security checks and airport-style metal detectors that guard the labyrinth of buildings beyond.[3] The home of many of the institutions involved in the humanitarian response in northern Iraq and a central coordinating hub, it is a different world to the field from my earlier travels.

Deep inside the compound, with its corridors of offices and conference rooms, the protection cluster has been meeting for a good two hours, planning and coordinating their response to the Mosul crisis. About 20 UN and INGO representatives sit around the long table, including Vito, as comfortable here as at the desert outpost days earlier. These meetings and related working groups are about ensuring a "system wide" response, "leadership" and "accountability" among UN agencies and INGOs. Like meetings in large bureaucracies around the world, minutes are taken, working groups are formed and action points are circulated. On today's agenda are the constant risk of the undermining of the humanitarian principles and the delivery of protection services at the sub-national level. With the need for government authorisation and a heavy reliance on military escorts to reach at-risk communities close to the front line, there is concern that state forces are unduly influencing where aid is being delivered.

This is the official world of humanitarianism, demonstrably different to the informal space where I previously travelled with Vito as he worked to build trust and a working partnership with the Kurdish soldiers. Rather than individual relationships, the humanitarian sector views the world primarily in terms of preformed entities, such as state actors, donors, affected communities and aid organisations themselves. Interactions between these recognised entities are guided by a range of mechanisms – whether it is legal frameworks, principles or codes of conduct. As outlined in Chapter 2, they are the product of humanitarianism's Western, state-focused tradition, where relationships are between state entities and are guided by legal frameworks. This approach has been further reinforced over recent decades as humanitarianism has become increasingly institutionalised, continually establishing professional standards and codes of conduct in an effort to better coordinate their response efforts. Humanitarian policy makers embedded in this world of established entities and frameworks are guided by this philosophical plumbing, further ensuring that humanitarianism is represented in these instrumental terms.

Many field workers, who travel to "the field" from "the centre" with strong institutional ties and knowledge, also think this way. For them, humanitarian response is primarily carried out according to official frameworks, which focus on the actions of official entities. It is mechanisms – whether legal frameworks or minimum standards – that matter. This is reinforced by the recruitment of people and professions who can be predisposed to think this way. Many protection staff have a legal background, with a Masters of International Law almost a mandatory accoutrement for young protection delegates on their first mission. For them, at least at the outset, protection focuses on frameworks and institutional identities rather than an understanding of people and social relationships. Furthermore, in the increasingly professionalised aid sector, technical experts have a substantial voice in policy development and decision-making in the field, which in turn promotes structures over relationships.[4] Whether architects, logisticians or civil engineers, they often bring an instrumental lens to the field due to the nature of the work they do, which is about quickly establishing services in difficult environments. In this technical mind-set, social relations between people take a secondary position; rather their needs – or rights – are already identified and are met through following pre-established frameworks.

Compounding this professional leaning, in the results-driven environment of humanitarian response the focus is ultimately on the *outcome*, which can be measured and reported on, rather than the *process*, which is the place of relationships. Success needs to be measured and reported back to head office and then onto donors, in line with the increasing professionalisation and bureaucratisation of the sector over recent decades. Even those who see the importance of unmeasurable processes pay a disproportionate attention to outcomes in order to meet the measurements of success. As one ICRC field delegate observes, "As we professionalise more, we spend more time behind our computer screens entering data and spend less time interacting with people." In a self-fulfilling circle, this feedback from the field, written and measured in purely instrumental terms, then reinforces the approach of policy staff at headquarters level. They see that the language and approach of the field is similar to their own, reinforcing that it is the correct, and only, approach.

Relational thinking

Back at the UN headquarters, the meeting is starting to draw to a close and Vito's phone vibrates in his pocket. It is a Peshmerga officer, about 80 kilometres away in the outskirts of Mosul. Vito knows the soldier from his earlier visits to the front line. The young lieutenant's platoon has just taken control of a small village from ISIS after a brief fire-fight and they now have some 30 civilians in their care. Short of food themselves and needing to move quickly, they do not have the time or resources to deal with them. The conversation is brief – Vito says he can help, and will call back soon.

He hits the speed dial on his phone, and is quickly in touch with a contact from one of the local humanitarian organisations his agency has partnered with in recent weeks. These local gypsy humanitarian organisations have adapted to the needs on the ground; once many were human rights agencies or civil society activist groups, now it is front-line emergency relief and evacuating civilians. The conversation with the young Kurd he met informally a few weeks ago is brief. They know the village and can be there in half an hour with relief supplies and transport back to one of the camps that surround the besieged city. Minutes later, Vito has the young officer back on the phone. "We'll be there in 30 minutes," he says with certainty. This is Vito's day-to-day business; unlike his more instrumental counterparts establishing services such as water and shelter or others who fill the plethora of coordination roles represented in the cluster meeting, he builds relationships.

In this he reflects an alternative mode of thinking practiced by some aid workers, which sees relief and protection as more than frameworks and guiding principles, but rather the result of a particular pattern of social relationships shaped by the context. "If you think of the material that they shape and build, it's relationships," explains a senior ICRC delegate with extensive experience in central Africa, Yemen and Iraq. Farouk, an ICRC protection delegate with mediation experience in Iraq, Yemen and Somalia agrees, saying it is about people talking to people as individuals, not as representatives of structures. "If you talk to people as structure-to-structure you lose that human connection which is very important. You can't build trust amongst structures; you can build trust amongst people." Emphasising the importance of relationships in achieving outcomes, Farouk goes on to explain that "while the relationship is not the end goal – which is ultimately some form of transaction or agreement that promotes the protection of civilians – the relationship is the enabler for this goal."

My friend Tom tells a similar story about his first mission in Pakistan with the Norwegian Refugee Council and the relative importance of structures and relationships. In his book, *Deep Field*, he recounts:

> Understanding this "personality-driven" context was as important as knowing about the guiding principles and best practises of humanitarian assistance. Each night, I climbed into my sleeping bag with two books: the sections of the various humanitarian guides that I felt I needed to learn about and a copy of Tolstoy's *Anna Karenina*. In the end, it was probably *Anna Karenina* that provided the better guide, with its intensely complex and fractious set of embedded social relationships that reflected the way that disasters and conflicts, too, are social phenomena.
>
> (Bamforth, 2014, pp. 11–12)

A student of arts and part-time travel writer, Tom has spent a career moving between development programs and humanitarian operations. Most recently a shelter coordinator for the International Federation of the Red Cross, he quickly concedes he has little knowledge about the technicalities of shelter compared to the architects and engineers who dominate the sector. Instead, his speciality – if it can even be called that – is establishing and sustaining the individual relationships that ultimately allow for protection outcomes in a world where agendas often differ.

The relational approach of humanitarian workers like Vito, Farouk and Tom is distinct from the institutional focus on entities and mechanisms. This is not to say that humanitarian agencies and policy makers are not aware of the need for building relationships. When prompted, policy makers acknowledge their relevance. Rather, relational practices are not institutionally promoted and supported in the same way as instrumental practices. People with an understanding of relationships are not recruited in the same way you would recruit a gender-based violence expert or legal adviser, but emerge incidentally among a sub-group of aid workers in the field. Relationships are the discretionary role of frontline aid workers. Furthermore, from the global level, conversations about relationships quickly focus on institutions and how staff can promote those relationships, with "bilateral" and "multilateral" relationships subsuming people-to-people relationships as they are understood by many field delegates.

Relational thinking and the humanitarian fix

Ultimately, there are two approaches to humanitarianism. The first focuses on pre-formed entities and mechanisms, reflecting the institutions humanitarians come from. It is a structured, institutional approach that works to help provide a unity of purpose among humanitarian agencies, which was once found wanting in the Great Lakes region of central Africa. It also links to the official protection frameworks, which have historically worked to guide the behaviour of a diverse range of actors in the humanitarian space. The second, somewhat hidden behind this official approach, are the relational practices of many individual humanitarian workers. This is not a discrete approach, as these relational actors also fully articulate the frameworks in their everyday work. Vito references human rights law in his work, Farouk builds his informal practices around the Geneva Conventions and Tom routinely turns to the humanitarian minimum standards. Instead, in the complex humanitarian arena these people work in, the relational approach informally accommodates some of the shortcomings faced by the institutional perspective.

The relational approach provides this humanitarian fix on three levels. First, while the instrumental approach favours consistency of context, relationships *acknowledge complexities*, including the messiness of the interactions with different actors, the mix of motivations and agendas they bring and the inevitability of political disagreement and debate. Second, while the institutional perspective seeks political consistency and works better when there is agreement, relations can accommodate this *disagreement and debate*, a necessary part of finding common ground from initially differing positions. Finally, in accepting this complexity, a relational approach also acknowledges there is *no single, universal response* to complex problems. Instead, the ongoing relationship ensures the response can be constantly renegotiated and adjusted as the environment changes. As Farouk explains, "I see the relationship as the most important part – at least as the most important enabler – for having impact. And when things haven't worked, it's been because the relationship stopped or was thin."

Building and maintaining relationships

Realising the importance of relationships, these humanitarian workers invest time and resources into building them. Often their approach is in line with other actors from the global world who work in the local arena, such as anthropologists or development workers. Like these actors they establish "messy partnerships" (Guijt, 2008, p. 14, cited in Eyben, 2010, p. 391), a relational approach that allows differently positioned actors to get a better grasp of the situation. These relationships begin in neutral spaces where people meet without any prior commitment, letting events develop at their own pace. Interestingly, this kind of approach has long been central to the work of diplomats. Cocktail parties and similar quasi-informal occasions are designed to provide such spaces.

On the front line of northern Iraq, these cocktail parties translate into "a lot of tea being drunk and a lot of family photos being shared". As Vito goes on to explain before one of his visits to the front line:

> You don't walk in and say this is my mandate, I want to help here, you have to give me access. The response will be, "Excuse me! Who the fuck are you? This is my town; this is my front line; you don't come and tell me what to do".

Instead he focuses on building a human connection over time. "It's about building a rapport, building trust, building an understanding of who they are; their motivations and needs," the Refugee Council program manager explains. Once you have established that personal relationship, it is about finding commonalities where the agenda of armed actors overlap with the humanitarian agenda and how the different actors can work together for a humanitarian outcome. This is not about establishing a formal agreement, which lack an element of flexibility that is required in the changing humanitarian environment, but a level of trust that each side will do their best to deliver on their promise. "In this environment trust is stronger than contract," Vito says after his desert meeting with the Peshmerga. As this trust builds, the messy partnership extends to include other, often more substantial, humanitarian outcomes.

ICRC delegates routinely practice a version of this, first building relationships with armed actors before establishing relatively small humanitarian projects that also match the needs of the armed actors, which in turn promote relationships built on trust. In Afghanistan, the ICRC's role of repatriating bodies has proven to be an avenue to establish relationships with the Taliban, and ultimately open the way for further access and more substantial programs.[5] "If the Taliban knew we were carrying the body of one of their own they would allow us through checkpoints; later they would start to let us through when we were doing other forms of humanitarian relief," explains Paul, an ICRC delegate operating out of Khost, a hotbed of insurgent activity in Afghanistan.

Similarly, the ICRC's role in restoring family links allowed them to build relationships with Taliban leaders, whose communities wanted to be in touch with their detained relatives, whether in Afghanistan or Guantanamo Bay. Rather than travelling along dangerous roads, through multiple government checkpoints where they would often be harassed, and then being searched at a military base before making a call to the prison, the relatives of detainees would go to the local ICRC office in Khost. As Paul highlights, "It was a meaningful service that not only built trust with the families, but with community leaders and the Taliban." He goes on to explain to me:

> There were some really hard-core guys who had made serious threats [to us] but eventually came around to the ideas of the humanitarian organisation

> after they had seen us in action with our mortal remains and restoring family links activities.

But it is not all cocktails and frocks, or tea and cigarettes. These are powerful actors with firm agendas who are used to resorting to threats and actual violence. In this context, the messy partnership approach still holds, building relationships and an understanding of the motivations of different actors, but in the context of potential violence. Another ICRC delegate working in Afghanistan explains how he developed relationships between the humanitarian organisation and the Taliban, who were demanding medical supplies. "They are not developing a relationship with us because of my Ukrainian charm or because I'm a good-looking guy," says Alexi. "No, these relationships start with demands and threats of violence. This is the language they understand; the language of people who have been at war for 30 years." For the Farsi and Pashto speaking Ukrainian, establishing a messy partnership was about holding the line and standing by the agency's principles, while slowly establishing a common understanding between the ICRC and the Taliban. While the humanitarian agency would not unilaterally hand over medical supplies to an armed group, they could supply health services themselves. As the blunt-talking Ukrainian explains:

> Our job is to care for civilians in the desert who don't have access to health care; this isn't at odds with the Taliban's agenda, who are also the only ones who can give us access to some parts of the country.

In this way, aggressive demands for medical supplies to be handed over to the Taliban opens up a conversation about the role of the humanitarian agency in providing health care to affected communities. This conversation does not involve the assertion of any humanitarian right to access affected communities, nor a lecture to the Taliban about international humanitarian law. According to my interviews, such approaches have often proven ineffective when dealing with the hard-line Islamic movement, which relies on and promotes a version of Sharia law rather than accepting Western laws and traditions that sit at the heart of the normative frameworks. Instead, it is a two-way conversation that starts with demands, moves on to roles and ultimately leads to a mutually beneficial relationship. For the ICRC, this is humanitarian access to provide relief to affected communities, which, while unspoken in this context, is in line with their mandate. Meanwhile the communities under the Taliban's control receive much-needed health services, which benefits them as the local authority.

Relationships and trust

These are not relationships built on a formal contract, or an agreement over mandates and frameworks, but an informal agreement sustained by mutual benefit as well as the central element of trust. As Vito explains of his approach to building relationships with non-state armed actors, "I don't make things too formal; in this kind of environment, trust is stronger than contract. You build trust by delivering on what you say, which then opens the way for further negotiations." Rasul from the ICRC has a similar personal mantra in his engagements with non-state armed actors: "Say what you cannot do; say what you can do, and then do it. In both cases you build credibility, you build trust." For Rasul, reflecting on his time negotiating with insurgents in Yemen, it is about starting out with a small, agreed issue to work together on, such as mortal remains repatriation or restoring family links, and then establishing trust by delivering on this, before moving on to more complex, contentious issues that earlier could not be agreed on, such as the treatment of detainees, "pushing the envelope further and finding common ground." Here we can see the interplay between building a messy partnership that benefits both sides, and the trust involved in establishing, sustaining and growing these partnerships.

This personal value of trust sits behind the institutional principles that have historically been at the centre of interactions between humanitarian organisations and armed groups. Historically, humanitarian intermediaries endeavoured to maintain a dialogue and engagement with other actors by being seen as principled, neutral and impartial actors. Abiding by these values worked to create trust that no agenda other than humanitarian ones were being pursued. However, these institutional values have lost some of their power over recent years, particularly in contemporary conflicts where insurgents increasingly see humanitarians as an extension of the state. The very nature of their role as intermediaries and disseminators of the official frameworks can reinforce this, positioning them as agents of the Western, state-based humanitarian framework. Also, despite dissemination efforts the institutional humanitarian values of neutrality, independence and impartiality that were meant to lay the ground rules for relationships with state actors are not widely understood. Semi-formal codes of conduct and institutional norms, they were written in a specific time for a specific audience, which in turn can make them difficult to fully understand, especially across cultures. Even Western humanitarian workers often struggle to clearly articulate the meaning of the latter two, despite them being fundamental to their work.

Trust, meanwhile, is a personal value recognised across borders. Bridging cultural, social and political divides, trust is more relevant in the multitude of personal relationships humanitarian workers establish in the complex arena they operate in than are the official principles. This is not a rejection of the institutional principles of neutrality, impartiality and independence, which have institutional trust between humanitarian agencies and non-state actors as their underlying goal. Rather, it is an effort to make these principles work in the local environment where the formal codes are not necessarily embraced or understood. Similarly, the relational approach that trust facilitates is not a direct alternative to the more instrumental approach that is the foundation for the normative frameworks, but a humanitarian fix carried out by humanitarian workers to operationalise these frameworks in different contexts.

Knowledge brokers

Knowledge is central to humanitarianism and to the professional identity of humanitarians. Institutionally, the ICRC has long been described as the guardian of the humanitarian frameworks, the official protector of this knowledge. As this often-repeated phrase implies, they watch over these laws to protect them from those who may undermine them, continually reaffirming their meaning through dissemination efforts, their lawyers correcting misinterpretations by the international community, and literally storing this knowledge in their library and archives. It is an institutional role that extends out to other humanitarian agencies, whether it is the UN as the source of the treaties and conventions designed to protect people's rights, or non-governmental organisations systematically articulating these international laws. This formal humanitarian knowledge resides in "the centre", notably in key humanitarian, political and legal institutions from whence it was exported around the world along with the state system. Even 150 years after the Conventions were first published, Geneva remains the home of the official humanitarian frameworks that sit at the centre of this formal knowledge. It is where many humanitarian lawyers and policy makers reside and where field workers often begin their journey into the field.

Humanitarian fieldworkers in general, and protection staff in particular, are an extension of this formal knowledge. As the official disseminators of the humanitarian frameworks and principles, tasked with sharing it as widely as possible, this knowledge sits at the heart of their professional identities. These delegates are expected to have a sound understanding of the humanitarian principles and the legal frameworks relevant to their agencies. As outlined earlier, many have legal backgrounds and can articulate in fine detail the intricacies of these official norms. This is continually reinforced through the thematic workshops and formal trainings that are a substantial part of the professional lives of aid workers. Weeks are spent studying PowerPoint slides, drawing on butchers paper and sticky notes with coloured markers, and negotiating group exercises in conference rooms around the world. In the process of this research alone, I attended similar protection workshops in a Swiss chateau overlooking the Alps, a lake-side Norwegian ski resort and a disused agricultural college in rural Australia. Ultimately, the aim is for humanitarian workers to carry this knowledge into the field, sharing it with other actors in the form of official dissemination efforts and putting it into practice through providing relief.

Here, many develop the second type of knowledge – the informal knowledge of direct experience.[6] To be discussed in more detail in the subsequent chapter, this field knowledge is developed while visiting the local context, where humanitarians have immediate and unmediated access to the network of actors that occupies the humanitarian arena. It can be knowledge of local cultures, beliefs and practices, or knowledge of the motivations and agendas of different actors. In this, they reflect development workers – and anthropologists for that matter – who develop their knowledge of local beliefs, cultures and community structures by spending time in communities. It is a knowledge highly regarded by field workers as it has been tested by experience and is context specific. "Of course, an understanding of the frameworks is important," Alexi, the straight-talking Ukrainian, explains. "But it's also important to understand the local culture and language, to know what drives people. You find this out by talking to local communities and local staff; by spending time with them." Gabriel, who has worked in places as diverse as the Congo, Colombia and Afghanistan, agrees, adding that:

> It's important to acknowledge that every context is different, that every context has its own difficulties and challenges; Colombia is different to Afghanistan, the groups are different, the dynamics are different. There is a need to learn and adapt to each environment.

A lawyer, articulate in humanitarian frameworks and principles, he actively develops the local knowledge which is central to navigating complex environments where he has worked during more than six years disseminating these laws for the ICRC. His approach to these official dissemination efforts "depends on the group, depends on the context, and depends on the formal concepts involved." Here we start to see how humanitarian workers adapt their presentation of the formal knowledge in response to the contextual knowledge they build while living in the local environment. At one level, as intermediaries, they may streamline the message for a local audience not educated in the nuances of humanitarian laws and principles, while essentially ensuring it remains unchanged. As will be discussed in more detail in the following section, they also act as translators, modifying the formal knowledge they carry to the field in order for it to be more relevant to the local context.

Yet despite this interaction between these two forms of knowledge, the local knowledge remains the unofficial knowledge of humanitarianism. It is overshadowed by the powerful discourse of the normative frameworks and restricted to the field and informal networks of humanitarian practitioners. As one long-term UN delegate now working in Geneva explains, this field knowledge is respected in informal conversations, but in formal forums it is reduced in status compared to the "real" experts, who are policy and legal experts. "Here the expert from the field becomes the supporting act, providing appropriate anecdotes that support these 'real' experts." The formal knowledge is the main game at headquarters level. Knowledge produced elsewhere is used in specifically defined contexts by researchers and policy makers who operate as a knowledge-elite that reinterprets local realities within the frameworks of global science.

There is an underlying purpose to this, for the informal knowledge of the field is sometimes contradictory to the formal knowledge of the centre. One is about fixed laws and frameworks, which are deemed to be universal across all contexts. Like development narratives (see Roe, 1991), the relative simplicity of the formal humanitarian frameworks allows them to guide the behaviour of a host of different actors. These strategic simplifications (see Roe, 1991) generate consensus among actors with different agendas, making an agreed form of action possible – in this case a unified approach towards civilian protection. The other operates in the murky area of the local, occupied by a diverse and changing set of actors, with differing cultures and agendas to those imagined by the formal frameworks. It is a world at odds with the universal narrative. To acknowledge this complexity is to undermine the universality that sits at the basis of formal knowledge. Thus, there is an advantage to keeping the two separate, with local knowledge remaining informal and off the books.

Sharing knowledge

As a result, humanitarians adopt an informal knowledge broker role, developing relationships and personal networks to share this unofficial knowledge. In this informal network they are both the creators of this local knowledge and the ultimate users. After collecting knowledge through direct experience, they then make a conscious effort to share it with colleagues through informal networks, private conversations and various after-hours social occasions. Away from formal documents and reports – the preserve of the official language – they share their personal strategies, successes, failures and the wide variety of contradictions they grapple with.

There is a great deal of respect for this informal network. "One of the best ways of learning is not through somebody giving you a lecture with a PowerPoint, but is what you extract from your colleagues, from your peers," explains Francisco, a protection delegate working in east Africa whose contact details have been passed to me through this same informal knowledge network.

> For me this is critical in an organisation like ours, like the ICRC, and something critical to any humanitarian actor. I mean, understanding how others are engaging with other non-state armed groups, how they are managing the security, how they are portraying protection discussions.

He goes on to explain how he increasingly turns to this local knowledge community to ask for advice when faced with a problem, most recently drawing on other people's experiences with the Taliban to guide his own engagements with Al Shababb in east Africa. "I believe more and more in this [community] than having a very nice 80-page report about our engagement with the Taliban; I want to talk directly to the head of delegation who was there at that moment." Francisco then linked me up with Farouk, "who has some really interesting things to say on the topic". An ICRC delegate currently working on developing a networking platform for field staff, Farouk explains the importance of creating a semi-formal network:

> Where colleagues can talk about the full density of their experience, not just go over the minutes of a meeting, an operational report, or whatever other institutional mechanism we have been provided. It's another space where you really bring in this personal, contextual side, and then share it and talk about it.

Knowledge chains and local agents

Effective humanitarian knowledge brokers also tap into local networks to further expand and supplement their own knowledge. Local staff become valuable partners in developing this dual knowledge, often holding long-term positions in country offices and providing context to expat staff who rotate through on assignments of two years, or often much less. Experienced delegates will recognise where their knowledge ends, whether it is due to the short time they spend in the field or an inevitable cultural distance. "You've got to recognise where your reality stops and the reality of local staff in that same context starts," explains a senior NRC protection delegate, whose resume lists Chad, the Democratic Republic of Congo, Liberia and South Sudan among others conflict zones. "What you bring to the context in terms of knowledge, experience and how you address problems is really advantageous, but there is also a certain disconnect; local staff help bridge this divide." As Sebastian, an Australian working with the ICRC, explains:

> A boy from Sydney going into the heart of Jonglei State in South Sudan wouldn't have a clue where to start asking or talking about humanitarian issues when it comes to relating to the Dinka, the Nuer, the Murle or the Shilluk populations. The big lesson for any humanitarian, or aspiring humanitarian, is to ensure that they work alongside and benefit from the intimate knowledge of local or national staff.

As experience grows, so does the realisation of the importance of this link between local and expat. "I think that's an error that every international delegate makes – to think that somehow they have the answer," Sebastian continues, reflecting on his time in the field from Geneva, where I have met him in his office at the Carlton. "With the high rotation of international staff, that local understanding, experience and knowledge is too often underused." It is a theme that repeatedly emerges, with experienced delegates almost universally answering the question, "How would you have done it differently on your first mission?" by saying they would engage with local staff and local communities more. As Alexi adds: "They have memories of what has happened in the past … what has worked, what hasn't. They have an intimate understanding of the culture and the political situation."

Significantly, there is also a slowly increasing number of international humanitarians who originate in the local context who later developed this dual knowledge by spending time in the West. Vito, who developed his ability to relate with different cultures moving between Muslim and Christian communities in the Philippines, later studied international development in Australia before going on to work for INGOs in Sri Lanka, Afghanistan and Iraq. Rasul is from Lebanon, where he worked with the local Red Cross National Society for ten years before joining the organisation's Swiss-based international arm. Occupying the border between two civilisations, with cultural knowledge and language skills reflecting this, Lebanese have increasingly been recruited by the ICRC as it seeks to diversify its membership. Similarly, there is a high representation of Colombians, who grew up in conflict but also have a strong Western education. With local roots and formal knowledge later developed in the centre they bring the dual knowledge that is central to the professional and personal lives of many aid workers.

Knowledge and the local fix

From this collection of knowledge through their own direct experience, personal networks and life experiences, these field workers develop their own models, versions of the operational models on the ground. Like development workers, who have a similar practice (see Desai, 2006), these personal approaches and ways of working diverge from the official frameworks, handbooks and codes of conduct. Unlike their development counterparts, however, humanitarian workers do not position their models in a specific world they are located in at the time. Rather, as humanitarian workers are continually shifting, they develop broad models that can provide guidance in different contexts. In effect, they carry a set of local workarounds that have previously proved successful in accommodating shortcomings in the official approach.

At its most simplistic, these local workarounds help them more efficiently carry out the more technical work of relief in complex, changing environments. But as discussed earlier, relief is only a small part of humanitarian protection, which extends into their other, arguably more influential role. For as discussed, humanitarian protection is first about disseminating the message of the normative frameworks and humanitarian principles, about maintaining the discourse that sustains humanitarian space and a common understanding of what is appropriate behaviour. To this end, their workarounds go beyond the technical to focus on ways to share the official message, making it accessible to a more diverse range of actors. This can involve ways to break it down to its simplest components for a poorly educated teenager, or using an understanding of local belief systems to articulate the humanitarian norms and principles through comparison, as described in Chapter 4. Importantly, as will be discussed in more detail in the subsequent section, these local workarounds also involve brokerage not just between actors, but between the two knowledge systems themselves. In this they move beyond direct dissemination to include the act of translation, modifying the message to suit the local context.

Humanitarian translators

At the end of one of the narrow corridors that run throughout the Carlton, Rasul pours a cup of Turkish coffee as he thinks through my question about the effectiveness of the normative frameworks in today's conflicts. The books lining the shelves are a seemingly random mix of English, French and Arabic; a Middle Eastern rug shares the space with small north African statues and family photos from Beirut. Behind him, a builder walks past the second story window as renovations of the 19th century building continue. "Of course, the law is important in front line negotiations," explains the *Chef Adjoint de Operation*, known in the building as "the CADO", a quaint title originating from the ICRC's French speaking history.

> But it's not to be rigidly dropped on people. You want to take the spirit of the law and make it more understandable and comprehensible to your average fighter and your average commander, who's not necessarily educated to start with. And if they are educated, they are educated in different ways, in different norms and different values.

After some 20 years working with the Red Cross Movement across the Middle East and Africa, the Lebanese national is now half way through a three-year stint in Geneva as a *CADO*, a role that acts as the liaison between the head of a region based in Geneva and the various heads of countries in the field. These classic go-betweens attempt the often-complex task of linking up the field offices to senior management in Geneva, and the various legal and policy units that surround them in the Carlton's tight office space.

On the surface, he is an intermediary between the field and head office, facilitating conversations between these two locations and groups – the field workers implementing the legal frameworks and the lawyers and policy makers in Geneva. But there is also more depth to this. Reflecting on the previous section, the CADO brings the dual knowledge of the field and the frameworks to his role. Having spent two decades negotiating with armed actors in the field with Red Cross, he has an intimate understanding of how the formal frameworks play out in the local context. This is the world of non-state armed actors who do not necessarily embrace the official narrative; who are increasingly asserting their own cultural or religious authority and acting according to their own institutional agenda rather than according to the established formula of state agents. "They are educated in different norms and different values; that doesn't mean there is only one set of alternative norms and values, there are many," Rasul explains, articulating the culture and religion of the part of the world he grew up in, some 4,000 kilometres from the lake-side town.

> You cannot just come and say, "This is the law. You have to follow the law." "Whose law?" they will ask. "By whose means? Is it the North's law? The South's law? Is it Christian law? Is it Islamic law? Because we all have laws and norms and values that we follow. But which law are you talking about? And why does it have to be that law that is applicable to me? I don't recognise it. I don't subscribe to it. I don't belong to that society, to that Western identity".

There is a knock, and a neatly dressed man in a suit puts his head through the door. Rasul smoothly switches to French to organise a meeting with the legal team later in the day, before returning to English, his coffee and thoughts on the

Middle East. "I think for a long time organisations, especially in the Western world, did not necessarily grasp that," he continues.

> They thought that these laws were universal, which they are in a way. But in their perception, they just had to go and say, "This is the law. You have to follow it as it is. You cannot even question it, because these are agreed upon." But they were not agreed upon by this person or by this region. They were not necessarily part of the initial reflection.

He goes on to explain how the laws that protect civilians were written and codified by central Europeans. "These are good laws, representing good values – I'm not questioning that," he says.

> I am saying that it doesn't smoothly transfer to other parts of the world. You cannot go and talk purely about the Geneva Conventions, and how global and international they are. It doesn't make any difference to this fighter or that commander. For them you have to make a relation to what they understand.

As Rasul explains it, his approach in the field is more that of mediator than intermediary, using knowledge of both worlds to translate the frameworks to suit the context.

> I go and say, "Listen, let's sit down and have a conversation. What do you believe in? What are your values? What is it that you will abide by? Please inform me, enlighten me and let me know." And then once they explain it, you'll find out that at the spirit of it, at the core of it, it's not that different. It's just different in the way it's presented. It's different in the way it's packaged.

Translating the global to the local

Unlike the official disseminators of the previous chapter who share the normative frameworks without altering them, these humanitarian translators modify the message to suit the context. In other words, they translate the official discourse of the frameworks in a way that makes sense to each of the multitude of actors situated in the local arena. "You have to adapt because you are the guest. You are the stranger in this land. You're the one going to them, so it's up to you to adapt to them," Rasul explains.

> So in that way I think the spirit of the law is the most important, not the text of the law. The text is just to explain those ideas, to explain that spirit of the law. The reality is these are ideas, these are thoughts, and you only take those ideas and thoughts and translate them to the ideas and thoughts that are the closest to the minds of the people you want to talk to.

It is a message reiterated by protection delegates in conflicts around the world. Katelin, an NRC protection adviser and cluster coordinator in South Sudan, says: "We have to be able to take the frameworks and look outside of them; look at what they are trying to say as opposed to what they say [on paper]". Dalai, an ICRC delegate working in the Niger Delta, says that even concepts humanitarian workers may find self-explanatory do not necessarily cross cultural boundaries. "You can't go to a group and say, 'We are neutral, impartial and independent'; they will be like, 'What the fuck does that mean?' You need to break it down into terms they understand," the Iranian explains. This is not necessarily simplifying the frameworks to make them more understandable, for no matter how simplistic you make them, they are still the same frameworks, but "turning to underlying reasoning and values", she says.

Ultimately, these aid workers are using their knowledge of both the global frameworks and local context to establish a coherent representation of the normative frameworks that is relevant to non-state armed actors. They do this through the process of translation, which allows for a negotiated meaning that bridges cultural and political divides. They are attempting to find a meaning that is both faithful to the official frameworks, yet also resonates with other actors. In doing so they are attempting to recruit these actors – who sit outside the Western legal tradition – into the overall humanitarian effort.

Translation tactics

In essence, these humanitarian workers are introducing their own unofficial tactics into the humanitarian narrative. In the same way that non-state armed actors introduce unofficial tactics to redefine the official strategy of the normative frameworks – introducing their own agenda and acting according to their own motivations (see Chapter 4) – some humanitarians counter with tactics designed to bring these actors back into accord with the official frameworks. In translating these frameworks, I posit that humanitarians adopt three broad approaches.

i) Reasoned arguments

First, they present reasoned arguments that bring about behaviour that is in line with those of the frameworks. This extends beyond providing reasons to comply with the normative frameworks, the official approach in which humanitarian intermediaries argue that they are international, universal laws that apply to all actors. Rather, this alternative approach provides actors reasons to behave in a certain way without referencing the official norms. Here the reasoning moves away from law talk and is tied in with the agenda of the armed actors.

These often focus on the pragmatic arguments that pro-civilian behaviour will enhance community support. As Rasul explains, reflecting on his work in Yemen and central Africa, contemporary conflicts are generally fought on the land that belongs to the non-state armed group.

> Predominantly they belong to that land, they belong to those tribes, or they belong to those social units within. These are their families, their communities. They want the best for their people regardless of how they see it. What they really want is to provide them with basic needs, to protect them, to make sure they're not targeted as such.

In Yemen, with the state government and institutions all but evaporated, Houthi rebels were competing for domestic legitimacy in their local territories. In this context, the protection delegate went to tribal leaders with a specific ask: "Let's start cooperating. I know we disagree on many things, but what we agree on is that we want to help your people". In this way, a legal conversation becomes a practical conversation about community support. It then evolves into a broader conversation about helping all communities, recounts Rasul.

> Just as the other side shouldn't prevent us from helping your communities, you shouldn't prevent us from helping theirs. So rather than an opaque conversation about neutrality and impartiality, we start to envisage Western law through really practical, pragmatic examples.

Staying with the Yemen example, Farouk tells a similar story from the south of the country. The ICRC protection delegate talks of engaging with radical Al-Qaeda jihadists who had exploited the power vacuum to take control of Abyan Province.

> A lot of these groups as a point of pride were trying to fit into the narrative of being a provider, so would make a point of talking about services to the community, what they were doing for the civilian population, and not just about their ideological struggle. So that was the beginning of, or at least an entry point to a discussion that could move towards a wider definition of protection. So not just distributions and providing assistance, but to protection in terms of ensuring that these negative effects of fighting a conflict don't end up harming them.

There is a certain utilitarian component to these reasoned arguments, reflecting the foundational arguments that led to the establishment of the official frameworks (see Chapter 2). They line up with the "humanitarian imperative" that innocent communities should be protected and the desire to protect one's own community from the ravages of war. While the legal frameworks may have formalised this into a European tradition, translating them to these underlying arguments crosses societies and borders.

Political arguments are an extension of this utilitarian translation of the normative frameworks. Just as non-state armed actors use the frameworks as a tool for legitimacy – recall the Alabama Room in Geneva and the formal signing of Deeds of Commitment – it appears as part of the reasoning of humanitarian translators promoting civilian protection. However, unlike the argument of community support, aid workers are cautious when addressing these reasons for civilian restraint, often leaving them unspoken. Speaking after the Alabama Room ceremony with the Free Syrian Army, a Geneva Call legal advisor is at first cautious when discussing the legitimacy it imbues on the rebel group. "I'm not sure about that … yeah, I guess it is," the former field delegate muses, before going on to concede:

> A commander of a group comes to Geneva and meets with the chancellor of the Canton of Geneva, with the head of Geneva Call, and we are all in the Alabama Room, and then they take pictures and then they bring these pictures to the community, so I can see there is a matter of legitimacy.

Across town at the ICRC building, another delegate-cum-headquarters-lawyer is also cautious in acknowledging the utilitarian purpose of the legitimacy narrative, referring to armed actors signing up to Deeds of Commitment.

> We'd like to think that part of their signing these Deeds of Commitment is just purely to show their interest in the good of the civilian population. But also part of it, and we need to be pragmatic and realistic, is because it gives them some sort of credibility and political legitimacy because they're shown to respect international or national norms.

A colleague down the hallway is similarly cautious, accepting legitimacy as part of the narrative of humanitarian protection, while leaving it an unspoken component of dissemination work.

> I don't like to speak for all of my colleagues, but I think most of them would accept that everything we do, whether it be with states or armed groups, might be perceived by them as having some degree of advantage. And frankly, if an armed group thinks that speaking to the ICRC is going to get it somewhere, that's its perception. If it perceives it will get a degree of legitimacy, I don't always see that as a bad thing. Meaning to say, anything that is a door opener to a meaningful humanitarian discussion, or ultimately even humanitarian ends is okay.

For the time being we will just put a marker on this caution and return to its significance in the next section, but what is clear from speaking to humanitarian fieldworkers and lawyers is that legitimacy is a part of an alternative humanitarian narrative, if only in the background.

ii) Human values

Second, humanitarian translators turn to values when putting their case. For Rasul, it is about finding some initial common ground with armed actors. "We can agree on values," he explains. "We might not agree on different ways of writing down these values, but we agree on values in their essence, in their *raison d'etre*." As already discussed, the human value of trust emerges ahead of the institutional principles of neutrality and independence. Similarly, other personal values that formed the foundation of the normative frameworks emerge in initial discussions with armed actors. "We may come from different cultures, but we still have common concerns for civilians," explains Paul from Khost, Afghanistan. "Every humane person thinks about that; let's just work with that and forget about the Geneva Conventions, forget about the law for a moment."

These values are often part of the personal ethic of the humanitarians involved, who still predominantly come from the same world as the normative frameworks. However, these basic values arguably exist across many different cultures and religions, allowing humanitarians to refer to their use in the local context. "We wouldn't necessarily refer to international law during negotiations," explains an NRC humanitarian access delegate operating in Afghanistan. "Instead, we'll try and make the same point by referring to the Islamic principle of charity." Rasul follows a similar approach, breaking down the legal frameworks into their core values that are similar across cultures. "You break the law down to smaller pieces that are digestible and understandable rather than the bulk that you start with."

iii) Local customs and principles

Third, closely linked to this notion of universal values, humanitarians turn to customary arguments when translating the normative frameworks. At one level, this is used in the official intermediary sense, with humanitarian organisations like the ICRC trawling through local customs to find ones that relate directly to humanitarian law and then using them as a reason to follow these international laws. As Rasul explains, cutting through the jargon and detail of customary law, all doctrines have a similar list of commandments as IHL.

> You don't have to project Western law onto them. You just come and say, "Listen, this is the law that you believe in; well, believe it or not this coincides exactly with these texts of IHL. All I'm asking you to do is abide with what you say that you believe in or that you follow or that you subscribe to".

In east Africa, Alfonso reiterates how customary law is working to reinforce the Geneva Conventions. "We try to combine these two frameworks in order to identify common patterns. The common principles we have in the Geneva Conventions and in Sharia Law in order to engage with a narrative that makes sense to them."

Here it is about using customary law to highlight the supposed universal nature of the Geneva Conventions and so remaining faithful to the state-based legal system. The act of translation comes from a slightly different position, adapting the official message so it is in line with local customs and beliefs. For humanitarian translators, there is no reference to the official frameworks in these conversations – it is not about comparing different laws and pointing out they are the same. Rather they translate the humanitarian laws and principles to the language of local customs to put the same case. In this subtle but important distinction, the often-rejected Western frameworks and the idea of universal laws are not part of the conversation. "Of course there are the international norms, of course there is domestic law, of course there are the policies, procedures and practices, but equally important are the traditions and customs of each given society," explains Alfonso, an ICRC head of country in east Africa who works at the local end of Rasul's go-between role.

Alfonso and his team in Somalia are turning to knowledge and customs unique to the region to discuss and promote humanitarian protection, incorporating *Biri ma Geid* into their narrative. Literally translated to "spared from the spear", this oral tradition defines categories of innocent people that deserved mercy, in particular women, children, the elderly and the sick (see Bangerter, 2011). It forbids rape as a tool of war, promotes the sanctity of medical structures and argues that prisoners must be treated with dignity and be taken care of – all common themes for students of international law. But importantly for Alfonso, they are non-legal arguments. "The value of these frameworks is we don't perceive them as legal, we don't use them as legal, we don't portray them or use them in a utilitarian way. For me they are not legal, they are something else," he says to me from Somalia.

> If we put it in a legal way, it would automatically be perceived by the group as a legal framework that has a Western, liberal agenda behind it, so this is where we have to play a little bit with the different systems.

While clearly not presented as part of the normative frameworks, this reasoning and moral narratives do not stray far from the official discourse. They somewhat unintentionally reflect the foundational arguments that led to the establishment of the official frameworks, which, as outlined in Chapter 2, were meant to bring a level of restraint to the increasing violence of industrialised warfare.

The official and unofficial scripts

Ultimately, humanitarians are using two scripts, both of which serve a purpose in protecting civilians. These two scripts align with the notions of official and unofficial knowledge introduced earlier. On one level, the official narrative is effective in unifying some actors who make up the humanitarian network, notably states, their militaries and humanitarian agencies. These actors are substantially invested in the normative frameworks, which were originally established to bring a level of order to the conflicts they were part of. Some non-state armed actors also respect the letter of the law on occasion, particularly when they aim to be part of the international system. This is why the role of the disseminator or intermediary is still important and why humanitarians consistently remain loyal to these frameworks. As Sebastian, a Geneva-based ICRC lawyer, explains, "Legal arguments remain central to the response with more organised militaries that clearly work within a framework of international law, including international humanitarian law, and whose training, doctrine and operational procedures reflect these laws." From this global perspective that sees the world as made up of sovereign states, this formal, legal approach makes sense and has proven to be somewhat effective.

Meanwhile, viewed from the local level, fissures start to appear. Here, the local arena of contemporary wars is revealed as far more complex and includes actors who do not sit neatly inside the normative vision. The response from some humanitarian field workers is to translate the official frameworks to meet these local challenges, drawing on their local knowledge in order to develop and sustain an alternative, unofficial script. While at the core it may be the same, explains Rasul, "It's different in the way it's presented, it's different in the way it's packaged, it's different in what is being represented."

To reiterate, this alternative script provides a humanitarian fix in complex contexts where armed groups act according to their agendas and beliefs rather than the codified norms of state agents. To reflect on the critical theory of Scott (1990) introduced in Chapter 3, the official script helps maintain consensus among the different actors in the humanitarian arena. Meanwhile, the act of translation provides aid workers room to manoeuvre outside of the official narrative, allowing for compromise and accommodating shifting agendas. These translations form an unofficial script, effectively helping to sustain the official frameworks without undermining them.

There has long been an awareness of the capacity of alternative narratives to undermine the official frameworks. This is reflected in the words of some humanitarian lawyers and policy makers who urge for caution when presenting alternative arguments for the protection of civilians. As one ICRC report into the challenges of contemporary conflict argues:

> Strategic argumentation should be used carefully, as it carries a risk of possible backlash. It should not lead to setting aside respect for IHL in favour of pragmatic concerns or opportunistic outcomes. Furthermore, strategic argumentation should be employed with discretion and with an awareness of the political sensitivity of some arguments.
>
> (ICRC, 2007)

It is a concern also expressed by many humanitarian field workers, who see the potential of this alternative narrative to undermine the formal frameworks. Sebastian, who has worked with the ICRC on three continents, puts the case for caution:

> I think if we become overly flexible we compromise the frameworks; it's easy to cross the line and not realise you've crossed it. And so I think sticking to the legal fundamentals as the core guiding principles and then deviating only in exceptional circumstances is a safer approach.

The concern is that articulating alternative narratives undermines the efforts of disseminators to promote the normative frameworks as the conventional wisdom.

Also, turning to more flexible ideas like human values, political legitimacy or practical reciprocity acknowledges the limitations of the frameworks and opens the way for more flexible, selective behaviours by all actors. As Sebastian explains, laws are not something to be negotiated:

> Laws should be respected full-stop; respecting IHL isn't about ensuring your soldiers will be welcomed with open arms by the civilian population, or you have a better chance of signing a good peace deal with the government; it's not part of a political bargaining tool or for gaining political legitimacy.

This puts humanitarian translators in a complex situation. On the one hand they promote the normative frameworks as being the conventional wisdom. Meanwhile, they use their local knowledge to navigate the milieu of the space they work in, translating this universal message so it is suitable for the local context, all the while realising that it may undermine their official role.

To account for these two sometimes-conflicting narratives, humanitarian translation remains unofficial, carried out informally by individuals rather than being institutionally driven. To borrow from Scott (1990), it remains a "hidden transcript" that operates alongside the "public transcript". While they will acknowledge the work they do in translating the frameworks, it is not part of their public identity. This unofficial tactic is kept for personal conversations or reflection workshops. In their formal engagements with their global counterparts they will often translate their messaging back to fit the official narrative. There is no subterfuge in this. This open secret allows the two narratives to coexist. Here we can return once again to Scott, who speaks of concealed personal, community and institutional "system goals" that coexist alongside the official goals. In this way humanitarian translators can preserve the authorised view of themselves and their institutions while actively translating the message to suit the multitude of local actors they engage with.

Furthermore, to help these two scripts to coexist, there are self-imposed limitations to the interpretations. As Rasul explains, emphasising the importance of balancing the unofficial translation and the official narrative: "You have to look within the range of what's an acceptable interpretation. How much can you adapt the rule to the cultural situation or the factual situation? That's a very difficult question." Latimer, a colleague of Rasul, says it is important to approach alternative strategic arguments with a great deal of awareness in order not to compromise the frameworks. According to the ICRC policy adviser on non-state armed actors, it is about being flexible enough to make the frameworks relevant, but not going so far as to undermine their normative value. "If you are over pragmatic it will probably backfire; if you are over flexible and just adapt to whatever you need to in order to reach a goal it will also backfire," he explains.

Thus, alternative interpretations do not digress too far from the official narrative, which has the normative frameworks at its foundations. It is about translating the meaning of these frameworks to another language, rather than developing a new meaning. In this the humanitarian is like the interpreter who does not make a literal translation but still produces the same meaning. This helps ensure that the unifying narrative still has a level of consistency across the network. There are similar expectations for all actors; it is just that these expectations are expressed differently according to the context.

Conclusion: brokers, translators and the humanitarian fix

Another mode of humanitarian practice has emerged in contemporary conflicts. As we have seen, political authority has fragmented in these so-called new wars, where non-state armed actors have increasingly asserted their authority, challenging the state's monopoly of violence and weakening state-centred notions of power. This is particularly the case in parts of the Middle East and Africa, where a combination of state fragility, conflict and instability have enhanced the military, political and social importance of non-state armed groups (see Chapter 1). These powerful actors have also made their presence felt in the humanitarian space, disrupting the original narrative that has guided the behaviour of armed actors. Humanitarians, already positioned along these fault lines, have responded with a series of unofficial fixes in an effort to recruit these new actors into the humanitarian effort, which this chapter outlines.

First, relationships are a central component to this unofficial mode of humanitarian protection. Instead of solely focusing on protection mechanisms such as legal frameworks, this mode of thinking recognises that humanitarian protection is the result of a pattern of social relationships shaped by context. It is informal, adaptable relationships between people that ultimately enable protection outcomes in complex environments where agendas often differ. This is not a discreet approach, as relational actors also fully articulate the frameworks in their everyday work and recognise their capacity to guide the behaviour of different actors (see Chapter 4). Rather, relationships are deployed to accommodate the shortcomings of formal frameworks in complex environments. They help smooth over differences and uncertainties, and allow for constant renegotiation and adjustment to contextual changes.

Second, this alternative mode of protection complements the formal, global knowledge with informal, local knowledge. The long-established global knowledge of the official frameworks is a key part of humanitarian protection and relief, with aid workers carrying it from "the centre" and sharing it as widely as possible in the form of dissemination (see Chapter 4). Aid workers in the field often complement this with a local knowledge, whether it is local cultures, beliefs and practices, or knowledge of the motivations and agendas of different actors. However, there are tensions between these two knowledge systems – with one acknowledging complexity and the other deemed to be universal across all contexts. Because of this they remain separate, one in the official world of institutional policy, the other in the informal world of everyday practice. It is left to field workers to mediate between the two, using their knowledge of both worlds to adapt official frameworks to the local context. In other words, they act as knowledge brokers between two sometimes-contradictory systems – between the global international protection frameworks they have traditionally represented and the non-state armed actors of the South who have been digressing from these official frameworks.

As the third section of this chapter explains, these knowledge brokers translate the official discourse of the protection frameworks in a way that makes them relevant to the multitude of actors that occupy the humanitarian arena. They do this by turning to comparative reasoned, moral and cultural arguments that represent both the foundations of the normative frameworks, and the motivations and belief systems of actors who are not historically part of this Western, legal tradition. This in turn enrols a broader array of actors from outside the Western, state tradition into the collective humanitarian effort. However, these alternative scripts are often conflicting, with one representing universal frameworks and principles and the other acknowledging contextual complexity. Because of this they are kept separate, with the translation remaining unofficial, an open secret coexisting alongside the official discourse. This allows the act of translation to accommodate contextual variations in conflicts, while not undermining the universal frameworks.

This chapter argues that it is this practice of translation that has allowed the established humanitarian protection frameworks to be sufficiently successful in contemporary wars to ensure they remain the focus for state and humanitarian actors. They are in essence an unofficial humanitarian fix to the challenges of transferring these official frameworks to contemporary wars where the traditional institutions of power these frameworks rely on are weak. They resolve the problem without undermining the power of the official frameworks in more traditional contexts and ensure that they are sustained.

In this we can reflect on the theories of everyday practice and resistance introduced in previous chapters (de Certeau, 1984; Scott, 1990). In his nuanced account of agency, de Certeau (1984) reveals the subversive "consumer practices" which are "not manifest through [their] products, but rather through [their] *ways of using* the products imposed by a dominant economic order" (p. xiii, emphasis in the original). Scott (1990) describes "hidden transcripts" that exist alongside the "public transcripts" of development policy. To reiterate from Chapter 3, "The hidden transcript is produced for a different audience and under different constraints of power than the public transcript" (Scott, 1990, p. 5). Just as recent development ethnographers have extended these ideas of agency and resistance from those at the receiving end of aid to include development professionals and their relationship with the organisations they work in (see Fechter & Hindman, 2011; Mosse, 2011), this chapter takes a comparable step to include humanitarian workers and their relationship with the official frameworks. Humanitarians are agents in both these scripts. As intermediaries, they promote the official script – the humanitarian frameworks and principles. Meanwhile, as brokers and translators they are also purveyors of unofficial scripts, modified versions of the official discourse designed to recruit disparate, non-state actors into the humanitarian protection effort.

Notes

1 Harvey's (1982; 2003) "spatial fix" addresses the inherent contradictory nature of capitalism, which has explicit geographical dimensions. It describes the geographical expansion needed to "fix" the inevitable crisis of over accumulation, which leaves surplus capital and labour underutilised. These surpluses are first absorbed by the activities required to open up space and establish the necessary physical and social infrastructure. Then, once this space is "produced", capital and labour are directed into production efforts made profitable by this spatial expansion of the system of capital (Harvey, 2003, pp. 109–112).
2 Harvey (2001) clarifies these literal and metaphorical ideas in another article. To "fix a problem", he explains, is to resolve a difficulty. Things are returned to normal functioning again. This literal meaning has another metaphorical derivative, "as in 'the drug addict needs a fix', in which it is the burning desire to relieve a chronic or pervasive problem that is the focus of meaning. Once the 'fix' is found or achieved then the problem is resolved and the desire evaporates. But, as in the case of the drug addict, it is implied that the resolution is temporary rather than permanent, since the craving soon returns" (p. 24).
3 As Duffield (2012) points out, risk management has led to the aid industry bunkering down in fortified compounds, limiting their physical and psychological engagement with local populations. "Care of oneself involves a psychological distancing that complements, and requires, the physical walls and razor wire of the fortified aid compound" (p. 29).
4 Eyben (2010) makes a similar case regarding the role of technical experts in development during the 1980s when the focus was on "things", while the social relations of those using them was ignored.
5 Under the Geneva Conventions, mortal remains must be disposed of according to the cultural and religious instructions of the deceased person. In addition to its traditional activities tracing those missing in armed conflicts, the ICRC searches for, identifies and repatriates mortal remains.
6 While not wishing to delve into the philosophy of knowledge, according to Russell (2004) there are two types of knowledge, "knowledge by description" and "knowledge by acquaintance". These can be equated to the formal knowledge of institutions and the informal knowledge of direct experience.

References

Bamforth, T. (2014). *Deep field: Dispatches from the front line of aid relief.* Abrams.

Bangerter, O. (2011). Reasons why armed groups choose to respect international humanitarian law or not. *International Review of the Red Cross*, 93(882), 353–384.

Bierschenk, T., Chauveau, J.-P., & de Sardan, J.-P. (2002). *Local development brokers in Africa: The rise of a new social category* (Working Paper No. 13). Institute for Ethnography and African Studies.

de Certeau, M. (1984). *The practice of everyday life.* University of California Press.

Desai, B. (2006). Inside out: Rationalizing practices and representations in agricultural development projects. In D. Lewis & D. Mosse (Eds.), *Development brokers and translators: The ethnography of aid agencies* (pp. 173–194). Kumarian Press.

Duffield, M. (2012). Risk management and the bunkering of the aid industry. *Development Dialogue*, 58, 21–35.

Eyben, R. (2010). Hiding relations: The irony of "effective aid". *European Journal of Development Research*, 22(3), 382–397.

Fechter, A.-M., & Hindman, H. (Eds.) (2011). *Inside the everyday lives of development workers: The challenges and futures of Aidland.* Kumarian Press.

Guijt, I. (2008). *Seeking surprise. Rethinking monitoring for collective learning in rural resource management.* Wageningen University and Research.

Harvey, D. (1982). *The limits of capital.* Basil Blackwell.

Harvey, D. (2001). Globalization and the "spatial fix". *Geographische Revue*, 2(3), 23–30.

Harvey, D. (2003). *The new imperialism.* Oxford University Press.

ICRC (2007). *International humanitarian law and the challenges of contemporary armed conflict.* 30th International Conference of the Red Cross and Red Crescent, Geneva, Switzerland.

Lewis, D., & Mosse, D. (Eds.). (2006). *Development brokers and translators: The ethnography of aid and agencies.* Kumarian Press.

Mosse, D. (Ed.) (2011). *Adventures in Aidland: The anthropology of professionals in international development.* Berghahn Books.

Roe, E. (1991). Development narratives, or making the best of blueprint development. *World Development*, 19(4), 287–300.

Russell, B. (2004). *The problems of philosophy.* Oxford University Press.

Scott, J. (1990). *Domination and the arts of resistance: Hidden transcripts.* Yale University Press.

6 Humanitarian travellers and local fixers

Introduction

It has become clear that this ethnography is a journey, first travelling across northern Iraq with Murshid, examining the humanitarian intermediary and the nature of humanitarian space. Then travelling with Vito in the previous chapter, which revealed the humanitarian broker and the unofficial scripts they turn to. Other humanitarian workers on their own journeys between countries, continents and cultures have also been a fundamental part of this ethnographic story. Their knowledge, collected from different contexts, is central to what has been revealed. As a participant observer, this book has also been about my own travels, from the Goma refugee camp to the roadblock near Sinjar, and then on to the Mosul operation some two years later.

The emergence of travel is not incidental to this book but, as this chapter will articulate, is central to the roles humanitarians play. For humanitarians are, to borrow from Clifford (1992), a "travelling culture", identified as much by their movement between worlds as where they reside. Defined through the idiom of temporary crisis, their work is not about sustained engagement, as is the case with development workers. Rather they shun commitment to place, moving on quickly once urgency has passed, in effect maintaining a constant state of transit. This chapter considers this mobility and its established place in the humanitarian endeavour through three interrelated ideas: the expatriate humanitarian traveller; the local staff they work with and rely heavily upon; and "the field" where they work, which is constructed in relation to "the centre".

This chapter will begin by exploring the local field, which can only be fully understood through its relationship with the global centre. The centre and the field – a concept closely related to the notion of the "margins" – can be identified as much by their discursive relationship to each other as the geographic locations that come from this understanding of the world. The centre – rooted in colonial, European history – is the perceived hub from which power and authority radiates outwards, bringing political order to the supposedly less developed margins (see, e.g., Said, 1978; Scott, 2009). It is also the geographic centre, with the sources of power that unite the international system emanating out of the Western hubs as a historical consequence of colonial expansion. This same process that assigns power to the centre, articulates the margins as the underdeveloped space at the edges of state authority (see also Meehan & Plonski, 2016; Thomas & Wilkin, 2004). The so-called "new wars" (Kaldor, 2006) can be seen as disruptions to the unifying authority of the centre over the margins. Geographically located at the periphery of earlier colonial expansion, away from state centres of power, they are the result of competing forms of power asserting their authority (see Chapter 4). Humanitarianism is one of the centre's responses to these disruptions, providing relief and promoting the discourse of humanitarian space in an effort to bring temporary order.

The very distance created by this imagery has cast the humanitarian as a traveller, of the centre travelling to the field to provide relief to vulnerable populations caught up in this violence and state breakdown. This notion of travel is woven into modern humanitarianism, providing significant functional effects. That is, it facilitates key components of the humanitarian endeavour. As this chapter will explain, by continually travelling humanitarians retain a level of distance from other actors who occupy the local space, which in turn facilitates their much-cited status as neutral and impartial actors. Travelling also has important structural effects on knowledge. The capacity to move freely between the centre and the margins allows humanitarians to transfer knowledge between these spaces, central to their role as intermediaries discussed in Chapter 4. Furthermore, travel facilitates learning and allows expatriate humanitarian workers to develop some level of the local knowledge required to adapt these frameworks to the local context, as discussed in Chapter 5.

Simultaneously, however, this separation from the local has inevitable negative effects. While travel promotes neutrality and facilitates dissemination and the development of some local knowledge, it is also responsible for creating the humanitarian as a transient figure, limiting contact with the local population and the substantive contextual knowledge that this interaction would provide. Furthermore, I argue that it impacts the flow of knowledge within humanitarian organisations and promotes a degree of ignorance about the local context in which humanitarians work. In a complex set of interactions, the very quality of physical distance between the centre and the field, which creates the need for the humanitarian traveller and helps ensure their useful outsider status, simultaneously isolates them from local knowledge.

In a further extension of these interactions, the humanitarian traveller and the limitations of transience have created the need for a counterpart solidly embedded in the local world. As this chapter goes on to discuss, the humanitarian traveller's necessary other emerges in the form of the national staff member. I argue that this somewhat hidden figure provides a local fix to the problems that emerge from humanitarian travel and the transience of the humanitarian endeavour. At the same time, the local figure and their international expat counterpart represent persistent racial hierarchies and power inequalities. I argue that while these local humanitarians are central to the modern humanitarian project, providing an unofficial fix to some of its limitations, they are simultaneously marginalised by a system that is structurally invested in the official protection discourse and the humanitarian as traveller and political outsider.

Reflecting on these interlinked components, the broader conceptual argument I pursue in this chapter is that established notions of the centre and the field, the subsequent humanitarian traveller, and the structural separations between international and local staff are constitutive parts of the modern humanitarian project. There is a systematic utility to these different elements, which are necessary components of the modern humanitarian philosophy and the mechanisations of humanitarian protection. Yet at the same time these necessary components produce inevitable problems, often inherited from the colonial system from which modern humanitarianism emerged and that established the centre/margins world view.

The global centre and the local field

Sinjar sits between the city of Mosul and Syria, on the vast expanse of the barren border region of northern Iraq. For me, sitting on the top of Mount Sinjar looking down at the town for the first time, the desert plain stretching off into the distance, it feels like the edge of the world. Once a stopover on the caravan trading routes beyond the edge of the Roman Empire, through the historical region of Mesopotamia, today it separates ISIS enclaves in Iraq and Syria. The invisible straight line across the desert, drawn after World War II when these two nation states were created, stretches some 50 kilometres to the west of the town. A temporary safe haven for many of those who have fled Mosul in recent days, Sinjar now simmers under the intense summer heat and the pressure of accommodating thousands of displaced families. Under the temporary security umbrella of the Kurdish Peshmerga, religious charities, community groups and the local Red Crescent do what they can to provide food and water to people now holed up in mosques, community halls and unfished buildings around the town. Weeks later, Sinjar will become the focus of the world's attention, when ISIS overruns the town and begins its brutal attempts to wipe out the local Yazidi population, forcing thousands to flee into the surrounding mountains. It is a world away from my home in inner-city Melbourne and my regular work at Australian Red Cross headquarters.

Humanitarians and the global centre

Humanitarians occupy two worlds, "the centre", and "the margins", which they articulate as "the field". The centre can be understood as the interface of the international system, facilitating the relationships between the nation states that form the global community. Key components of this are the international frameworks that guide behaviour between states, whether it is the interactions through trade, aid or commerce. Humanitarianism is represented in this global picture by the international humanitarian norms that guide behaviour during armed conflict, as explained in Chapter 1. Humanitarians themselves are key protagonists in this international system, actively disseminating these norms to reify this coherent vision of the world. In this sense they are the classical humanitarian intermediaries of Chapter 4, reinforcing the frameworks through constant repetition. I recall colleagues at Australian Red Cross constantly on the road, with brochures and PowerPoint presentations, visiting universities, schools, government departments and the array of civil society institutions, promoting these frameworks. It is a role repeated in almost every nation state around the world. And while INGOs may not have been officially granted this state-mandate to disseminate, they too are continually reinforcing the humanitarian frameworks that form a component of the centre's unifying effort.

As the name implies, the centre is also centrally located geographically, with sources of power emanating out of predominantly Western centres to bring a unity of order to the international system, with national capitals serving as hubs of this power. This abstract map is a product of colonialism, with the nation state system having radiated out of Europe through a process of exploration, conquest and colonisation, and then later decolonisation and the post-colonial state-making processes. As discussed in Chapter 2, the geography of colonialism lingers in our international system to this day. Humanitarians, reflecting this geography, predominantly originate from these same Western capitals and regional hubs, gravitating as part of their careers to key humanitarian centres such as Geneva and New York. The same recent graduates and early career Red Cross staff disseminating the frameworks across Australia, for example, almost invariably had one eye towards moving to Geneva, the original source of the knowledge they disseminate.

This is not to say they are all graduates of the Western political science, international relations and law schools that defined many international aid workers of two decades ago. Reflecting the multiple hubs that make up the centre, an element of national diversity has slowly spread across the sector. Now aid workers are just as likely to come from institutions in Latin America and parts of Africa, Asia and the Middle East as from Europe. Yet while representing a more diverse cultural mix, they are still of the centre, or more specifically the regional hubs that reflect the centre and its institutions. This is represented in the interview subjects that make up this study, with many starting their education and careers in these regional hubs, often heading to places like Geneva before spreading out into the field and the front line of humanitarian response.

Humanitarians and the field

This introduces the second world that humanitarians occupy, which exists at the margins of the centre's authority. Humanitarians – and anthropologists for that matter – often describe this other world they travel to when they leave the centre as the field. The term is rooted in European history and colonial-era geography. For late 19th and early 20th century anthropologists, research came to involve leaving the comfort of university libraries and one's own society to go into the field and engage with local communities outside of Europe (see Gupta & Ferguson, 1997; Kuklik, 2008). Similarly, post-Dunant humanitarians, imbued with Western notions of charity, philanthropy and limits on the conduct of war, travelled out from European centres, living and working in the field and providing relief to those in need, before returning to their lives in Western centres (see Davey, 2012; Hutchinson, 1996; Redfield, 2013). Whether a colonial-era anthropologist or humanitarian, the field was the place one travelled to, occupied by an alien or different culture, and characterised by temporary outposts, encampments, primitive living conditions and hardship. Thus, the field existed entirely relative to the European centre and those who conjured this imagery. It is the place that exists beyond the centre and its civilising effect.

The colonial-era term continues to this day, part of the humanitarian vernacular when describing that taken-for-granted space where "fieldwork" is carried out. It is a term of the centre, of home, that describes the world beyond the capital cities and regional hubs where humanitarian institutions are situated. "Are you going to *the field*?" "How was *the field*?" "I just got back from *the field*," "I'll be away in *the field*," are common refrains of humanitarian workers that articulate this different world where they work. In part, these descriptions help sustain earlier simplistic understandings of the centre and the field, reifying the field as somewhere beyond the civilising effects of the centre and its institutions.

It is this fieldwork and the personal hardship involved that makes one a "real humanitarian". Indeed, if there is a single factor that determines someone's experience and credibility as a humanitarian it is their experience in the field. It is often one of the first points of conversation, with aid workers listing their recent "missions" to demonstrate their credibility, highlighting the time spent in more geographically remote and politically complex places. My own references throughout this book to various field missions in part represent this same assertion of professional credibility. Six months in Iraq is credible, but not of the same order as two years in the politically complex Yemen or time in the remote mountain regions of Afghanistan when measuring humanitarian experience.

Yet this idea of the field, although central to humanitarians' identity, remains a largely ill-formed concept in humanitarian literature and practice. This mysterious space, situated over the horizon from the centre, has been left to common sense. It is, to borrow an earlier critique of anthropologists' understanding of their field, "beyond and below the threshold of reflexivity" (Gupta & Ferguson, 1997, p. 3). The field thus remains a mysterious place, simply understood as the space of humanitarian work that is outside or beyond the centre where the institution resides, both in its geographical terms and in terms of the reach of the institutional frameworks that define the global system. It remains, to use earlier attempts to understand the world, the ill-defined space that exists at the margins of the centre's authority.

While the ambiguity of the term leaves this space quite ill-defined, there are related descriptions that bring some texture to how humanitarians and humanitarianism understands the field and its relationship to the centre. It is reflected in descriptions of complex emergencies, the key field site for humanitarians, as opposed to their development worker siblings, who use the same all-encompassing term. As the term complex emergency implies, these humanitarian crises are "complex sites", characterised by "total or considerable breakdown of state authority", reflected in the Inter-Agency Standing Committee's official definition (see, e.g., IASC, 2008, p. 24).

This description that defines the field they work in as being at the margins of state authority is also reflected in the words of humanitarian workers themselves. Speaking from the field in the Central African Republic, Simon, an International Rescue Committee (IRC) delegate, describes the world in which he works in terms that reflect those of many others I spoke to and the official definition:

> There's been a break-down in state authority as a result of years of internal conflict, leading to ever increasing hunger, displacement and disease.... The state government hasn't the capacity to reassert control outside the capital.... [I]t remains at the margins of international interest, with little or no concerted outside intervention to restore stability.

Here we see how the field emanates out from hubs of authority. For Simon, the field is not the capital of Bangui, which forms his centre, and the centre of operation for the IRC in the Central African Republic. Instead, it is the contested areas beyond the capital's authority, where a weak state government is failing to contain the violence between Muslim ex-Seleka rebels and anti-Balaka Christians. Further south in the Democratic Republic of Congo, another aid worker describes a weak government failing to assert its authority from the capital to the country's east, where a confusing cast of characters are battling for economic and political power. "From the west coast of a country two-thirds the size of Europe, with little or no infrastructure, the state government simply does not have the ability to police the contested peripheries of its eastern borders," he explains.

These descriptions by humanitarians also bring a geographical understanding to the marginal areas where complex emergencies occur. They are frequently geographically located both away from international centres, but also away from "nodes" of state authority. Viewed from Geneva, places like Bangui, Kinshasa or Erbil are the field, but to call it that in any of these regional capitals would attract eye-rolls from those humanitarians based there. Rather, these are hubs of stability, with the actual crisis usually occurring further *afield*, beyond the centre's control. This shifting understanding of the field continues as you move out to regional centres, away from these state capitals, reflecting a model of state power which gradually fades as you move from administrative capitals to the remote margins.[1] It positions the field as predominantly geographically remote from the centre and its hubs, where the state frameworks have failed to sufficiently embed.

Complicating this discursive field

This conceptualisation of the field as being at the margins of the state, where there has been a breakdown of state power, reflects the long-established humanitarian discourse that emerged from the centre. It is part of a broader discourse that sees power emanating outwards from the centre to the periphery, where the margins are seen as unruly places needing to be pacified (Goodhand, 2018, p. 6).

Humanitarians are one of the centre's responses to this disruption to state authority, travelling to the margins to provide relief and promoting the discourse of humanitarian space in an effort to bring temporary order (see Chapter 4). However, this conceptualisation also conceals a more complex story, for the margins where humanitarians work are not simply a space of fading state authority. They are complex sites of their own, which share common characteristics of state breakdown, but also their own unique, local variations and power structures. "There certainly are consistencies between different conflicts," Simon explains from Bangui, reflecting on the three places he has worked over the past six years.

> State failure is clearly part of this. But it's also important to acknowledge that every context is different. Every context has its own history and a unique set of actors with their own power dynamics. Rebels in Colombia are clearly different to the Taliban in Afghanistan, who have little in common with the Muslim rebels in CAR.

As the IRC delegate alludes to, the field is more complex than a place beyond the margins of state authority. For state fragility or failure also sees the emergence, or re-emergence, of competing religious, cultural and political visions that were temporarily veiled by the state-making process that spread out from Europe (see Chapter 2). These local legacies appear across the former colonial world, but can be seen quite clearly in the Middle East, where the Islamic world is mounting a form of colonial resistance against Western expansion (see Barkawi, 2004, pp. 18–22). Here I think of the Taliban's ongoing efforts to establish an Islamic state across Afghanistan, ISIS establishing a version of the state in large parts of Iraq and Syria, or the Kurds flexing their ethnic authority in the border areas of Iraq, Syria and Turkey.

Instead of a place that lies beyond the glow of state power and its unifying frameworks, the field in which humanitarians work is revealed as a site of competing power sources struggling for the control and allegiance of the population. It is a complex world partly reflected in recent analyses of war and peace transitions, where contested areas between states appear as "frontiers" and "borderlands", while "peripheries" form in space distant from the centre's power and competing "enclaves" emerge where local power sources attempt to supplant the state (see Korf & Raeymaekers, 2013; Meehan & Plonski, 2016). Rather than hard boundaries between the centre and the margins, states and failed states, these contested margins appear as hybrid sites, in which law and other state practices are actively transformed and colonised by alternative power sources (see Das & Poole, 2004). At the same time the centre continually works to assert and reassert its authority over these contested margins (Das & Poole, 2004).

The systematic effects of the centre/field relationship

These layered understandings of the global centre and the local field have significant and inherent effects on modern humanitarianism in general and humanitarian protection in particular. As discussed earlier, humanitarianism emerged from the European centre, radiating out to provide relief and to promote a particular notion of limited war. This dualistic world-view is not incidental to modern humanitarianism, but remains deeply embedded in our understanding of humanitarian practice, part of the established discourse and related lexicon of humanitarians themselves. This discursive force positions the humanitarian frameworks as the accepted protection mechanism and privileges the knowledge of the centre. As I go on to discuss, it also creates the need for the international humanitarian, travelling between these two worlds to disseminate the centre's frameworks and provide relief. This mobility weaves its way further into humanitarian practice, facilitating the neutral, outsider position so central to modern humanitarianism. However, I argue that these effects of the centre/field discourse also lead to some of humanitarianism's seemingly intractable shortcomings. For the field ultimately emerges as a far more complex world than the established discourse portrays, creating a parallel need for proximity and contextual understanding, which are in many ways incompatible with the position of travelling outsider.

Humanitarian travellers

Humanitarianism attracts particular kinds of people; confident and assertive travellers for one. Humanitarian organisations also recruit for this personality type, requiring prospective field staff to have experience traveling and working across remote locations. In fact, it was a record of independent travel across Africa and the Middle East, rather than any professional qualification, that largely precipitated my own entry into the humanitarian sector. However, the reason for the centrality of travel to humanitarianism goes beyond the geographic isolation and complexity of working in the field, already described in popular first-hand accounts of humanitarian fieldwork (see, e.g., Alexander, 2013; Bamforth, 2014; Cain et al., 2006). More significantly, I argue that continuous circulation facilitates humanitarians' detachment from the political context in which they work, allowing them to demonstrate and sustain a level of neutrality and independence. Furthermore, it is central to developing the local, contextual knowledge that allows them to work effectively in the field. Yet, as the following section will go on to discuss, this continual mobility is also responsible for some of the most problematic parts of humanitarian practice – the temporary expatriate, implementing global frameworks, devoid of contextual concerns.[2]

Travel and neutrality

For humanitarians operating in the politically contested arena of armed conflicts, the veil of neutrality has long helped protect them from attack and facilitated access to affected communities. It is a pragmatic principle that sees humanitarians agreeing not to interfere – whether intentionally or unintentionally – if they are given access to affected communities (see Chapters 1 and 4). For humanitarian institutions representing themselves as neutral actors, this comes through the eschewing of politics and a focus on "the impartial, independent, and neutral provision of relief to those in immediate danger of harm" (Barnett, 2005, p. 724). As Redfield (2012) explains, it is an approach that "shuns commitment to place", defined "through the idiom of temporary crisis" rather than sustained, long-term engagement (p. 359). This classical approach to humanitarianism stands in contrast to long-term approaches intended to improve life circumstances, such as economic development, an inherently political endeavour that works to restructure underlying social relations (Barnett, 2005).

This is further reinforced by the outsider status of the international humanitarian. Without local religious, ethnic or political affiliations, the argument goes, international humanitarians are better positioned to withstand the pressures of established power relations. Furthermore, as outsiders, international staff are not pressured by expectations of family and community, so are better positioned to withstand undue expectations and attempts to manipulate aid delivery (Schenkenberg, 2016). Humanitarian delegates themselves articulate this idea of the humanitarian as the consummate outsider. As Sebastian, the Australian ICRC delegate first encountered in Chapter 5, says:

> The role we fill – or more specifically the role of the international delegate – is to be perceived as absolutely neutral and not representing, through perception or otherwise, the views, beliefs, goals or ambitions of one side to the party of the conflict or another.

Other interviewees reinforce this idea of the need for outsiders in the highly charged political environments of armed conflicts. As another ICRC delegate explains: "You have to be perceived as being neutral, and not responding to the pressures of government authorities, armed groups, or tribal leaders. That sometimes is just easier when you're not from there."

The humanitarian expat's local counterparts, the argument continues, face critical challenges adhering to the humanitarian principles of neutrality and impartiality when armed conflicts are taking place in their own countries (see Schenkenberg, 2016).[3] This may involve a deliberate choice to favour a specific population, or the unintentional consequences of established affiliations with institutions, groups and communities. While my travelling companion on the road to Sinjar, Mohamed, is a humanitarian professional, he is also a Sunni. In a country long-riven by sectarian divides, in a war waged in the name of religion, in a part of the country controlled by a Kurdish minority long repressed by Sunni political leaders, he is intrinsically bound up in the politics of the conflict. It is a story reflected in conflicts around the world, many of which are driven by ethnic and religious violence. Speaking from Afghanistan, riven by religious and tribal war for generations, one ICRC delegate articulates a certain inevitability of local actors becoming part of the political world.

> They may come from a certain family with political links, or they may come from a certain tribe that is perceived in some way by its own tribe or other

> tribes. Whereas being a Swiss or Lebanese delegate in South Sudan or Afghanistan, you can be perceived as neutral just because of the colour and origin of your passport.

This outsider position cannot be maintained, the argument goes, if humanitarian workers become too closely linked to a place or culture. There is often criticism from classical humanitarians of those who cross these boundaries, embedding in the local world and "going native". For these critics, not belonging to any local faction, whether cultural or political, is a professional obligation. "Some people cross that threshold and start to become part of the local culture, identifying with the local culture; that's a choice they make," explains Rasul. "For me, that's a red line we should never cross; you cannot be neutral anymore."

Some humanitarians make a conscious choice of merging into the local culture, told in striking detail in *Emma's War* (Scroggins, 2002). Similarly, Jennifer, speaking of her ten years working with the UN in Sudan and South Sudan, explains:

> I wasn't there to stay in a camp and mix with foreigners. I was there to immerse myself in the local community. That's what I always do when I go overseas. I don't want to be removed from it; I want to be part of it in every way.

The aid worker talks of spending extended time in the community, building trust and establishing lasting relationships in a country that eventually "started to feel like home". Ultimately, she was given her own Dinka name as an acknowledgement of how close she had become to one of the tribes of South Sudan.

The professional justification – to be discussed more in the next section – reflects that of development workers (and anthropologists) who feel that to understand a community it is necessary to embed in it over a period of time. But perhaps more significantly, there is also a certain inevitability to this politicisation, even for the humanitarian traditionalists. According to the political geographer Relph (2008), while the degree to which people become involved may be a matter of choice, to live somewhere for any period of time is to be caught up in matters of politics. As an ICRC delegate with 12 years' experience explains to me, "Neutrality is crucial when working in conflicts." However, reflecting the thoughts of Relph, she says:

> The longer you are in a conflict, and particularly if you work on one side of the conflict, you almost inevitably become affected by it. You increasingly start seeing the world from the position of those who surround you and may stop appreciating the view from the other side.

To maintain their outsider status, humanitarian workers, unlike their more sedentary development colleagues, are highly mobile, continually moving between field sites and humanitarian crisis. In the era of protracted crisis, this is not simply the inevitable result of the humanitarian relief cycle, but institutional policy.

Institutional reliance on outsiders and their regular rotation is a classical organisational and governmental technique to prevent the development of detrimental alliances and biases on the ground. The Ottoman Empire used this strategy with its international representatives as early as the 16th century (Autesserre, 2014). In modern times, diplomats are regularly moved between theatres in order to ensure that they do not develop links in the host country that might compromise their allegiances (Autesserre, 2014). Similarly, the ICRC routinely rotates its delegates every two years, and limits their stay to a maximum of three years in a single place, in part to ensure that they remain neutral. While not as institutionalised, many conflict-focused INGOs like the IRC, NRC and MSF supplement the natural churn by rotating career staff to promote a fresh perspective and reduce bias, with the average of a year in a country.

It starts to become apparent that continual movement has important systematic effects, positioning the humanitarian worker as the political outsider in highly contested environments. Separation from local politics – whether real or perceived – comes in part from being an outsider, not belonging to a particular place or its community. Humanitarians sustain this outsider status through transience. Travelling between field missions, sometimes for as little as a few months, rarely working in any one place for more than a year or two, they are continually in transit, never fully embedded in the local space and drawn into its political machinations.

Travel and knowledge

Humanitarians' movement between different worlds is also functionally linked to their knowledge. Through travel they are able to develop two layers of knowledge; that of the centre where they predominantly originate and that of the local margins where they travel for field work. Importantly, as this book argues, their local knowledge allows them to translate the protection frameworks to suit these different contexts.

As discussed previously, humanitarianism has its roots in the centre, intrinsically linked to the European state experience and the international frameworks that guide behaviour in times of war. It is perhaps unsurprising that these frameworks and related principles are the focus of humanitarians working at the global level. They are the global leavers that help guide international behaviour. They also form the foundations of a systematic global approach to humanitarian protection at the local level. Hence, they are the first tier of knowledge for perspective humanitarians, serving as the academic or formal knowledge that is often a required step to working in the international humanitarian sector. Humanitarian workers develop this knowledge on a global circuit, first through educational institutions and then while working in humanitarian offices around the world. They go on to deploy this knowledge in their professional capacities, whether as a guide to building relevant policy, as a traditional legal tool, or in disseminating and promoting what has been described elsewhere in this book as the official humanitarian discourse, or unifying narrative, in the field. As discussed in

Chapter 4, in their official capacity humanitarians are intermediaries, promoting the official international laws and principles to bring a level of order to conflicts and in turn promote the protection of at-risk groups.

Yet this global perspective is only part of the formula of the humanitarian knowledge that guides protection. It is their dual knowledge that allows humanitarians to respond to the complex environment of contemporary conflicts, allowing them to move beyond disseminators to become the active brokers described in Chapter 5. As mentioned earlier, the field in which they work is not a singular, homogenous state-like space. Instead it is made up of multiple and varying contexts, where state authority is supplemented and colonised by competing religious, cultural and political power sources. In order to operate in their unofficial capacity as brokers, translating the global frameworks to fit the context, they need to have some understanding this local environment.

Experienced humanitarian workers reflecting on their first mission inevitably highlight their lack of local knowledge when they arrive in the field for the first time and the limitations it places on their ability to operate. "I was completely unqualified for this," explains Rebecca of her arrival in Sierra Leone as a first-mission protection delegate, "equipped with a law degree, some volunteer experience and a well-thumbed copy of the minimum standards." Or as Simon reflects from the Central African Republic, "No matter how much you prepare, no matter how many books you read, no matter how many language lessons you take, you will not be ready for a place like CAR, for mediating between the different factions." They highlight the need to understand the local context and the significance of the differences between the world they come from and the local field in which they work. As Rasul also explains:

> In this job you are coming from a totally different background, with different cultural benchmarks. Does that mean we cannot negotiate in these contexts? You can, but you have to adapt; you have to learn about the specific context; you have to take your time to study the culture and understand its differences.

Alongside the rise in the professionalisation of the humanitarian sector, there have been efforts by humanitarian organisations to institutionalise the development of this local knowledge. Early career humanitarians take part in cultural awareness workshops and courses in a spectrum of foreign languages are provided to extend skills beyond the traditional UN languages. Before deployment – time permitting – efforts are made to provide detailed briefings of the local context. But as humanitarians know, cultural awareness workshops are a poor substitute for the lived experience. With time often pressing, few aid workers arrive in country equipped with more than a cursory understanding of the historical background of the context. Few still speak anything other than the international languages, hardly a personal failing considering the number of languages and dialects that the local environment presents.

Instead, much of this knowledge comes through spending time in the local context. "You may have read the books, you may have learnt Pashtu, but when you first arrive in Afghanistan, you don't know anything about the country, about tribal relationships, about using that language to build relationships," says Alexi, speaking from Afghanistan where the Ukrainian leads ICRC negotiations with the Taliban leadership. "That understanding can only come through talking to people, through taking an interest in the local culture, through being on the ground." As the Arabic speaking Rasul explains of his first time working in Yemen, simply understanding the language is not enough.

> People appreciate it, but there is a whole cultural basket of things to understand – language being just one item in this basket. Then you have to add the contextual knowledge, the cultural knowledge and the many local variations of these. That comes through sitting down with local people, talking with them, sharing a meal with them.

In broad terms, this is what Russell (2004) describes as the "knowledge of acquaintance", which can only come through the direct, unmediated interaction with people or place. For humanitarians, this informal knowledge complements the "knowledge of description" (Russell, 2004) that comes through their formal education and the official workshops and trainings that aid workers continually receive.

Informal knowledge

So how does this informal knowledge of direct experience develop? From speaking with experienced delegates across the humanitarian spectrum, there are three preconditions: experiencing multiple contexts, spending time in the field and interacting closely with other field staff. To talk to humanitarians is to be provided a geographical and historical map of the world's conflict zones. "From Colombia, to Sudan, then Afghanistan, I was in Geneva for a while, then Syria," lists one. "I started in the Congo with the UN, then Chad, before going to Afghanistan with the ICRC. Now I'm taking a bit of a break here [in Geneva] before going out again," another recites. These are more than lists of travel destinations, but a resume of experiences and knowledge collected. There is the unspoken belief that these different missions are part of the journey to becoming an effective humanitarian worker, practiced at engaging with diverse actors and adapting to complex environments. Reflecting on six years moving between "South Sudan, Colombia and Afghanistan, before returning to Geneva", Sebastian explains to me:

> It's about the experience in engaging with a diversity of people and groups. Sitting down with armed groups in the South Sudanese bush, or in the Colombian jungle gets you used to bringing up humanitarian concerns in a way that is hopefully understandable and relevant to the person in front of you in Afghanistan. The broader and more diverse the range of contexts that you've worked in, the easier it gets.

Contextual knowledge also comes through time in the field. This particularly includes the human interaction and communication skills that are seen as central to humanitarian protection and related practices of dissemination and mediation. This almost mythical journey to a place of understanding is reflected in the words of many aid workers, who talk of their increasing confidence in adapting to each new context. In the early stages of their careers, with minimal field experience, they turn to the certainty of institutional policy and official frameworks to guide their actions; the knowledge and skills collected at the centre. As Farouk explains, reflecting on his earlier work with MSF in Somalia:

> At the beginning it is just so overwhelming. At the beginning you are far less willing to go off the books, to operate outside the official framework. With experience, you start to extend what you do, modify your approach, adapt to the context.

This is not about learning and implementing concrete "tricks of the trade", but having the confidence to adapt to complex, changing situations and to introduce more personal approaches. Farouk continues:

> For our job, experience means you get to a certain point where the situation and the circumstances you are in are no longer overwhelming, or the degree to how overwhelming they are starts to reduce. So you can start to bring in a more personal, more conscious way of working.

Finally, humanitarians collect this local, informal knowledge through continual engagement with other humanitarian workers who are on a similar journey. This in effect supplements the direct experience that constant travel provides, with knowledge from people who have spent time in related contexts or in the area of operation. As Farouk continues: "While [mechanisms] are important, there also needs to be a space for personal experience, a space to discuss personal approaches to contextual challenges that don't have universal solutions." Rasul, his friend and colleague currently based in Geneva, has a similar philosophy: "When you start out, and whenever you arrive in a new country, you almost need tutoring by the people around you, people who know the context well, on how to adapt to each new context." Local staff also form an important component of this informal knowledge network. It is a complex relationship, as will be discussed in detail in the next section, but this local network is invariably seen as an invaluable avenue to developing an understanding of the context.

Here we see how travel provides local, contextual knowledge on multiple levels. It allows direct experiences and the knowledge gained from these to be shared across different field locations, which is then further reinforced through the network of travellers who share these experiences with each other. Importantly, it places humanitarian workers in the field, where the interaction with people and place provides the local knowledge required to adapt to the context. These repeated experiences allow humanitarians to more effectively adapt to the context of each subsequent humanitarian crisis. In this way, mobility forms a necessary component of the modern humanitarian endeavour, facilitating neutrality, the dissemination of the official frameworks in the field and the development of a level of contextual knowledge. But there is more to this mobility; after all, some of the problems of the humanitarian endeavour are intrinsically connected with continuous travel and the temporary nature of humanitarianism. It is those I turn to now.

The problems of humanitarian transience

There is much more to travelling then the neutrality and knowledge it helps facilitate. To extend the analogy further, privileged travellers and expats have fundamental flaws: "living in a bubble" and "disregarding the local", they often possess only a peripheral knowledge of the culture around them, explains Fechter (2007, pp. 41–43). As the anthropologist notes, expats are perceived as lacking everything anthropologists stand for, "such as speaking the local language, being knowledgeable of local cultures, and having contact with local people" (Fechter, 2007, pp. 18–19; see also Amit, 2011). It is hardly surprising that the expat humanitarian traveller is similarly flawed. Indeed, many of the problems of the humanitarian sector are linked to its temporary nature and the transience of humanitarian workers, notably the lack of contextual knowledge for humanitarian workers and their institutions, the reproduction of the colonial system and its biases, and the related power divide between international humanitarians and their local staff.

Developing a sound contextual understanding is important for humanitarian workers. As discussed in the previous section it allows them to make informed operational decisions and engage with local actors from a position of knowledge and understanding. Similarly, for development workers a contextual understanding is important for establishing relevant, sustainable programs. "If people feel that you are showing a respect for their culture you will have more acceptance," one development worker explains to me, as we compare her local Kurdish dress with the Western camping aesthetic favoured by many humanitarian workers. "This acceptance helps you engage with the community, which in turn helps build an understanding of their needs, which you don't get from looking in from the outside," she continues.

Development workers, like anthropologists, portray themselves as being part of the local world in which they work, attempting to blur the boundaries between themselves and the local population. Their wardrobes incorporate local dress, they shop in local markets, learn regional dialects and socialise with the local community wherever possible. Embedding in the local population and building strong relationships with the community, the argument goes, is the most effective way to build an understanding of the context. As development anthropologists have articulated, it is only through extended contact with others "that one can learn … about their codes, expectations, modes of action and resources" (Bierschenk et al., 2002, p. 20).

It is a philosophy often at odds with the operational culture of humanitarian organisations and their staff, who in the pursuit of neutrality seek to remain separate from the local world and its political fractures. Unlike development workers, they do not seek to blur the boundaries between themselves and the communities they work among. Displaying their outsider status, humanitarians tend not to adopt local dress, instead often choosing the Western humanitarian field chic of khaki chinos and blue work shirts. Beyond this operational culture, security concerns of armed conflicts function to separate humanitarian workers from the affected community, enclosing them in walled compounds or restricting their movements to large towns and cities, the more stable regional hubs described earlier. This sees them spending large amounts of their time in offices that are not too dissimilar from those at headquarters, sitting alongside other international delegates, before being driven back to their residences at the end of the working day. Furthermore, they tend to spend their free time socialising with each other, congregating at the collective residence, or gathering in hotel bars and restaurants, with only fleeting encounters with the local environment and its people (see also Redfield, 2012).

Significantly, as discussed in the previous section they live impermanent lives, their time in a country often counted in months rather than years. Two-, three- or six-month responses are still prevalent across the humanitarian sector, partly due to short-term funding cycles and the related reliance on short-term contracts. The pressures of the work environment, the isolation of unaccompanied missions and the day-to-day routine that is the reality of compound life also promote a rapid turnover of staff (see also Loquercio et al., 2006). Furthermore, the respect attached to multiple missions, including the latest high-profile crisis, often sees humanitarians move quickly from mission to mission as part of a career strategy. As one senior protection adviser explains, reflecting on her earlier work with the UNHCR, "A variety of experiences through temporary assignments helps propel a longer-term career trajectory; even more so if they are larger, high profile missions." As a result, humanitarians are rarely in place long enough to build their local knowledge and establish the relationships that are central to the mediation efforts described in the previous chapter.

The double bind of humanitarian mobility

As the previous section argued, the temporary nature of humanitarianism is both an ends and a means, helping to facilitate the perception of neutrality and impartiality that allows access to highly charged political environments. It is an intrinsic part of the established philosophy, which defines humanitarianism as apolitical, providing temporary support during moments of crisis, before moving on. While it is possible to argue the extent to which modern humanitarian agencies embrace this position, as discussed in Chapter 1 it remains a core component of humanitarian practice in general and protection in particular. Yet, as explained in this section, this same transience inhibits building relations with the local population and developing an understanding of the local context. It materialises in some of the worst aspects of humanitarianism, such as the West imposing its belief systems on the global South without regard to context, or in the form of the "ugly expat" imposing a set of outside values and norms on a world that they have little understanding of, before quickly moving onto the next crisis. For the transience that helps facilitate the humanitarian's status as the neutral outsider also impedes the development of contextual knowledge.

In what Redfield (2012) identifies as a classic double bind, humanitarianism is left attempting to balance the benefits of knowledge that comes through time in a place, with the politicisation long-term placements bring, with each negatively impacting on the other.[4] In a true double bind, humanitarian practitioners and policy makers are left oscillating between incompatible alternatives. As one aid worker succinctly articulates, "There is the constant challenge of building inside knowledge of the local context, while retaining the benefits of being an outsider." Should they choose to remain in place in order to develop contextual knowledge and a local network, humanitarians can ultimately be seen as political actors; should they pursue the neutrality of the impermanent outsider, local knowledge and relationships become elusive. In a complex interaction, the mobility that is a central part of the modern humanitarian endeavour – linking the centre to the field, allowing for dissemination, facilitating neutrality and promoting contextual knowledge – is also responsible for many of its most persistent problems. This complex interaction is further reflected in the unequal relationship between international and local staff. In this further contradictory dilemma, I will argue that this relationship both provides an unofficial fix to the problems of humanitarian mobility, while simultaneously sustaining long-established inequalities between the international humanitarian and their local counterpart.

The local fixer

Faisel, our driver on the road to Sinjar, also fills the unofficial fixer role of his position. Fluent in local languages, gatherer of local information, and provider of any necessities we need from local markets and stalls along the way, he is the perennial figure of any humanitarian operation. Mohammed, my local counterpart, his skill-set reflecting my own, but with the benefit of contextual knowledge, fills a similar role as a bridge to the local network. This fixer role is not original to humanitarianism. My first encounter was in journalism, where the fixer, usually a local journalist, has long held a supporting role. An actual descriptive title commonly used by journalists, fixers are routinely hired by foreign correspondents to act as translator and guides, and to gain access to interview subjects. Held in high regard, but rarely credited, these fixers are crucial to the final outcome. It is an apt description for national staff like Faisel and Mohammed.

National staff members are significant actors in any humanitarian operation. They carry a depth of knowledge that can only come from being settled in a place, knowledge that so often proves elusive to the travelling expat. Furthermore, local staff are a consistent presence in a humanitarian response. Aware of the successes and failures of previous international staff who have long moved on, they are well placed to ensure that these past experiences guide future decisions. As ICRC delegate Alexi explains from Afghanistan, "The local staff have stories, the local staff have memories, good memories and bad memories of your predecessors, of what expat staff tried before. They have an intimate understanding of the political situation, of the history." Or, as Redfield (2012) poetically describes, "Materially light and socially heavy, the national staff member remains stolidly set, a repetitive actor in local history" (p. 360). They are firmly anchored in the local world, in contrast to the humanitarian expat, who, "materially heavy and socially light … appears ever contingent, swept away by distant concerns" (p. 360).

These sharp distinctions between the international expat and the national staff member are a direct result of our understanding of humanitarianism itself. As discussed earlier, modern humanitarianism emerged from the European centre during a specific time in history. Developing in the context of colonial expansion, and imbued by Christian notions of charity and philanthropy, humanitarianism radiated out from the global centre to limit the conduct of war and provide relief to deserving victims in the global South. As Redfield (2012) explains, "Little thought was given to the possibility of other geographic trajectories, or the implications of [this outward movement] across unequal economies" (p. 362). This approach remains embedded in humanitarianism today, part of the colonial discourse that has maintained the centre/periphery relationship and has produced a specific understanding of helpers and victims.

There are substantial consequences to this accepted understanding. For while humanitarianism may no longer be a collective of Europeans, having absorbed aid workers from other global hubs, this colonial history lingers in the accepted categories of humanitarians. It has created two groups of humanitarian: international humanitarian "experts", fluent in the humanitarian frameworks and principles, travelling out into the field to help the so-called vulnerable; and national staff, the inevitable "other" of the international aid worker, who are part of the marginal space created in opposition to the centre, and part of the population that lacks appropriate resources and is in need of assistance. This discursive distinction, established from the centre, privileges Western forms of knowledge over others. As a result, national staff are inevitably marginalised, usually hired in supporting roles to the international "experts" (Roth, 2012, p. 1462). Furthermore, unlike the neutral and independent outsider, local staff are perceived as "not entirely neutral and impartial", part of the political or cultural milieu of the crisis, further justifying their relegation to more subordinate roles.

The subsequent inequalities of this largely colonial heritage have been the subject of much introspection among humanitarian organisations and scholars (see, e.g., Fassin, 2012; Redfield, 2012; Roth, 2012). Large pay disparities remain a constant point of difference between well-remunerated expats and national staff on local salaries. While expatriates occupy privileged positions as technical experts, project leads and country managers, national staff members predominantly fill positions as interpreters, drivers, assistants and office administrators. Furthermore, there is little opportunity for local staff to graduate to the more lucrative international circuit (Redfield, 2012, pp. 365–366). Although vital to day-to-day operations, locals remain relatively invisible in the public profile and organisational charts of humanitarian organisations. In contrast, expats receive ample media attention and occupy core positions in field sites, acting as highly visible conduits between the field and headquarters (Redfield, 2012).

While the humanitarian work of expats is repeatedly highlighted, it is the local staff who carry out many of the most direct humanitarian activities, the expats' foreign status partially insulating them from the risks that come with front-line humanitarian work. Their safety a priority, in the event of a direct threat or personal emergency expats are immediately evacuated, while frequent attacks on local staff receive little attention (Fassin, 2012, pp. 233–242). Here we can reflect on my own departure from Sinjar when ISIS approached, or the front-line role played by Iraqi Red Crescent staff during the Mosul operation. Meanwhile, as the international spokesperson, I fielded media interviews from a relatively safe distance, somewhat inadvertently casting the front-line local staff in a supporting role for the international audiences of CNN and BBC.

Roth (2012) has made a particularly detailed study of the ongoing asymmetry between international and national staff. Her work, which includes extensive interviews with national staff, suggests that the problem is one of unequal power and culture clashes. Summing up some of her findings, she says:

> National staff were critical of international experts who overlooked their competence and expertise and did not take them seriously. Furthermore, national staff criticised international aid workers and organisations that did not consult the local population and beneficiaries about their needs and interests, ignored local culture, dressed inappropriately or distributed food and other items that were unwelcome.... National staff perceived international staff not only as arrogant and ignorant, but also as unqualified and superfluous. Unsurprisingly, they were critical if inexperienced and – in their view – ignorant young international aid workers were assigned to do jobs that national staff felt quite capable of doing themselves.
>
> (pp. 1464–1465)

It is a complex debate which oscillates between the need and value in empowering local humanitarian actors (see, e.g., Roth, 2012), a process which is well underway in international development, and understanding how to overcome the operational complexities this brings for humanitarian response (see, e.g., Shevchenko & Fox, 2008). Promoting greater equality between nationals and expatriates, it is argued, "cannot be dissociated from the fact that there are components of humanitarian action that may call for the maintenance of certain differences between the two sets of humanitarian workers, which are less unifying, and less likely to foster equality" (Shevchenko & Fox, 2008, p. 119).

The argument I pursue here is that this structural separation between the local and international is a constitutive part of modern humanitarianism. This, I argue, is why these imbalances have remained so persistent in the face of on-going policy initiatives. The discursive forces that privilege the knowledge of the centre, positioning the humanitarian frameworks as the accepted protection mechanism and casting the international humanitarian as the expert and neutral outsider, does so at the expense of local voices and knowledge. Those not versed in the European tradition of humanitarianism are cast in the supporting role, a relationship that conjures imagery of colonial officers and their local intermediaries.

Understanding the local humanitarian intermediary

To understand the role of local staff and their place in the modern humanitarian endeavour it is worth reflecting on earlier studies of figures that operated between the local community and the state apparatus. Before the term broker was introduced into scholarship, the colonial system was dependent on local guides, translators and intermediaries. This colonial-era go-between later became evident in anthropological studies into the links between colonial and European political authority. Redfield (1956) observed the existence of "hinge groups", a cluster of cultural intermediaries who provide a link between local communities and state representatives. In the same year, Wolf (1956) introduced the concept of the cultural brokers, "groups of people who mediate between community oriented groups in communities and nation-orientated groups which operate primarily through national institutions" (p. 1075). These colonial-era intermediaries facilitated important links between the local community and the European emissaries of the day, necessary for local knowledge and cross-cultural engagements.

While the later development broker – explored elsewhere in this book – "activates the continuing interplay between apparently irreconcilable discourses and practices" (James, 2011, p. 335), these earlier conceptualisations are also highly pertinent for this research. They broadly reflect local staff members and their relationships with their international counterparts. Largely separated from the local context, international humanitarian staff develop their understandings of the local world and its people through local staff members. Similarly, the relationships that are central to the international humanitarian's work are established through these local interpreters and fixers. As Sebastian, an Australian working with the ICRC, explains to me, echoing other aid workers I spoke to:

> One of the errors almost every international delegate makes is that you think you have the answers. Yes, that's partly true, but it misses the central role of local staff to any operation. Local staff have the contextual knowledge, know the history of the operation and have an established network.

In other words, local staff members act as a link or hinge between the international aid worker, who has a specific type of knowledge, and the local context. The steady stream of expatriates passing through a country assures a constant need for these latter-day cultural brokers, their knowledge and their networks.

In a further reference to other work into brokers and brokerage, this relationship between international humanitarians and their local counterparts is reminiscent of the function of collective brokerage described by French anthropologists.[5] Bierschenk, Chauveau and de Sardan (2000) extended the research of development brokers to include the idea of "collective brokerage", in the sense of a "brokerage chain", in which brokers are linked in contiguity, or a "brokerage club", a collective of brokers acting in symbiosis (pp. 29–30). These connections could extend from the city to the district level and on to the village, allowing the development broker to be part of a regional, national or international network (see also Bierschenk et al., 2002).

This brokerage chain, described in relation to development brokers, is a useful metaphor to further understand the relationship between international and national humanitarian staff. International humanitarian brokers, predominantly from the centre, translate the official frameworks in order for them to align with the agendas of local non-state armed actors, as discussed in previous chapters. However, while the best brokers have the ability to operate on their own, independent of other intermediaries, many brokers do not enjoy this type of autonomy and are obliged to call on external agents (see Bierschenk et al., 2002). This, I argue, is even more pertinent for the highly mobile humanitarian broker, who must rely substantively on national staff, embedded in the local world, for access and their contextual knowledge. Linking the international humanitarian into the local system, this act of collective brokerage facilitates the transfer and translation of knowledge from the global centre to the relevant local actors in the local context. In other words, many humanitarians rely on their local counterparts in order to carry out the humanitarian fix described in the previous chapter.

This broker chain, while it links the national with the international, is quite problematic, as it is not a relationship of equals. Like the local brokers, fixers and translators of the colonial era, national staff predominantly remain outside the central power structures, firmly part of the local world (see also Redfield, 2012). While they are important to the everyday practice of humanitarian protection, national staff remain largely invisible, the international humanitarian's necessary but hidden other. In this way, while their contextual knowledge and networks help ensure the effectiveness of the established protection philosophy, their significance is not formally acknowledged beyond the immediate international field workers involved. At the global level, it is the frameworks that drive protection rather than these somewhat invisible relationships between local staff and their global counterparts.

Furthermore, operating as the interface between the expatriate humanitarian and local community, they remain removed from the global system. From their place firmly anchored in the local world, the global system remains somewhere over the horizon, distant and unknowable. This detachment from the knowledge of the centre ensures their subordinate position. They remain a supporting act, providing contextual knowledge to the real experts, the international humanitarians educated in the official frameworks. Clearly, there are those who have crossed this divide, starting out as national staff and moving onto expatriate positions, some of whom we met in Chapter 5, but this alternative trajectory remains the exception (see also Roth, 2012). Rather, the patterns that defined the relationship between the colonial officer and local staff are largely sustained in humanitarian practice today. While national staff members are pivotal to the effectiveness of humanitarianism in contemporary wars, their roles remain a continuation of humanitarianism's Western, colonial history.

Conclusion

The global centre and local field, international humanitarians who cross this discursive divide, and their national counterparts, solidly set in the local, form a complex, interconnected ontology. This relationship can be traced back to modern humanitarianism's foundations and a certain vision of the world that is rooted in colonial expansion. In this world view, power and authority radiated out from the centre, bringing political order to the less developed periphery. Similarly, modern humanitarianism, a distinctly European creation, radiated out from the centre, providing relief to deserving victims and promoting a particular vision of how war should be conducted. This geography of colonialism lingers in humanitarianism to this day, with humanitarian agencies still largely of the centre, deploying their representatives to complex emergencies in the global South, providing relief to certain categories of victims, and disseminating Western norms and principles.

As discussed in this chapter, the very quality of distance between the centre and the field also created the need for a traveller to move between these two worlds, providing relief and disseminating the official frameworks. In turn, this movement has significant structural effects on modern humanitarianism. It facilitates the humanitarian outsider, the so-called neutral and impartial actor, not of the local place and its politics. Furthermore, constant travel maintains this outsider status, as the international humanitarian never stays long enough to develop political affiliations or allegiances with local actors. In this way, the centre/margins conceptualisation of the world and the humanitarian traveller that has emerged from this world view are intrinsic to the modern humanitarian endeavour.

However, the quality of distance that works to create the outsider, separate from local politics, also creates a need for proximity (see also Redfield, 2012). It is proximity to the place and its culture that makes the local knowable. This local knowledge is a necessary part of humanitarian protection, even more so in the fragmented spaces of contemporary wars where there exists a complex mix of actors with diverse, shifting agendas. As discussed earlier, this contextual knowledge is a necessary component of the humanitarian fix that makes the official frameworks relevant to these diverse actors. This leaves humanitarians in a classic double bind, oscillating between incompatible, yet necessary alternatives, with the relative immobility required for local knowledge conflicting with the mobility required to maintain the position of outsider.

This dilemma has in part been patched over by the international humanitarian's local counterpart – the national staff member. The emergence of the international humanitarian traveller, of the centre, in transit through the local, providing relief and disseminating the official frameworks, created the need for this humanitarian other. In contrast to the international humanitarian, the national staff member is firmly anchored in the local world, intertwined with its political and cultural machinations, but also possessing the local knowledge and networks that comes with this permanence of place. It is this local knowledge and established networks that has made them an important component of the modern humanitarian endeavour and necessary partner to the international humanitarian. They are important facilitators for the international humanitarian intermediary and broker described in earlier chapters.

Yet this is not a partnership of equals; despite constant attempts to decolonise the relationship, the local humanitarian remains largely the hidden other. Just as the unofficial fix applied by international humanitarians is somewhat hidden (see Chapter 5), so is its local facilitator. Their local knowledge remains secondary to the formal expertise of the humanitarian traveller and somewhat contradictory to the idea of universal norms that guide a global system. Furthermore, in a system invested in political outsiders, local insiders are further disempowered. In a somewhat ironic twist, by facilitating the temporary humanitarian fix of the official frameworks in contemporary wars, and so making them more effective, local staff also sustain the colonial antecedents that are the source of the system's inequalities.

Notes

1 It is an understanding that is echoed in work on everything from the European state system (Tilly, 1990) to studies of South East Asia (Scott, 2009) and sub-Saharan Africa (Boone, 2003). These studies highlight that the capacity and costs of state penetration are directly linked to the distance and accessibility of the targeted regions. In other words, the more geographically isolated the territory, the greater the cost of imposing revenues from trade and taxation, the less incentive to build state infrastructure and project state power.

2 I acknowledge that the academic usage of the term expatriate can be controversial in some areas of study. While the term technically refers to a person living outside their native county, the majority of contemporary migrants are not referred to as expatriates. Rather, the term instead tends to be reserved for Western migrants, which is the way I use it here (see Fechter & Walsh, 2010).

3 It is important in this regard to differentiate between different types of crisis. As Schenkenberg (2016) points out, the role of local actors in natural disasters is much less controversial than in armed conflicts (p. 6).

4 As Wilden and Wilson (1976) explain, "A true double bind – or a situation set up to be perceived as one – requires a choice between two states which are equally valued and so equally insufficient that a self-perpetuating oscillation is engendered by any active choice between them.... It is the result of the fact that one must choose, and moreover choose between incompatible alternatives" (p. 276; as cited in Redfield, 2012, p. 361).

5 As Jacobs (2014) explains, brokerage research has fallen into two clusters. On one hand there is the British-Dutch-Anglophone cluster around Mosse and Lewis. On the other hand there is the German-French-Francophone, post-colonial network, which since the 1980s has been working on "*courtage*" and in particular on the "*courtier local en developpement*" (p. 308).

References

Alexander, J. (2013). *Chasing chaos: My decade in and out of emergency aid.* Broadway Books.

Amit, V. (Ed.) (2011). *Going first class? New approaches to privileged travel and movement.* Berghahn Books.

Autesserre, S. (2014). *Peaceland: Conflict resolution and the everyday politics of international intervention.* Cambridge University Press.

Bamforth, T. (2014). *Deep field: Dispatches from the front line of aid relief.* Abrams.

Barkawi, T. (2004). On the pedagogy of "small wars". *International Affairs*, 80(1), 19–37.

Barnett, M. (2005). Humanitarianism transformed. *Perspectives in Politics*, 3(4), 723–740.

Bierschenk, T., Chauveau, J.-P., & de Sardan, J.-P. (2000). *Courtiers en developpement: Les villages Africains en quete de projets* [Development brokers: African villages in search of projects]. Kathala.

Bierschenk, T., Chauveau, J.-P., & de Sardan, J.-P. (2002). *Local development brokers in Africa: The rise of a new social category* (Working Paper No. 13). Institute for Ethnography and African Studies.

Boone, C. (2003). *Political topographies of the African state: Territorial authority and institutional choice.* Cambridge University Press.

Cain, K. Postlewait, H. & Thomson, A. (2006). *Emergency sex (and other desperate measures): True stories from a war zone.* Ebury Press.

Clifford, J. (1992). Travelling cultures. In L. Grossberg, C. Nelson, & P. Treichler (Eds.), *Cultural studies* (pp. 96–116). Routledge.

Das, V., & Poole, D. (Eds.) (2004). *Anthropology in the margins of the state.* School of America Research Press.

Davey, E. (2012). *New players through old lenses: Why history matters when engaging with Southern actors* (No. 48; HPG Policy Brief). Overseas Development Institute.

Fassin, D. (2012). *Humanitarian reason: A moral history of the present.* University of California Press.

Fechter, A.-M. (2007). *Transnational lives: Expatriates in Indonesia.* Ashgate.

Fechter, A.-M., & Walsh, K. (2010). Examining "expatriate" continuities: Postcolonial approaches to mobile professionals. *Journal of Ethnic and Migration Studies*, 36(8), 1197–1210.

Goodhand, J. (2018). *Borderlands, brokers and peacebuilding: The political economy of conflict and development in the borderlands* [Working Paper No. 2]. University of London.

Gupta, A., & Ferguson, J. (Eds.) (1997). *Anthropological locations: Boundaries and grounds of a field science.* University of California Press.

Hutchinson, J. (1996). *Champions of charity: War and the rise of the Red Cross.* Westview Press.

IASC (2008). *Civil-military guidelines and references for complex emergencies.* United Nations.

Jacobs, M. (2014). Development brokerage, anthropology and public action: Local empowerment, international cooperation and aid. *Volkskunde*, 3, 299–318.

James, D. (2011). The return of the broker: consensus, hierarchy, and choice in South African land reform. *Journal of the Royal Anthropological Institute*, 17(2), 318–338.

Kaldor, M. (2006). *New and old wars: Organised violence in a global era.* Stanford University.

Korf, B., & Raeymaekers, T. (Eds.) (2013). *Violence on the margins: States, conflict and borderlands.* Palgrave Macmillan.

Kuklik, H. (2008). *A new history of anthropology.* Wiley-Blackwell.

Loquercio, D., Hammersley, M., & Emmens, B. (2006). *Understanding and addressing staff turnover in humanitarian agencies* (No. 55; Network Papers). Overseas Development Institute.

Meehan, P., & Plonski, S. (2016). *Brokering the margins: A review of concepts and methods* (Working Paper No. 1). University of London.

Redfield, P. (2012). The unbearable lightness of ex-pats: Double binds of humanitarian mobility. *Cultural Anthropology*, 27(2), 358–382.

Redfield, P. (2013). *Life in crisis: The ethical journey of doctors without borders*. University of California Press.

Redfield, R. (1956). *Peasant society and culture: An anthropological approach to civilization*. University of Chicago Press.

Relph, E. (2008). *Place and placelessness*. Sage.

Roth, S. (2012). Professionalisation trends and inequality: Experiences and practices in aid relationships. *Third World Quarterly*, 33(8), 1459–1474.

Russell, B. (2004). *The problems of philosophy*. Oxford University Press.

Said, E. (1978). *Orientalism*. Pantheon.

Schenkenberg, E. (2016). *The challenges of localised humanitarian aid in armed conflict* (No. 3; Emergency Gap Series). MSF.

Scott, J. (2009). *The art of not being governed: An anarchist history of upland Southeast Asia*. Yale University Press.

Scroggins, D. (2002). *Emma's war: An aid worker, a warlord, radical Islam, and the politics of oil – a true story of love and death in Sudan*. Pantheon Books.

Shevchenko, O., & Fox, R. (2008). "Nationals" and "expatriates": Challenges of fulfilling "sans frontieres" ideals in international humanitarian action. *Health and Human Rights in Practice*, 10(1), 109–122.

Thomas, C., & Wilkin, P. (2004). Still waiting after all these years: "The Third World" on the periphery of international relations. *The British Journal of Politics and International Relations*, 6(2), 241–258.

Tilly, C. (1990). *Coercion, capital and the European states, A.D. 990–1990*. Basil Blackwell.

Wilden, A., & Wilson, T. (1976). The double bind: Logic, magic, and economics. In C. Sluzki & D. Ransom (Eds.), *Double bind: The foundation of communicational approach to the family* (pp. 263–286). Grune and Stratton.

Wolf, E. (1956). Aspects of group relations in a complex society: Mexico. *American Anthropologist*, 58(6), 1065–1078.

7 Conclusion

In the preceding pages I have used ethnographic methodologies to tease out the contradictions and tensions of humanitarian protection in contemporary conflicts. These are inextricably linked to the very foundations of modern humanitarianism, a tradition of European origin that revolves around a set of international laws and universal principles. In simple terms, these work to limit the behaviour of armed actors towards civilians and facilitate relief to affected communities. Humanitarians fill a scripted role in this protection philosophy, disseminating and promoting the laws and principles to ensure they are understood, and providing relief to selected communities in line with the provisions of these laws. This state-centred approach has been broadened throughout the 20th century in order to incorporate civil wars and emerging non-state armed actors, but the fundamentals remain.

However, tensions exist between these state-based frameworks and the complex context of contemporary wars. These tensions have only grown in recent decades as non-state armed actors have increasingly asserted their authority. Rather than the proto-states assumed by the established protection philosophy, these are arguably best understood as hybrid actors, who reflect some of the attributes of a state, but are also influenced by political, cultural and religious traditions that are at odds with the Western norms that guide humanitarian protection. As a result, they selectively accept or transgress these laws, sometimes following the established norms, while at other times asserting their own strategic, political or cultural justifications to target civilians, manipulate relief aid and deny humanitarian access. The previous three chapters have explored how protection works in these complex, contradictory contexts, using the international humanitarian practitioner as the focal point.

How does protection work in contemporary wars?

Humanitarian space and its network of actors

Humanitarians are commonly portrayed as neutral and impartial actors operating in a humanitarian space, apart from politics. This space is not primarily a physical space set aside for humanitarian activity, but as field workers are only too aware, it comprises a complex network of actors with often-competing motivations and agendas. Humanitarian space is synonymous with these competing actors accepting the role that humanitarians play, allowing them the metaphorical space to provide relief without fear of attack or interference. Furthermore, it involves an acceptance that parts of a population – notably civilians – are not part of the fight. In the official representation, this comes through armed actors accepting the official legal frameworks that oblige them to practice restraint towards civilians and allow for neutral and impartial humanitarian relief. In this vision it is these laws that create humanitarian space and drive humanitarian protection.

This direct link between legal frameworks and protection outcomes emerges in protection policy initiatives (see, e.g., Caverzasio, 2001; Slim & Bonwick, 2005), research commissioned by humanitarian agencies (see, e.g., Fresard, 2004; Niland & Polastro, 2015) and is the starting point for much scholarly literature (see, e.g., de Torrente, 2004; Donini et al., 2004; Rieff, 2002). Theirs is a rational approach that identifies problems and then turns to established mechanisms to find solutions, often at the expense of examining the relationship between these frameworks and complex local practices that have been described by other humanitarian scholars (see, e.g., Hilhorst & Jansen, 2010; Hilhorst & Serrano, 2010). Hilhorst and her followers have envisioned humanitarian space as an *arena* where multiple actors shape the everyday realities of humanitarian action. This research takes this conceptualisation further, examining the relationship between this network of actors and the official protection frameworks.

Protection frameworks as a discourse

This book acknowledges the importance of these official frameworks in guiding the behaviour of these actors and promoting protection, just not in the way that has previously been assumed. Rather than normative laws to be followed and prosecuted if breached, this book recognises the humanitarian frameworks as a discourse, which guides the behaviour of armed actors and creates the metaphorical humanitarian space described here. As critical analysts of policy discourse have argued, a simple, coherent narrative can be a powerful force in creating a level of tactical consensus among disparate actors. Reflecting on Roe (1994), policy narratives generate consensus around major policies and make political action possible. Similarly, as Mosse (2005) argues, broad development narratives create a far better framework for maintaining relationships in the program space than contradictory development realities. In a similar vein, this book reveals that humanitarian laws and principles act as a protection narrative, stabilising a particular interpretation of humanitarian protection that is able to encapsulate the often-competing positions of different actors. A product of the international state system, this narrative represents a broad agreement on what is accepted behaviour by all actors in armed conflict. This facilitates a coordinated approach among a set of competing actors that provides for the protection of affected communities and access for humanitarians.

Humanitarian intermediaries

Like the policy narratives outlined by Roe (1994) and Mosse (2005), protection relies on a community that recruits and retains these actors by promoting the central narrative. As this book has revealed, the task in part falls on humanitarian workers, who fill a number of interconnected roles as promoters of the humanitarian protection narrative. In what I describe as their official role, humanitarian intermediaries actively promote the frameworks and principles in order to ensure that they are widely understood and accepted. In other words, as described in Chapter 4, they reify the official narrative through constant repetition, whether through their dissemination efforts, advocacy on behalf of at-risk groups or the everyday performance of their prescribed role as neutral and impartial actors. In these efforts, these humanitarian intermediaries do not modify or distort the message, but remain faithful to the language of the frameworks. This ensures a consistency that encourages their universal application and minimises any uncertainty about what is accepted behaviour. Clearly humanitarians do not always, if ever, hold to this ideal type, as this book has articulated, but to initially frame them this way provides useful insights into these supposedly neutral, impartial actors and the roles they fill.

While humanitarians have not been articulated as the intermediaries more commonly described by anthropologists (see, e.g., Latour, 1993; Lindquist, 2015), this role has always been a central part of the humanitarian endeavour. From the very outset of modern-day humanitarianism, it was understood that for the protection frameworks to be effective they had to be embedded into the everyday behaviour and knowledge of actors involved in armed conflict, which was initially assumed to be state actors. The official humanitarians of the day were mandated with the task of promoting these frameworks and protecting them from being undermined. Neutral, impartial actors, positioned between warring parties and sharing a consistent message, they were classic go-betweens and intermediaries.

Contemporary wars and the disruptions to the discourse

Historically, these dissemination efforts tied state actors to the established narrative. They have broadened over recent decades in an effort to recruit non-state armed actors into the narrative as they increasingly asserted their authority in contemporary conflicts. The official narrative of humanitarian laws and principles clearly has some relevance to these non-state armed actors. Insurgents and rebel organisations often behave like proto-states or states-in-the-making, reflecting the internationally recognised entity they seek to replace (see, e.g., Mampilly, 2011; Schlichte, 2009). Many sign on to the humanitarian norms, as it is often to their advantage to do so, providing a level of local and international legitimacy they ultimately seek in their quest for statehood or state rule (see Stanton, 2016). In other words, the official humanitarian discourse ties these "new" actors into the established network.

These actors, however, are far more complex than this understanding implies, demonstrating shifting patterns of behaviour that do not necessarily conform to international norms (see, e.g., Arjona et al., 2015; Kalyvas, 2006; Schlichte, 2009; Staniland, 2012). As this book outlined earlier, drawing on these and other researchers of insurgent violence, many non-state armed actors are also invested in cultural, religious and political traditions that were temporarily subsumed by the Western state-making process. Furthermore, as they were not part of the original conversation that established the international norms that guide the behaviour of state actors, they feel – and to some degree are – less bound by this official narrative and more likely to act according to their own institutional agenda. As such, they can be seen as hybrid actors, reflecting some of the attributes of states, while also selectively rejecting international frameworks, often to the detriment of civilians.

Humanitarian brokers and translators

The response to these complexities has been two-fold. At the official level, there have been continued efforts to assert the normative frameworks, bolstering and extending them to accommodate these new actors. Humanitarian workers continue to play a significant part in this effort, as intermediaries actively promoting the official script. This official effort holds the traditional state-based actors into the established humanitarian protection order and has some effect in recruiting new, non-state armed actors. However, as narrative theory attests, the broader the network and more disparate the interests, the more difficult it is to unify them under a single narrative (see Roe, 1994).

This has seen the emergence of a second, alternative modality of humanitarian protection, which can be understood through comparative research into development brokers and translators (see, e.g., Bierschenk et al., 2000; Lewis & Mosse, 2006; Mosse, 2004). Rather than acting solely as intermediaries who disseminate the official message unchanged, humanitarians have emerged as brokers who straddle the different worlds of humanitarian protection. In an acknowledgment that a complex network of actors drives protection, these humanitarians are relational, seeing the world primarily as a series of relationships rather than pre-formed entities or institutions that are the focus of the more normative vision of humanitarian protection. These relationships are built around a level of trust that each side will deliver on what they promise as well as a mutual understanding of the motivations and needs on both sides of the relationship. From there, it is about finding commonalities where the agenda of armed actors overlaps with the humanitarian agenda. These overlaps allow for the establishment of messy partnerships between armed actors and humanitarians that bring about positive protection outcomes. Furthermore, humanitarians using this unofficial approach to protection strategically use both the knowledge of the official frameworks and an informal knowledge of the local context to engage with a diverse spectrum of actors. In doing so, they reinterpret the humanitarian laws and principles in order for them to be relevant to a wider network of actors. In other words, they translate the meaning of the official narrative so that it reflects the interests, agendas and belief systems of actors outside of the Western, legal tradition, and in so doing give them a reason to participate in the established humanitarian order.

Importantly, these efforts are not about creating an entirely new discourse. Rather, as the term translation implies, they are providing a negotiated meaning that resonates with local actors, but also attempts to remain faithful to the official frameworks. In order to establish the crucial relationships that promote protection, they present reasoned arguments that reflect the foundational arguments that led to the establishment of the humanitarian norms. Rather than citing the need to follow the law, these logical arguments focus on the benefits of protecting the community or of mutual restraint. Furthermore, they turn to the human values that underpin the legal frameworks, such as moral values of human life or notions of trust and reciprocity. Finally, they turn to local customary norms that instil imperatives of securing civilian welfare that are in fact similar to the frameworks of international law. In these translations, they are neither rejecting the established structures nor establishing an alternative narrative. Rather, they are creatively adapting the narrative in order to accommodate its shortcomings in contexts where non-state armed actors do not necessarily relate to the official frameworks it rests on. It is this unofficial fix that sustains the viability of the official frameworks in the complex context of contemporary wars.

Humanitarian travellers

Yet there are complexities to humanitarian brokerage and the fix it provides, which this book reveals through an examination of a related humanitarian figure, the traveller. For unlike brokers of the past, who were quite sedentary figures, embedded in the local community, humanitarians are intrinsically mobile. This mobility is rooted in the history of humanitarianism, which originally radiated out of Europe, propelled by colonial expansion, to provide charity to the deserving poor of the global South and promote a particular philosophy of restraint in war. This very notion of distance between the giver and the receiver of aid created the need for the humanitarian traveller. These notions of distance and travel in turn have significant structural effects that sustain humanitarianism as we understand it. Being of the centre, travelling to the field, helps ensure humanitarians' outsider status and so their position as neutral emissaries operating independently from local politics. This travel between the centre and the margins also facilitates the transfer of knowledge that is central to their official role as intermediaries. Furthermore, travel facilitates learning, allowing expats who understand the global frameworks to develop some level of the local knowledge they require as brokers.

However, this same mobility that is necessary to international humanitarians' official and unofficial roles also limits their capacity. The very act of movement that allows them to transfer knowledge between different worlds and helps ensure their outsider status simultaneously works to isolate them from local knowledge. As anthropologists and development workers have long argued, it is only through extended contact with the local community that one can understand their motivations and build substantive relationships (see, e.g., Bierschenk et al., 2002,

p. 20). Such sustained engagement is at odds with the foundations of modern humanitarianism and the humanitarian as the neutral, impartial outsider. As explained in Chapter 6, this leaves humanitarianism in a classic double bind, permanently oscillating between the need for local knowledge and relationships that come through time in a place, and the need to retain distance and avoid the kind of attachment that long-term placement brings. Furthermore, this mobility works to sustain some of the colonial power imbalances that have historically been part of the humanitarian system, reifying the power of the centre over the local. This emerges perhaps most clearly in the relationship between international humanitarian experts and the local staff they rely on.

The local humanitarian fixer

The colonial discourses that created two distinct worlds has a contemporary cognate that creates two groups of humanitarians: the international humanitarian, of the centre, travelling out into the field to help the so-called vulnerable, and the local staff member, who belongs to the marginal space created in opposition to the centre. Furthermore, the local staff member emerges as the international humanitarian's necessary other, embedded in the local context and possessing the depth of contextual knowledge that so often eludes the travelling expat. The very notion of distance that created the humanitarian traveller created a need for the proximity that is required not only to deliver relief and disseminate notions of limited war, but to build an understanding of the local. For as discussed earlier, it is proximity that makes a place knowable. The local staff member fills this role, acting as a necessary link between the humanitarian outsider and the local system. This proximity, and the knowledge it provides, is even more significant in many contemporary conflicts where actors do not necessarily follow the norms understood by international aid workers, but selectively act according to local customs and their own shifting agendas. I argue that the local humanitarian provides a fix to the problems that emerge from the transience of the humanitarian endeavour and the humanitarian traveller. This act of "collective brokerage" (see Bierschenk et al., 2000, pp. 29–30) between international and local staff facilitates the transfer of knowledge from the global centre and the act of translation that makes it relevant to actors in the local context.

At the same time, the local figure and their expat counterpart represents persistent racial hierarchies and power inequalities. The discursive distinction between the two groups, established by the centre, privileges the Western knowledge of the international humanitarian over the contextual, cultural knowledge of their local counterpart. Privileging the centre and the expertise it provides also promotes outward movement over alternative trajectories, helping to ensure the global system remains distant and unknowable to local staff, sustaining these established inequalities. This subordinate status is further reinforced by the value placed on the outsider position of international staff, itself a product of the centre-periphery relationship, with local humanitarians perceived as being part of local politics and influenced by established affiliations. As a result, they remain a supporting act, providing contextual knowledge and links to established local networks, a necessary but largely hidden fix to the shortcomings of the international humanitarian traveller.

The humanitarian fix

What emerges in this book are two interlinked modalities of humanitarian protection. The first, which I refer to as the official approach, focuses on pre-formed entities, the relationships between which are guided by formal mechanisms. It is the product of humanitarianism's Western, state-focused tradition where interactions are predominantly between states and official institutions. Interactions between these bodies are guided by a set of norms or mutually agreed standards of behaviour. At one level, these norms are underpinned by a series of rules, the specific application of these norms, for which violation has a price. At the same time, as this book articulates, these official frameworks also operate as a discourse, a simple, coherent narrative that creates a level of consensus among actors on what is agreed behaviour in times of war. The humanitarian intermediaries of Chapter 4 play a significant role in this, reifying this narrative through constant repetition of the official frameworks as they were laid out. It is a universal system that operates on a global scale, and is transferrable between contexts, which are seen as reflections of the state view of the world.

The second, partly hidden behind these official mechanisms, is a pragmatic approach to humanitarian protection that stresses the need to understand and adapt to the specific context and the motivations of different parties. It is an informal response to the contextual challenges that the official approach has faced in the complex environment of contemporary conflicts. Unlike the official approach, which relies on frameworks, this alternative modality puts relationships, which have been identified in this book as being central to protection, at the forefront of practice. This relational approach is able to acknowledge complexity, accommodate disagreement and debate, and in turn ensures that the response can be constantly negotiated and adjusted to suit contextual changes. Reflecting on the challenges the normative frameworks face in contemporary conflicts, the relational approach is able to smooth over the differences and uncertainties between actors that can disrupt established protection efforts.

Furthermore, this unofficial modality turns to alternative translations of the official frameworks in order to overcome contextual challenges. In other words, the original unifying narrative is adapted to suit each context and the diverse mix of actors that have made their presence felt in contemporary wars. In this approach, discussed in Chapter 5, humanitarians draw on a toolbox of reasoned arguments and value systems in order to make their pro-civilian case to actors outside the Western tradition. These alternative translations align with reasons for restraint held by non-state armed actors, revealed in Chapter 1 in terms of top-down arguments such as legitimacy and the bottom-up motivations of cultural norms and value systems. Importantly, as the term translation implies, these interpretations do not digress far from the official narrative. Instead they reflect the underlying reasoning and values that sit behind the official framework, whether garnering legitimacy and community support, or values of restraint and compassion.

The unofficial modality of protection is not a discrete approach as the relational actors who articulate these alternative translations are also invested in the official protection frameworks. Rather than a dichotomy of practice, the two approaches complement each other, with humanitarian actors at times prioritising the frameworks, while at other times turning to comparable reasoned arguments and values if the context requires. The parallel script is an attempt to accommodate the shortcomings of the formal frameworks in complex environments occupied by actors who selectively digress from the Western, state-based protection frameworks. Furthermore, in articulating this alternative argument, they draw from a repository of reasoned arguments and values that are not at odds with the official protection frameworks, but rather exist underneath these legal norms.

Moral transaction

Reflecting on this, it is too simplistic to say that the humanitarian protection frameworks stand in opposition to established belief systems in cultures outside the European tradition, for they are drawn from a set of underlying principles and values. While derived from European principles, values such as trust, innocence, compassion, reciprocity, restraint and the moral value of human life cut across cultural, religious and political systems. Though rebel organisations may not be consistently invested in the European state system and its laws, they do have an underlying set of values. No matter how radical a rebel organisation, its practices are embedded in the values, norms, beliefs and forms of governance of the community that it emerges from. Indeed, as discussed in Chapter 1, reflecting these common cultural and political values is integral to an organisation's long-term viability, for it brings legitimacy. In practical terms, with this legitimacy comes the crucial community support for recruitment, intelligence, taxes, supplies and labour that helps sustain and build a rebel movement. In ideological terms, these values combine to form a narrative that sustains a group's power and authority over a community.

Taken as a purely instrumental approach, the established protection philosophy is incompatible with these diverse belief systems. However, as this book has revealed, the practice of protection is far more complex than this legal view would indicate. As we have seen, these frameworks are being adapted to the local context using the underlying values they were initially built on. These underlying values are more flexible and ultimately more compatible to those of actors who are emerging in contemporary conflicts. These values arise out of the range of beliefs that cross different cultures, whether Western, European values or those of people in the once colonised South. Taking into account both its official and unofficial modalities, humanitarian protection can be seen as a moral discourse that can interact with other moral discourses.

Public and hidden scripts

To reiterate, I hold that humanitarian protection consists of two scripts. First, there is the official script, which is built around fixed laws and frameworks that are deemed to be universal across all contexts. As discussed earlier, humanitarians routinely invoke the laws and principles when communicating with governments and armed groups, cite the Geneva Conventions and human rights law in response to violations, and have an ongoing program of disseminating these laws and principles to ensure legal obligations are widely understood. The other, unofficial script is contextual, adapting to the disparate, ever changing mix of actors who occupy the humanitarian arena. These two scripts are not independent of each other; they interact. The unofficial script is a translated version of the official frameworks, relying on the pragmatic arguments and moral values that underpin the humanitarian frameworks to present a similar case for pro-civilian behaviour.

Yet, at the same time the two scripts remain separate. The frameworks, supposedly universally relevant across all contexts, remain the formal, public representation of humanitarian protection, while the alternative translations remain off the books, an informal response to local challenges. There is resistance to incorporating these alternative messages, built on reasoned arguments and moral values, into the official protection discourse. They are left in the realm of everyday practice, rather than being formalised. It is left to field workers to learn through experience, build contextual knowledge and adapt the frameworks as best as possible to different audiences.

There are operational reasons why the two are not integrated. It is difficult to formalise such practices and still allow them to be flexible enough to cover the diverse, changing contexts of contemporary conflicts. While practices are often formalised for very good reasons, this can cause them to lose their flexibility. This can be seen in the institutionalisation of the humanitarian sector, which, while providing a coherent response, also reduces flexibility and contextual relevance. Those at headquarters are more invested in the official frameworks, as they match the environment they operate in – that of institutions – while it is those in the field that need to deal with contextual realities, thus sustaining this divide.

Yet there are also underlying reasons for this divide that are only partly articulated by discussions with aid workers about the relationships between formal frameworks and their everyday practices. There are reasons why the legalists press the need to focus on the frameworks, for to do otherwise is to undermine their universality and consequently their power. To argue for more flexible interpretations of the official protection philosophy opens the narrative up to reinterpretation by the people they are meant to guide in ways that suit their agenda. This undermines the rules-based philosophy at the core of the official approach to humanitarian protection in favour of pragmatic concerns and strategic outcomes. The legalist position does not fall across simple headquarters/field or policy makers/operational staff divides, as some field workers certainly hold this legal view. Indeed, those who move between headquarters and the field often nimbly move between the two scripts, expressing support for both and never fully articulating a position that would integrate the informal positions into the formal protection frameworks. These humanitarian actors, some of whom we met in Part II of this book, clearly grapple with the relationships between the two approaches, how they interact and how they could compete with each other.

This book posits that there are underlying structural reasons for having two scripts – one formal, the other at least semi-formal. It argues that the tensions that aid workers experience between the two are an inherent part of the relationship. The unofficial narrative has the potential to undermine the formal frameworks, a case loosely presented by some people interviewed for this book, and more clearly articulated in the theories I have turned to. Like policy narratives, the simplicity of the humanitarian frameworks allows them to guide the behaviour of a host of different actors. As Roe (1994) articulates in regard to policy narratives, these strategic simplifications help in the face of situations whose complexity can paralyse policy making. By being broad and generic, policy narratives are able to unify different actors by allowing different positions to be held at the same time. Indeed, the more complexity decision-makers experience, the more pressure there is to generate broad, explanatory narratives to provide a unified course of action. This book extends this argument, articulating the official frameworks as a narrative that unifies often-competing actors behind a common protection strategy. Like policy narratives, its strength lies in a simplicity and vagueness that can be accepted by the disparate network of actors in the conflict space.

Meanwhile, the unofficial script changes and adapts to complex environments and actors. It is the response to complex realities that have been masked by the official script but can still prove disruptive. To formally incorporate this complexity is to undermine the universality that the humanitarian frameworks rest on and the simplicity of the official protection narrative. Thus, they are kept separate, with local knowledge and practices remaining informal and off the books. The informal nature of this system provides humanitarian workers with the room to manoeuvre without disrupting the official narrative. There is an unspoken acceptance of this, with humanitarian organisations providing these travelling representatives the freedom to steer their way through local scenarios and produce alternative interpretations of the official discourse. There is the unspoken assumption that aid workers will learn through experience and adopt the arguments that work with different audiences. By outsourcing this flexibility, the official global discourse is maintained while aid workers provide the local fix. At one level it remains universal, while at the other level it is diversified by a broad range of actors. At one level it remains a legal matter, rather than a moral one. These are clear, legal positions, rather than ambiguous moral positions, open to interpretation.

Decolonising protection

In looking to the scholarly debates about the efficacy of Western humanitarian protection frameworks in contemporary wars, can we still argue that protection philosophy is a Western experience that lacks relevance in many contemporary conflicts? This book agrees with this basic proposition, but also presents the complications underlying this argument. In everyday practice the protection frameworks have been partly decolonised and diversified by humanitarian actors drawing on local experiences. Many of these humanitarian actors are culturally ambiguous, often providing hyphenated explanations of their national and ethnic background – Palestinian-American, French-African, Middle Eastern-European – or come from cultural melting pots of former colonies such as Latin America, Lebanon and the Philippines. Others originally rooted in the West have studiously explored cultural and religious complexities, or have found themselves thrust into diverse cultural experiences through life experience. Furthermore, the brokerage that is part of protection in contemporary wars incorporates local humanitarian actors who bring their local knowledge and networks to the humanitarian endeavour. Drawing on this diverse knowledge base, humanitarians are able to go beyond framing protection in purely instrumental terms, instead paying attention to the social process of protection. As a result of these endeavours, rather than a Eurocentric approach based on the state system and its laws, protection comes down to how different humanitarian staff translate the frameworks to suit different contexts.

At the same time, however, the geography of colonialism still lingers in the humanitarian endeavour. Humanitarian agencies are still largely of the centre. The official humanitarian narrative remains an important component of humanitarian protection, influencing the behaviour of armed actors, whether state or state-like. Furthermore, the international humanitarian outsider remains an important component of this philosophy, reifying the frameworks as they were designed. Meanwhile, the alternative translations that partly decolonise protection, making it more effective in contemporary conflicts, remains largely hidden for functional purposes. As a result, many of the colonial era inequalities remain intact, sustained by the official discourse and its structural effects.

Directions for further research

This book has explored the complex set of interactions that exist between the official frameworks that seek to guide the protection of civilians and the way protection efforts take shape in actual practice. In revealing *how* protection works, I have combined critical theory analysis, notably the nuanced examinations of agency and everyday practice of de Certeau (1984) and Scott (1990), with ethnographic observation, which is best equipped to build a detailed understanding of everyday practices and social interactions. I have explored these interactions through the lens of the international humanitarian worker, a pivotal actor in the complex humanitarian space between the protection frameworks and protection outcomes. However, there are clearly other significant actors in this network that warrant similar attention. One such actor is the local humanitarian worker, who has appeared in this study as the necessary other of the international humanitarian. While there are ongoing policy initiatives to localise humanitarianism and empower local staff, these efforts remain constrained by the established humanitarian discourse identified in this book. An "insider-outsider" examination of the agency and everyday practice of the local humanitarian has the potential to tease out some uncomfortable realties about this power imbalance and how it is sustained, which would inform future policy initiatives. Furthermore, these local actors are increasingly complex figures, challenging the discursive rendering of local/international. Many are part of international diaspora communities, linked into the international, while a few others have returned home after time in the West, further blurring the boundary between national and international.

This book and its findings also have the potential to be a stepping-off point for further research into collective brokerage in relation to international and local humanitarians. The perspective I have adopted for this research – centred around the international humanitarian worker – allows for only a partial understanding of this relationship. There is space to explore it in more detail, whether in the form of the vertical "chain" linking brokers together, or the brokerage "club" in which the brokerage function is assumed by multiple actors in symbiosis (see Bierschenk et al., 2000, pp. 29–30). The power imbalance and how it is sustained would be a central theme of any such study. As discussed in this book, collective brokerage involving national and international staff is not a relationship of equals, rather those with contacts and knowledge beyond the immediate locale have emerged as leaders of the brokerage club, or occupying a place further up a hierarchical brokerage chain.

Brokerage chains and clubs are also likely to link together other actors in the humanitarian space, also warranting further research. For example, the pivotal relationships between humanitarians and armed actors could be explored through the concept of collective brokerage, with individual armed actors filling a broker function in their interactions with the humanitarian broker of Chapter 5. During my own travels for this research, I met such actors, including military personnel officially designated to act as links to humanitarian organisations and the growing number of "civ-mil" coordinators in the humanitarian sector. If collective brokerage is operating between humanitarians and armed state actors, one could assume similar agents emerge in non-state armed groups.

Applied implications

This research did not set out to provide clear policy recommendations. Such recommendations would follow in the tradition of instrumental scholars who identify failure before providing technical solutions. Instead, this is an attempt fill a gap in knowledge by opening the black box that exists between the official protection frameworks and protection outcomes. It is an attempt to reveal *how* these frameworks operate in the real world of contemporary conflicts. I leave it to policy makers to take this complex set of relationships further and explore concrete policy options. With this in mind, I offer three areas that warrant their attention.

People

I have argued that relationships are at the centre of humanitarian protection, ultimately driving positive outcomes for at-risk groups. Rather than a set of rules to be followed or prosecuted if breached, the official protection frameworks act as a narrative glue to establish the networks of alliances, coalitions and partnerships that drive protection. The broker has appeared as a key actor in establishing and sustaining this network in the complex environment of contemporary wars, translating the frameworks to recruit a more diverse network of actors and creating linkages where none exist. Yet this crucial agent in the success of the frameworks is not mentioned in operational directives by any name, nor are they recruited for. Instead they emerge incidentally from the pool of the usual interlocutors who are not necessarily fully equipped to take up such a task. Today's humanitarian brokers have collected most of their skills through happenstance and life experience, before testing them through trial and error.

Rather than relying on chance, I propose that a new professional should be recruited for and developed. That said, this would be no easy task. Mosse (2011) was correct when he drew attention to similar challenges in recruiting for the development sector:

> The participatory turn in international development has made the constitution of expert development identities more complex. Professionals of participatory programs have to deny or conceal their expertise and agency (and their practical role in program delivery) in order to preserve an authorized view of themselves as facilitators of community action or local knowledge, as "catalysts", hastening but not partaking in the reaction.... Where ... expertise requires self-effacement, it is harder to constitute professional identities.
>
> (p. 17)

To this end, it is time to think this role through. Ultimately, it is about recruiting and training a group of humanitarian practitioners who refuse to frame protection in purely instrumental terms, but instead pay attention to social processes of protection. It is not only about the fixed knowledge of the formal frameworks, but the varied knowledge of the local context and its actors.

Networks

When thinking of these actors and the relationships they establish, it is also worth further reflection on collective brokerage. Just as there is space for further research into these networks, the ideas warrant the attention of policy makers. This is no simple task, as brokerage "chains" and "clubs" (Bierschenk et al., 2000, pp. 29–30) are not easily recognisable. They are not necessarily permanent collaborations, instead constantly appearing, reforming and fading according to the needs on the ground and the actors available. Furthermore, they can be quite intricate structures, with their power deriving from the different positions taken by various members and their interactions. For the international and local staff, this comes through the complementary forms of knowledge held by the different actors in this network. Yet despite these complexities, the perspective of collective brokerage has the potential to provide new direction for policy makers grappling with the power imbalance between national and international staff. What policy initiatives, for example, would change a hierarchical vertical chain, into a club where complementary forms of knowledge are equally valued? This policy conversation can also extend beyond these particular actors, for collective brokerage is a prevalent social formula in institutional settings (see Bierschenk et al., 2002, pp. 25–26).

Knowledge

Reflecting on the value of both formal and informal knowledge, discussed in Chapters 5 and 6, there is space to promote peer-to-peer knowledge sharing among aid workers. This is not a call for expanding the already formidable raft of skills trainings and workshops. Nor is it a call to further duplicate established institutional efforts to share knowledge and experiences. Such formal systems are already in place where aid workers can share past experiences, such as end-of-mission reports and the ubiquitous reflection workshops. Rather, this is a call for spaces and channels where aid workers can share the dilemmas they are facing in a less structured and more spontaneous way.

This would be about further facilitating the informal community of practice that already exists, away from the institutional machinations that tend to undermine openness, collaboration and sharing, and away from the institutional hierarchy, professional competitiveness, career trajectories and organisational turf wars that have a similar undermining impact. There can clearly be structures that facilitate these conversations, but the conversations themselves need to be free to roam. This would also be about encouraging practitioners to recognise and be aware of the personal skills they are carrying from one place to another, about encouraging them to shape and recognise this work as a valuable set of personal practices.

What would such a space look like? I offer only sweeping thoughts drawn from the knowledge shared in the previous chapters. Reflecting on the private nature of the existing conversations, this is not a public place, but a closed community, given the freedom to openly talk about their experiences and thoughts. Reflecting on the informal nature of the existing communications, such a space would be about sharing personal stories and anecdotes. Stories have the power to embrace complexity; to borrow from anthropology, they are able to provide the thick descriptions of personal observation and experience that show how protection actually works in complex environments.

In closing

This book has been concerned with how humanitarian protection works, focusing on the complex relationship between the official frameworks that seek to guide the protection of civilians and how they actually take shape in practice. To this end, its approach has been ethnographic, examining the everyday practice of humanitarians tasked with disseminating and implementing these laws and principles. Viewed from the inside, it becomes clear that it is not the frameworks that guide protection, but rather it is first and foremost the relationships between the actors who occupy the humanitarian arena. This is not to say that the frameworks do not serve an important function, just not the one that is commonly articulated. Rather than laws to be followed, the frameworks act as a unifying narrative that establishes and preserves these relationships.

We have seen that international humanitarian workers fill two important and interconnected roles. First, they act as intermediaries who, through constant repetition of the frameworks and their everyday performances as neutral, impartial actors, reify the official narrative which works to unify state and state-like actors. Second, they act as mediators or brokers, who actively translate the official frameworks to make them relevant to actors from outside this European, state-focused tradition and who selectively transgress these frameworks according to their circumstances. They, in part, decolonise humanitarian protection by turning to a mix of reasoned arguments and moral values to recruit actors from other political, cultural and religious traditions. In other words, they provide a temporary fix that makes these Western-based frameworks relevant in a post-colonial world. However, the fix also sustains many of the colonial inequalities that are intrinsic to the protection frameworks.

References

Arjona, A., Kasfir, N., & Mampilly, Z. (Eds.). (2015). *Rebel governance in civil war.* Cambridge University Press.

Bierschenk, T., Chauveau, J.-P., & de Sardan, J.-P. (2000). *Courtiers en developpement: Les villages Africains en quete de projets* [Development brokers: African villages in search of projects]. Kathala.

Bierschenk, T., Chauveau, J.-P., & de Sardan, J.-P. (2002). *Local development brokers in Africa: The rise of a new social category* (Working Paper No. 13). Institute for Ethnography and African Studies.

Caverzasio, S. (2001). *Strengthening protection in war.* ICRC.

de Certeau, M. (1984). *The practice of everyday life.* University of California Press.

de Torrente, N. (2004). Humanitarian action under attack: Reflections on the Iraq war. *Harvard Human Rights Journal,* 17, 1–29.

Donini, A., Minear, L., & Walker, P. (2004). Iraq and the crisis of humanitarian action. *Humanitarian Exchange,* 26, 37–40.

Fresard, J.-J. (2004). *The roots of behaviour in war: A survey of the literature.* ICRC.

Hilhorst, D., & Jansen, B. (2010). Humanitarian space as arena: A perspective on the everyday politics of aid. *Development and Change,* 41(6), 1117–1139.

Hilhorst, D., & Serrano, M. (2010). The humanitarian arena in Angola, 1975–2008. *Disasters,* 34(2), 183–201.

Kalyvas, S. (2006). *The logic of violence in civil war.* Cambridge University Press.

Latour, B. (1993). *We have never been modern* (C. Porter, Trans.). Harvard University Press.

Lewis, D., & Mosse, D. (Eds.). (2006). *Development brokers and translators: The ethnography of aid and agencies*. Kumarian Press.

Lindquist, J. (2015). Brokers and brokerage, Anthropology of. In J. Wright (Ed.), *International encyclopedia of social and behavioral science* (Vol. 2, pp. 870–874). Elsevier.

Mampilly, Z. (2011). *Rebel rulers: Insurgent governance and civilian life during war*. Cornell University Press.

Mosse, D. (2004). *Is good policy unimplementable?* Reflections on the ethnography of aid policy and practice. *Development and Change*, 35(4), 639–671.

Mosse, D. (2005). *Cultivating development: An ethnography of aid policy and practice*. Pluto Press.

Mosse, D. (Ed.) (2011). *Adventures in Aidland: The anthropology of professionals in international development*. Berghahn Books.

Niland, N., & Polastro, R. (2015). *Independent whole of system review of protection in the context of humanitarian action*. Inter-Agency Standing Committee.

Rieff, D. (2002). Humanitarianism in crisis. *Foreign Affairs*, 81(6), 111–121.

Roe, E. (1994). *Narrative policy analysis: Theory and practice*. Duke University Press.

Schlichte, K. (2009). *In the shadow of violence*. Campus Verlag.

Scott, J. (1990). *Domination and the arts of resistance: Hidden transcripts*. Yale University Press.

Slim, H., & Bonwick, A. (2005). *Protection: An ALNAP guide for humanitarian agencies*. Overseas Development Institute.

Staniland, P. (2012). States, insurgents, and wartime political orders. *Perspectives on Politics*, 10(2), 243–264.

Stanton, J. (2016). *Violence and restraint in civil war: Civilian targeting in the shadow of international law*. Cambridge University Press.

Index